My Ancestral VOICES

*Stories of Five Generations of the
Blackburn Family from Slavery to the Present Day*

Dr. Joice Christine Bailey Lewis

ISBN 978-1-956696-49-3 (paperback)
ISBN 978-1-956696-50-9 (digital)

Copyright © 2021 by Dr. Joice Christine Bailey Lewis

All rights reserved. No part of this publication may be reproduced, distributed, or transmitted in any form or by any means, including photocopying, recording, or other electronic or mechanical methods without the prior written permission of the copyright owner. For permission requests, solicit the publisher via the address below.

Rushmore Press LLC
1 800 460 9188
www.rushmorepress.com

Printed in the United States of America

DEDICATION

My Ancestral Voices is dedicated to my ancestors, without whom this book would not have been possible. Personal dedication goes to my parents, L. S. Bailey and Annie Lee Bailey, for their hard work and God-fearing presence that taught me to be the best person I could be; Albert Lewis, my spouse for sixty-two years; my children Al Deric Lewis, Tamera D. Lewis Pettigrew, and Tari C. Lewis and their spouses, who believed in me and always urged me to achieve the highest levels of attainment possible; my sisters Mary Lois Dantzler Brown, Mable Wilson, Gladys Martin, and Gloria Bailey Cook, and my brother, James Dunnigan, for their encouragement and for their undying love.

A special dedication goes to my friends, especially Marian Graham Jenkins, who first read the book and declared it publishable, Jean Freeman Kliever, who edited the book, and other friends who loved me and those who enjoyed my stories when added to my speeches and letters.

Finally, I dedicate this book to my grandchildren and to my great-grandchildren who will continue the legacy of being better than they know how to be because they stand on the shoulders of their Blackburn ancestors.

CONTENTS

Introduction ix
Prologue xi

My Ancestral Voices 1
Life on the Plantation 2
Freedom, Freedom 6
Leaving the Plantation. 9
Going Home. 10
Land for Sale. Land for Sale. 15
Let My People Go 18
Cousin Sterling's Mountain. 22
Smallpox 24
Vignette: Retracing History. 28
Unconfirmed Historical Record 31
Uncle Louis Blackburn 32
The Unwanted Visitor. 34
Women of Grace and Goodness 37
Craziness with Common Sense 42
Tragedy Befalls the Family. 44
Uncle Bob Blackburn 45
A Short Life. 46
Uncle John Blackburn. 47
The Dare. 49
Grandpa and Grandma William and Annie Bailey 52
The Old Yellow Gal. 55
Grandpa's Land Was Stolen 57
Grandma Annie Bailey Died 59
The Quilt and the Traveling Ghost 60

Grandma's Lively Ghost 61
Grandpa's Virility at Ninety Years Old. 63
Ancestors, Aunts, and Uncles 68
Enemy in the House 73
Black Beauty. 77
The Funniest Man Alive 84
In Louis Bailey's Own Words. 85
Louis Bailey's Life Continued 93
Stack-O-Dollars 95
The Black Hand of Death. 97
Moody Swamp 100
Acts of Criminal Mischief? 102
Concern for Fair Treatment for Black People
  in the United States. 105
Black Is Beautiful 107
Howard Bailey. 109
The Second Herman Bailey. 111
The First Herman Bailey. 112
Aunt Lucille 116
Grandma Rebecca Reed. 119
Eula Reed, Our Birth Mother 122
Uncle Moody 126
Aunt Pladelle. 128
Zeke the Man 129
Moody Leaves Town 130
Sold into Slavery in 1943 132
Moody Returns. 134
The Deacon 136
The Day of the County Fair 140
Third Sunday in May Homecoming 157
The Naked Churchgoer. 162
The Nearly Naked Churchgoer 165
Arthur Prince from New Orleans 176
Daddy's First Girlfriend. 185
Daddy Marries Eula Reed 187
A Mother for Daddy's Children. 190
I Remember Well (At Nine Months Old) 192

I Saw the Moon	194
Vignette: In My Mind's Eye	197
Daddy Gathers His Children Home	198
My Birth Mother Puts Me Down	199
Daddy Picks Me Up	206
Life with Daddy	209
"Tho Me In De Bri' Patch"	216
We Are Our Brother's Keeper	225
Where Is Mrs. Julia?	227
Daddy, the Family Man	231
Working in the Fields	236
The Color of Freedom Is Red	238
Sister Lois	241
Mable	242
Mable and the Snake	245
The First Graduate in Our Family	247
Gladys	249
Gloria	250
The Bouncing Underpants	251
Three Holes in One Head	253
The Mule in the Bedroom	255
Southern Justice	259
Burying the Dead and Killing the Living	262
Hunger Knows No Race	265
Gloria Makes a Plan	267
Hot Lunches for Colored Students	271
Baptism in the Creek	272
Daddy Becomes Ill	277
Trying to Get Out of Debt	279
Mrs. Baby Ruth	281
We Move to Town	284
Unequal Education for Negro Children	285
Industrial High School	288
Albert Lewis Jr.	292
Going North in Search of a Better Life	301
Vignette: Before Rosa Parks, There Was Gloria	304
My Arrival in Detroit and Domestic Work Experiences	305

Vignette: The Swimming Pool..........................308
Domestic Service Goes North..........................312
Lewis Business College 314
California, Here I Come 316
When Is a Wedding Not a Wedding?....................317
Vignette: Being Ten Times Better 323
Freedom to Travel 326
Retirement Reflections 328
Vignette: "It Beats Picking Cotton"....................330
The Civil Rights Movement 332
Vignette: Personal 334
The Civil Rights Movement as Seen by White People........335
The Death of Eula Mama.............................337
The Death of Annie Lee Mama........................339
Land Ownership Makes a Man 340
Hushed 342

Appendix: The Holly Spring Missionary
        Baptist Church History......................343
About the Author 349

INTRODUCTION

My Ancestral Voices is a compilation of stories that cover five generations of Blackburns, beginning with the parents of Romeo Blackburn Sr. The stories end with the children of the fifth generation. Each story describes events that actually occurred and are interwoven with details that are either true, assumed, or plausible.

It is true that Great-Grandpa Romeo Blackburn and his parents were slaves on a Virginia plantation. It is true that Romeo's parents were sold to a slave owner in Alabama. It is true that Romeo traveled to Alabama to find his parents and sister. It is assumed that Romeo walked to Alabama to find his family as walking was the main mode of transportation for Negroes during that time. It is plausible that he traveled by way of the Cumberland Trail and Indian Paths as these were the routes most traveled by Negroes going north and south. Events that were witnessed by the writer are true and the details are true. The dialogue spoken by persons in these stories is either true, assumed, or plausible. Events occurring in the writer's immediate family are told without enmity with an understanding of the strains and stresses of the times and with appreciation that from such humble beginnings, family members lived to enjoy positive lives.

Names of persons in these stories are true. Names of persons involved in stories that may have been embarrassing to the individuals have either been omitted or their first names or titles such as "reverend," "deacon," "cousin," or "daughter" have been used. However, anyone living in the area at the time the events occurred will recognize the persons involved.

One exception of name omission involves the main character of the naked churchgoer, who told his story to the writer and gave his permission to include the story in this book. Details and dialogue have been added to this story by the writer.

The history of the Holly Spring Missionary Baptist Church is a true historical document that is updated and presented every year at the third Sunday in May church reunion ceremony.

Proof that many of my ancestors are buried in the Holly Spring Missionary Baptist Church Cemetery has been obtained from the gravestones as burial records have not been kept. Some ancestors described in these stories are known to be buried in *unmarked* graves.

Inherent in the legacy that was left by my ancestors are strong survival instincts, tendencies toward success, and defiance in never allowing other people and other races to define the destiny of family members in each generation.

PROLOGUE

Fog swirled and rose in spirals around the gravestones where my ancestors had lain for over a hundred years. It was as though the souls of friends and families rose from their graves and mingled together, greeting one another as if they were talking over the garden fence. They marveled over their survival, their triumphs, their trials, and they recounted many exploits that invoked tears and laughter down through the years while streams of sunlight pierced the surrounding forest, warming the morning dew.

I had come in the early morning to commune with my ancestors and to draw strength from the stories and their lives. I needed to connect with their strength, their perseverance, and their will to survive. I had returned to Alabama as superintendent of schools in the state that had denied me a college education and in which I had lived as a second-class citizen during the era of Jim Crow. I needed to hear the voices of my ancestors to be sustained for the long journey ahead. I sat in my car in the parking lot of the Holly Spring Missionary Baptist Church, facing the cemetery where my ancestors are buried. I closed my eyes and listened with my heart to the voices of my ancestors. They talked of slavery, of pain, of freedom, of joy, and of love. They sang old Negro spirituals that brought solace to the souls long dead. While I listened with my heart, I heard their stories and found that I knew them all. I had heard these stories while sitting by the roaring fire, walking in the woods, working in the fields, or just resting on the porch on a rainy summer afternoon.

These stories are about events that my ancestors and five subsequent generations lived and told: how my great-grandfather walked from Virginia to Romulus, Alabama, in search of his mother, father, and sister who had been sold and sent farther south during slavery; how he became the founder of Holly Spring Missionary Baptist Church; how and why the people buried in the church cemetery are arranged in a social hierarchy; how my ancestors, five generations of family members and I, have added our voices to these stories.

My ancestors, who are buried in the Holly Spring Missionary Baptist Church Cemetery, consist of conjoined families, beginning with the church founders, my great-grandfather, Romeo Blackburn, and Hiter Wells, and ends with my father, L. S. Bailey.

The conjoined families encompass the Bailey, Foster, Knox, Henderson, Stewart, Harper, Reed, Harris, McKinney, and Thomas families. The graves are situated in a social hierarchy that belies their closeness to Romeo Blackburn Sr. and Hiter Wells, the church founders. The Blackburn descendants are buried on the right, and the Wells descendants are buried on the left, facing the church.

Great-Grandpa Romeo Blackburn and Hiter Wells are buried in the middle of the cemetery on what was initially the front row. Since their burials, three longer rows of graves have been added, moving forward toward the church building. The cemetery has been expanded to the right and left sides toward the front road on the left and farther into the woods on the right side. Those persons who were not members of my ancestry are buried behind the fourth row.

I sat in the silent morning imagining in my heart the activity taking place in the swirling fog. I heard again the voices of my ancestors, telling their exploits and their stories. I am a storyteller who will tell our stories to coming generations and ensure that our history will not be forgotten. Listen, listen, listen and you will also hear *my ancestral voices*.

My Ancestral Voices

Romeo Blackburn, my great-grandfather, was born in the state of Virginia, the son of two slaves who lived on a plantation near Blackburn's Ford and Bull Run. His parents, Jack and Nancy, were descendants of slaves who were part of the cargo deposited at Manastoh, Virginia, located on the south bank of the James River, at the fall line opposite the state capital city of Richmond, on the north side of the river. The name of the city, Manastoh, was changed to Manchester and was an active city serving as the port of entry for slave ships principally in the eighteenth century.[1] The plantation, where Romeo and his family were enslaved, was situated in the area of the "first major land battle of the American Civil War."[2]

Jack and Nancy, a slave couple, were young and strong. Jack was eighteen and Nancy was thirteen when Romeo was born. The two slaves appeared so much in love that the owners named the baby Romeo after the male lover in Shakespeare's Romeo and Juliet.[3] Romeo was a strong baby, who was highly prized by the owners and greatly loved by his father and mother.

Great-Grandpa Romeo Blackburn told stories of his life when he was a slave on a Virginia plantation and how he came to Romulus, Alabama. He often spoke of the James River in Virginia. My father, L. S. Bailey, remembered the stories told by his grandfather. When Daddy was seventy-nine years old, he visited Virginia and was pleased to finally see the James River.

[1.] What//en.wikipedia.org/wiki/Manchester,_Virginia
[2.] Wikipedia, the free encyclopedia; "The First Battle of Bull Run"; page 1 of 12
[3.] http//shakespeare.miTedu/romeo_juliet/full.html

Life on the Plantation

Romeo, was eighteen years old when the slaves were freed in 1865. Now that he was a free man, he could go in search of his family who had been sold away from him eight years earlier.

Romeo lay awake in his cabin all through the last night of his life on the Virginia plantation. His eyes traced the lines of mud, chinking the crevices between the logs of the cabin in which he was born. The floor of the cabin was also made of packed earth that had been trodden under foot until it was as hard as brick baked in the sun.

This one-room cabin had been home for four people—his father, mother, sister, and him. For the first ten years of his life, they lived secure in their love for one another, believing that the slave owner would not sell any of them and that they would live out their lives together.

The bed upon which Romeo lay was once large enough for him to move around and curl up near his pillow. Now, it was two feet too short for his body. He placed a workbench at the foot of his bed upon which to rest his feet.

The firelight flickered in the old stone fireplace, throwing light and shadows upon the earthen floor and around the log cabin.

Here he lay, staring around the room. In the firelight, he imagined his mother making corn pones and boiling greens for supper. She cooked for her family after she spent the day in the big house, cooking for the plantation owner's family.

There was one window in the log cabin facing the open fields. A croaker sack, draped over the opening, was frayed from years of blowing in the wind. Through this window, Romeo could see where the years of toil and sweat of his people had taken place. This was where they tended the crops that were sold to make the owner wealthy. This was the place of drudgery and pain with no reward or succor for the slaves. This was their hell. This was their damnation, the place from which only death could free them. Their only hope of release was heaven. They would sing to relieve themselves of their hopeless lives.

Swing low, sweet Chariot, comin' fuh to carry me home.

They belonged to their slave masters. That fact was everywhere: in the subservient lives they lived, in the tattered clothing they wore, and in the constant search for enough food to keep body and soul together.

They were chattel, not men. They were expected to obey and never to challenge the words of their owners.

Romeo grew up in and out of the big house as a personal servant to the owner's children. From the age of five, he was required to minister to the children, to attend to their wants or needs, and to receive whippings in the children's stead when they committed behavior infractions. If the children broke a vase, Romeo received the punishment and was told he should have prevented the act of vandalism. If the children were not ready for supper on time or were not at the schoolroom when the tutor arrived or if they failed to keep their clothes clean, Romeo was punished because he had failed to take proper care of the children. Romeo tried to please Mr. Will, the slave owner, and his wife, but the children felt obliged to use him as the whipping boy as often as they could.

He saw himself entering the cabin, crying and rubbing his backsides. "She beat me 'cause Master Robert fell from the tree. I was 'spose to watch out for him," he sobbed. The mistress of the plantation had whipped him because her son had fallen out of the large elm tree in the front yard. It did not matter that the son was a year older than Romeo. As the whipping boy, he stood in the stead of his masters for any beatings that were meted out.

Romeo's mother folded him into her large lap and said, "Don't you fret none. It's goin' tuh be all right. Your mama loves you."

His mother would rub his body and kiss his face. Thus, she would wipe away his tears and soothe his hurt. He always felt better because he knew that his mother's love was unconditional and that no one could take it away.

When the slave owner's children were being tutored, Romeo sat quietly on the floor of the schoolroom. He absorbed the teacher's instruction with religious fervor. His mother told him to learn everything he could as quickly as he could and to impart his knowledge to his family. This he did, teaching his mother and sister to read and to write.

He was a bright boy, quick at learning and imbued with an intuition that kept him one step ahead of most troubles. Because of his quick wit and dexterity, he was very useful around the house. As a result, he was not sent to the field as the children grew old enough not to need him. Instead, he was given duties around the house and was required to run errands for the household.

During the early 1800s, mail was delivered on the waterways. The local settlement where Romeo lived was located on the James River.

Romeo was sent to the dock area on the James River to fetch the mail. This errand was beneficial to his physical and mental growth.

On his first trip, he was so engrossed in his surroundings—the trees, the animals, the flowers, the houses, and the shops—in the settlement that he was away from the plantation for several hours. When he returned, the mistress beat him until he could hardly sit down for several days.

When he was sent to get the mail again, he ran as far as he could and walked rapidly the remainder of the way. As time went by, he became a fast runner with enough endurance to take him to his destination and back to the plantation. Soon, he started running everywhere he went. He never seemed to walk; he just ran.

Romeo never lost his inquisitiveness regarding his surroundings. He still watched the trees, the flowers, the animals, and especially the lay of the land. He paid intense attention to the docks along the waterway. He was interested in the barges that traveled from the area up and down the James River. He watched as the barges were loaded from the docks. Negro men carried cargo onto the barges to be shipped to the Atlantic Ocean where it was placed on ships bound for other ports.

Every time he went to retrieve the mail, he stole glances at the comings and goings on the docks. He also practiced his reading skills by reading the addresses on the letters and packages obtained from the post. In time, his physical and mental characteristics were greatly enhanced.

Romeo's family remained intact for the first ten years of his life. His father worked in the fields and his mother was the cook.

It was the custom on the plantation that the owner and his visitors would play cards after dinner. On one occasion when guests were present at the plantation, the owner lost to his adversary, who exacted recompense of great value. The visitor demanded the ownership of the cook who had prepared the best meal he had ever eaten. To pay his debt, the slave plantation owner relinquished Nancy and sold her daughter and her husband to the guest but decided to keep Romeo as a servant to himself.

Mercifully, the couple and their daughter were taken away together, but they were extremely sad to leave Romeo behind. The family was taken to Gordo, Alabama.

Romeo was left without a family. The love and comfort experienced during the ten years that Romeo and his family had been together had ended. For the next eight years, he resorted to taking care of Mr. Will using the skills he had garnered while taking care of the slave owner's children. As a result, Romeo served as Mr. Will's valet and accompanied him to various destinations during the Civil War.

Freedom, Freedom

Freedom over me. And before I be a slave, I be buried in my grave, and go home to my Lord, and be free.[4]

The morning had dawned long ago, but the darkness lingered, shrouded in a cloudy mist. A horse and a man stood at the end of the lane, obscured by the misty haze, barely visible to the plantation owner who stood on the front porch of his plantation house.

Mr. Will, as he was called by the slaves on the Virginia plantation, was of the third generation of slave owners. During the years of slavery, one-hundred-plus souls had been owned and put to work on this plantation, making large profits on tobacco, rice, and cotton for the slave owner.

Times had changed for Mr. Will. The War Between the States had come and gone. President Abraham Lincoln gave consideration to the freeing of slaves in the new United States. According to public records, the US Senate passed the Thirteenth Amendment to the Constitution on April 8, 1864, to officially abolish and continue to prohibit slavery and involuntary servitude, except as a punishment for a crime. The Thirteenth Amendment was ratified in December 1865, thus freeing the slaves.

This amendment was the first of the Reconstruction Amendments.[5] When the field slaves realized that they were free to leave the plantation, they walked away toward the north. Now only a handful of Negroes were left on the plantation. Those who

---

[4.] Old Negro spiritual "Oh, Freedom"
[5.] Wikipedia

remained were experienced in housework. None could till the fields. The ex-slave owner stood musing over his plight.

The horse stomped his right front foot, pawing at the earth in frustration for having to wait in the cold morning mist. He was the last of a line of pure-bred horses that had been owned by the family over the years. Mr. Will rode this horse when he went "to help out in the war." He would be back very shortly, he told his wife as he rode away from his rich, thriving slave-holding plantation.

The Northern and the Southern soldiers fought the first major land battle of what became known as the American Civil War, not far from his home at a place called Bull Run. Mr. Will joined his fellow Southerners to repel the interlopers and to send them back up north.

Along with the other Southern soldiers who survived, he came home defeated to find nearly all of his slaves gone north. Although the plantation had been spared the usual burning, it had been looted and pillaged. The stock had been taken, and the interior of the house and its furnishings had been ransacked.

Mr. Will sighed as he looked down the lane. He was ready for his morning ride to look over the fields, a ride he and his ancestors before him had taken each morning. There was no good reason for him to check the fields and the workers because there was no work being done on the plantation. However, he would take the ride again because he must. It was the duty of the landowner to take the morning ride, to survey the land, and to know that he was "to the manor born."[6] He was a Southern gentleman.

The man who stood by the horse's head was as erect as a marble statue. He was six feet, four inches tall. His body was strong with taunt muscles. He was blue-black in color with straight black hair. His eyes were jet-black, large, and slightly slanted. The inside of his mouth and the inner parts of his lips were a perfect pink, which formed around pure-white teeth. This trait would be evident in his descendants for generations to come.

[6.] *http://www.phrases.org.uk/meanings/to-the-manner-born.html*

It was said that his ancestors were stolen from West Africa, in the country of Senegal, by Arab and white slavers, which explained the dark skin, the thick straight hair, the aquiline nose, dark slanted eyes, and his tall muscular build. His sculptured jaws depicted a tough, disciplined will. He stood with his head held erect, facing down the road away from the plantation. He seemed deep in thought. His name was Romeo.

The day would wait no longer. Mr. Will stepped off the porch and sauntered down to the man and the horse.

"Morning, Romy," he said, using a familiarity that subjected the man to a shortened version of his name.

"Morning, sir," Romeo replied without moving a muscle.

Leaving the Plantation

As the owner reached for his horse's reins, Romeo spoke again, "Sir, I am leaving today." Mr. Will dropped the reins and stared at Romeo who was the best worker left on the plantation and had remained with Mr. Will during the Civil War after his own spouse died and his other family members were either dead or had gone away.

"What will I do without you, boy?" he asked.

"I don't know, sir. I'm free now, and I must be going to find my family."

Romeo released the horse's reins and walked away. Footsteps could be heard receding in the fog. Faster and faster the footsteps went until they became the sound of running—running faster and faster. Romeo ran toward his future.

Going Home

Romeo Blackburn's destination was Alabama where he hoped to find his mother, father, and sister. Since the age of ten when his mother, father, and sister were sold to a slave owner in Alabama, Romeo had corresponded with his mother. They were able to execute this activity through his responsibility for fetching the mail and his mother's insistence upon being the slave who received the mail at the Alabama plantation. Because she could read and sort the mail to each recipient, she was afforded this privilege.

An old atlas left in the plantation library provided Romeo with the information he needed to prepare himself for his journey to Alabama. He knew his journey would be along the waterways and through the woods, towns, and cities. Romeo knew the dangers he faced, being a Negro man traveling toward the South so soon after the Civil War. White citizens were angry about losing the war, losing their homes, losing their way of life, and having lost their slave workers. He heard about an organization called the Ku Klux Klan, established in 1865 in Tennessee. It was founded as a local social club but quickly became a vehicle of resistance against Reconstruction. It focused on intimidating freed slaves, using terror and violence. Romeo knew that this group was his greatest enemy.[7]

Romeo needed money for his journey. He had been intrigued by the workers on the James River docks since he was a child. It was natural for him to want to become a dockworker on the James River docks.

[7.] http,//www.johnnyleeclary.com/files/page.php?p=21

The James River was situated near the Prince William County area where Romeo lived. The James River would not take him in the direction he wanted to go to find his family; it ran east and west. He needed to go south. However, he planned to work on the James River as long as it took to earn enough money to finance his journey. Then he would find his way to Alabama and to his mother, father, and sister. Wherever his family lived would be his home. Romeo was going home.

Romeo arrived at the docks. He stood staring at the Negro men loading cargo onto the barges. "Hey, you there, boy!" a voice called out. The shout was repeated until Romeo realized that the white foreman was calling him.

"Yes, sir," Romeo replied.

"You willing to work, boy?" asked the caller.

"Yes, sir," said Romeo.

"Well, come over here. What's your name?"

"Romeo."

"Romeo, what?"

"Romeo Blackburn, sir," he said.

Romeo's Blackburn surname was given to his ancestors when the plantation on which they lived had been owned by the Blackburn family. The Blackburn family moved from Virginia to North Carolina in 1779.[8] They left a legacy of the Blackburn's name, which was still used as the name of a river crossing called the Blackburn's Ford and as the surname of Romeo's ancestors.

Romeo Blackburn was hired to work on the docks on the James River. He was on his way. He had a job and he had a name. He would work and he would earn enough money to find his family. The day came when Romeo had earned sufficient funds to start his journey.

He would walk all the way. He exited Virginia and entered Tennessee near the area now called Bristol. He made his way to the Tennessee River where he took the Great Indian Warpath Trail called the Upper Creek Path from Bridgeport, which roughly follows the same route as the Tennessee River until he came to Alabama.

---

8. Francis Blackburn Hilliard, "Blackburns—Today and Yesterday," pages 16-17

He continued on the Warpath, following the bank of the Tennessee River. He traveled through Running Water Valley where he found the Cumberland Trail. There, he traveled south on the Cumberland Trail through the Cumberland Valley and reached Gadsden, Alabama.

Romeo left the Warpath Trail as it veered southeast, for he needed to go due south. He found the Black Warrior River and followed it south to Tuscaloosa, Alabama.

According to his atlas map, Romeo needed to travel west from the cities of Tuscaloosa and Northport. There, he was to cross a bridge between the two cities. Unfortunately, when he arrived, the bridge was in disrepair, having been destroyed during the Civil War by General Craxton's Raiders, a group of southern soldiers that approached Tuscaloosa through Northport.[9]

Romeo endured the stares and innuendoes as he was ferried across the river. He quickly lost himself in the underbrush when he arrived in Northport. There, he waited until night fell. It was October, and a big harvest moon lit his way. He had learned how to calculate his directions by the shadow of the sun or the moon or when the day was sunny and when the moon was bright enough to cast a shadow at night. This he learned when he traveled with Mr. Will in the war. He placed a stick into the ground at a level spot where his shadow was cast. He marked the shadow tip with a rock and he determined his direction going west from the first shadow mark.[10]

When Romeo could discern that the town had closed and everyone had gone home, he crept from his hiding place and headed west by the wagon road leading in that direction. He walked for miles throughout the night. Late in the night, he heard dogs barking in the distance. His mother had warned him about being caught in the woods by white hunters or the KKK. He began to run to place distance between himself and the dog owners. Being a fast and enduring runner, he covered many miles before he grew tired. On he ran until he could hear the dogs no more. He crossed the Sipsey

---

[9]. http,//spillerfurniture.com/store locations/1/Spiller+Furniture+of+Northp orThtml
[10]. http,//www.armystudyguide.com/content/army_board_study_guide_topics/land_navigation_map_reading/field-expedient-methods-of-determiningdirection.shtml

River and continued to run until he was utterly exhausted. He fell by the trunk of a large oak tree and was asleep when his head hit the ground.

Morning came. Above his head, bright colors flashed in a blinding light. Golden wings fluttered in a heavenly breeze. Bright golden beings moved up and down on golden strands. Their wings glistened in the heavenly light. They fluttered to and fro. As the angel-like beings flew up and down golden streets, they joined in a heavenly chorus, voices blending as only angels could sing. They sang to the glory of God. Romeo could hear his mother's voice singing in the choir. Had she died and gone to heaven before he arrived? Had he died in the night and joined her around God's throne? He lay there wondering, bathed in a golden glow.

Something fell upon his face; an angel touched him with its golden wing. Another angel, another wing, gently brushed his face. He slowly became aware of his surroundings. Golden leaves were falling from the large oak tree under which he had slept. Golden rays of the sun shone through the tree branches, illuminating brightly colored leaves that danced in the wind. Golden rays of sunshine reached from heaven to the ground below, creating a heavenly highway. He lay in golden splendor and listened to the heavenly choir. As he became fully awake, he realized he could still hear the angels singing. It was his mother's voice leading the choir.

> *Swing low, sweet chariot,*
> *Coming fuh to carry me home. Swing low, sweet chariot,*
> *Comin' fuh to carry me home.*

His mother's voice led the verses, and the congregation followed.

> Mother: *I looked over Jordan and what did I see?*
> Congregation: *Comin' fuh to carry me home.*
> Mother: *A band of angels comin' after me.*
> Congregation: *Comin' fuh to carry me home.*

His mother's voice rang out, loud and clear, even after he had fully awakened. He looked around. From where was her voice coming? He turned toward his left, and the sound became louder. He crawled toward the sound, and it became even louder, still. He jumped to his feet and began to run toward the sound of his mother's voice.

As he broke through the trees and the underbrush, there in an outdoor clearing, under a brush arbor, sat a congregation of Negro people singing and praising God. They were worshipping in what was called a Brush Arbor Church.

He halted in his haste to reach his mother for fear he would startle the people. He crept forward slowly. Then he began to run again until he was in the midst of the congregation. There, sitting on logs that had been felled and placed in rows facing a makeshift pulpit was the church congregation which included his mother, father, and sister.

The preacher was first to see Romeo. "Come forward, brother. We are free people, praising God for our deliverance. Join us," the preacher said.

The congregation turned toward Romeo. There were strange eyes in the group, and there were loving eyes upon his face. His mother, father, and sister shouted with joy and embraced him. "My baby done come home!" shouted his mother joyfully.

She sat down on the nearest log, and Romeo buried his face in her lap. She said, "Don't you fret none. It's goin' tuh be all right. Your mama loves you." She embraced him and wiped away his tears. It was then that Romeo knew he was home.

Land for Sale. Land for Sale

Signs were everywhere: Land for Sale. After the Civil War, former slave owners were land rich and cash poor. They needed money to survive. Their vast land holdings were like millstones around their necks. Without workers to till the land, bushes and brambles took over the fields.

During Reconstruction, immediately after the end of the Civil War, many Negro men earned the money to buy the unused land.

Romeo Blackburn remained with his mother, father, and sister for one year, working on the farm of his parents' past owner where they shared harvest crops. The new method by which white landowners made a living without slave labor was called sharecropping. Sharecropping became a system of agriculture in which a landowner allowed a tenant to use the land in return for a share of the crops produced on the land.[11] When he had acquired funds to buy land, Great-Grandpa Romeo paid 125 dollars for 250 acres of land at 50 cents an acre. He bought the land from an ex-slave owner named Fred Robinson. Before the Civil War, the Robinson family, from whom the land was bought, owned many slaves who farmed their plantation. Great-Grandpa Romeo bought the land that covered the western section of Robinson's holdings, which was located in Romulus, Alabama, between Romulus Road and Buhl, Alabama. The land was rich in timber and game. There were creeks, springs, a mountain, and ample flat land ready for farming.

[11.] http,//en.wikipedia.org/wiki/Sharecropping

Great-Grandpa Romeo Blackburn was not a recipient of the 40 acres suggested as a payment to former slaves who were freed and protected by the Union Armies, who occupied areas of the South, nor did he receive a mule[12] for plowing his land. Had Romeo remained in his original home in Virginia, he might have been in competition for receiving some of the lands under this plan that included the islands from Charleston to the south and the abandoned rice fields along the rivers for 30 miles back from the sea.[13]

However, the plan to give freed slaves 40 acres and a mule was vetoed after Abraham Lincoln's assassination by Lincoln's successor, President Andrew Johnson. The veto did not mention the 40 acres and the mule as if the offer had never existed. The former slaves had to find other means of starting their own family farms.

The day came when Great-Grandpa Romeo had established himself as a landowner and a family man. Romeo married Lucy Wells, the sister of Hiter Wells. Together, he and Hiter later founded Holly Spring Missionary Baptist Church. Romeo and Lucy had nine children.

Great-Grandpa Romeo built his home a half-mile from the main road and settled down with his wife and children. He built a large log home made from pine logs cut from his land. The logs were assembled to form a double-pen dogtrot-type house that was typical of southern log houses of this era. Unlike the one-room log cabins used by slaves, Romeo built his house to consist of four rooms. There were two rooms on each side, separated by an open breezeway—the dogtrot.

His mother and father lived with him until they died. His sister married a young farmer in Gordo, Alabama where she remained throughout her life, leading to other members of the family going to Gordo years later.

Trees were felled and the land was cleared during his first winter on the land. As years went by, the cleared acreage became a vast farm on which cotton and corn, as well as ribbon and sorghum cane, were

---

12. en.wikipedia.org/wiki/40_acres_and_a_mule
13. en.wikipedia.org/wiki/40_acres_and_a_mule

grown. Great-Grandfather Romeo also grew tobacco for his own use and for those in the community who did not grow their own. His large animal stock included cows, horses, mules, goats, hogs, turkeys, and chickens. Wild game grew in profusion on the mountain and in the surrounding forest.

At first, Romeo's parents, Jack and Nancy, lived on one side of the house. As the children were born, they slept in the backroom and the grandparents lived in the front room. Romeo and Lucy continued to occupy the front room across the breezeway. The kitchen was extended farther back on Romeo and Lucy's side of the house. The children grew up to occupy the two rooms on their side after the grandparents had passed away.

Great-great-grandparents Jack and Nancy were buried in the cemetery near the Brush Arbor Church that Romeo and Hiter Wells founded.

According to public record, it was the year 1874 when support from the Union Army and the Freedmen Bureau was ebbing in the Southern territory of the new United States of America. The Freedmen Bureau had protected the enfranchisement of freed slaves since 1866 during the era of Reconstruction by considering a freedman to be 100 percent of a man instead of three-fifth percent of a man. But by 1874, just eight years later, the freed slaves were being disenfranchised and reduced in standing once again.

With the Compromise of 1877, the disenfranchisement of the Freedmen was complete. The freedmen, again, became second-class citizens. White Southerners labeled the following period as Redemption. White-dominated state legislatures enacted Jim Crow laws and disfranchised most blacks and many poor whites through the enactment of a combination of constitutional amendments and electoral laws. It was during this time that the White Democratic Party imposed a system of white supremacy and second-class citizenship for blacks. Jim Crow became the law of the South.

Let My People Go

Go down, Moses, way down in Egypt land. Tell old Pharaoh to let my people go.

During slavery, balconies called slave lofts had been built in the rear of the white churches to accommodate those slaves who became Christians. Negro Christians attended white churches with their slave masters. Some joined the church with letters of Christian discipleship from the white pastors or their owners, and some joined churches based on their experience as Christians.

When they attended the white churches, the slaves sat in the slave lofts. After slavery, the free Negro people were excluded from white churches. Southern whites, who could no longer exploit the Negro people for their labor, refused to allow the freedmen to attend the white churches, therefore requiring Negroes to create churches of their own.

Romeo had found his family in a brush arbor, worshipping and praising God. It was to cathedrals in the woods that the Negro people had been relegated.

Tall pine trees formed the church spires, pointing fingers toward heaven. Oaktree trunks formed the colonnades through which they marched, entering their places of worship. Felled logs formed the pews upon which they sat, clapping their hands and stomping their feet to the rhythm of their songs. They read the scripture and prayed long heartrending prayers. They shouted and spoke in tongues as God commanded them. Into this holy place, God sent the Holy Spirit to accompany them on their journey.

Be not dismayed what 'ere betides, God will take care of you.

This they sang, and this they believed. When they left for home, they were fortified for the week ahead.

Romeo Blackburn was born a slave and lived in slavery until he was eighteen years old. Yet he had learned to read and write and to perform arithmetical calculations. He had been an aide to his slave master during the Civil War, and after his slave mistress died, had managed the household accounts on the plantation. He knew how to manage his affairs during these dark days.

Romeo Blackburn believed that God had blessed him with great bounty. He was a landowner in Romulus, Alabama. He had completed his journey from Virginia and had found his father, mother, and sister in Gordo, Alabama. He had taken his father and mother to Romulus to live with him and his wife, Lucy. His farm, bought from Fred Robinson, was now a thriving concern. He knew how blessed he was to have made a prosperous life for himself and his family.

He strove to demonstrate that he was thankful for his blessings and to fulfill the requirements of himself and his people, which were to acquire land, to work hard, to worship God, to believe in Jesus Christ, to pray, and to live Christian lives.

Great-Grandpa Romeo Blackburn, brothers Hiter Wells, Allen Foster, and Frank Knox joined in the establishment of a deacon ministry of which Great-Grandpa Romeo Blackburn Sr. was the first deacon.

The membership of the ministry grew. Meetings were held in a brush arbor or rotated from house to house. Revival meetings were held in the fall of the year when converts to Christianity were baptized in the nearby creek. Communion commemorating the body and blood of Jesus was performed whenever visiting ministers were in attendance.

Shandry C. Dorroh gives an account of the burial site for members of the first church of my ancestors, "Near the Brush Arbor Church location, there is a cemetery, marked by three gravestones, identified for members of the Harper and Foster families. There is evidence of many more graves in this cemetery. Some have field stones with no inscriptions. Some can only be determined by the indentions in orderly rows. This cemetery is overgrown with large trees."[14]

It is opined that great-great grandpa and great-great grandma, Jack and Nancy Blackburn, are buried in this cemetery. Their grave markers may have been made of wood and have since rotted away.

As the membership increased in the deacon ministry, more space and a suitable place of worship were required. Romeo was confident that with the help of visiting ministers and the cooperation of many faithful people, they could organize to build a house of worship.

The small congregation followed the dictates of the Bible in Psalm 127:1, "Unless the Lord builds the house, those who build it labor in vain."[15] They relied on their belief in God and their acceptance of Jesus Christ as their personal Savior to guide them in building a church. Ten acres of land, located in Romulus near Fosters and Ralph, Alabama, were bought from Deacon Hiter Wells. Upon this land, the Holly Spring Missionary Baptist Church was erected. The church was a wood frame edifice built on the order of the white churches. It had a slave loft which the Negro congregants called the Balcony. The congregation moved from the original site in the brush arbor to the new church in the year of our Lord 1874.

Great-Grandpa Romeo was born into slavery. He died a free man. He was not only a prosperous landowner; he was a leader of the Romulus community and the lead founder of Holly Spring Missionary Baptist Church. The church still stands as a monument to the accomplishment of Great-Grandfather Romeo Blackburn.

As Romeo's sons became adults, they were given portions of the farm for their families. The eldest son refused his birthright, went to Gordo where his aunt lived, and never returned home. He later went to Georgia where members of his family still live. Louis, the next eldest son, moved back to the home house, so-called as it was the first house built on the property. He inherited it when his father passed away. The land was divided between Louis, Romeo Junior,

---

[14.] Romulus, Historical and Genealogical Gleamings Concerning the Community of Romulus Tuscaloosa County Alabama, Compiled by Shandry C. Dorroh
[15.] Psalm 127:1

Robert, and John. The daughters did not inherit. They were required to marry well.

When Great-Grandma Lucy died and was buried in the Brush Arbor Cemetery, Great-Grandpa Romeo married an Indian woman. Children were born to the couple. However, they did not become a part of the Romulus family as they moved away and all contact was lost. I found a granddaughter and a great-grandchild from this marriage in the year 2005.

Public records show that Great-Grandpa Romeo Blackburn was born in 1841 and died in March 1926 at the age of eighty-five. He was buried in the Holly Spring Missionary Baptist Church Cemetery in the center of what is now the fourth row back from the church. His children and grandchildren are buried to the right of his grave and going forward to the first row is where the last of my ancestors, my father, L. S. Bailey, is buried.

Cousin Sterling's Mountain

As the Appalachian Mountain chain moves southward, it dwindles to a series of bumps on the national landscape. Some bumps are hill size and others are small mountains. One of the small mountains bearing Sterling Foster's name lies between Romulus and Ralph, Alabama.

Cousin Sterling Foster, son of Malinda Foster and Hiter Wells, bought the mountain and the surrounding land. It is not known how or why he bought the land and the mountain. However, it is suspected that it was to commemorate his mother's life.

When Malinda contracted smallpox, she was quarantined on the mountain. She was thankful to be a survivor of the epidemic. Malinda Foster, cousin Sterling's mother, was born a slave on the Bailey Plantation in Mississippi. This was the same plantation on which my grandfather, William Bailey, lived. Malinda's family moved to Romulus and lived at the foot of the mountain that cousin Sterling later bought.

When Malinda and her family lived on the Bailey Plantation, she was given the responsibility of taking care of the babies whose mothers worked in the cotton fields. The babysitting responsibility remained after the slaves were freed, for those workers who remained on the Bailey farm. It was during this time that Malinda took care of Grandpa William.

During her time as the babysitter of the plantation, several children became ill. Knowing that she would be blamed for the children's illness and that she was expected to keep the children safe, she gave four of the children medicine that she thought would make them well by the time their parents came home from the field. She gave three children a strong dose because they were more ill than the fourth child. The latter child was given a small dose to keep him from coming down with the illness.

When the parents came home, Malinda told them that she had given the children the medicine she took from the top shelf in one house. When the medicine was revealed, it was found to be strychnine. Instead of making them well, three of the children died and the fourth child was severely ill for some time. Malinda could not read.

Malinda was twelve years old when the slaves were freed. She outlived the scandal of the death of the three children to whom she gave strychnine. Malinda and her family moved to Romulus in an area near the mountain. There was a creek that ran at the base of the mountain along which the Foster, Wells, and Reed families established a postslavery community for Negroes.

Smallpox

According to historical records, there was a smallpox epidemic in Alabama in 1874–75, during which 990 cases of smallpox were reported with 262 deaths. Of this number, 204 of the deaths were among the Negro population. There were cases of smallpox in Tuscaloosa, Alabama. Aunt Malinda was one of the victims.

Malinda awoke experiencing fever and chills. Her muscles ached and a flat reddish-purple rash covered her chest, abdomen, and back. After three days, her fever dropped. This respite lasted for two days. During which time, the doctor was summoned.

The doctor treated the white people with tender loving care but provided only consultation to the Negro people. He asked about Malinda's symptoms. The family told the doctor that she had had chills and fever for three days. Now after a respite of two days, the fevers had returned and she was covered over with a bumpy rash on her feet, hands, back, and face. The doctor immediately concluded that she had the dreaded smallpox disease. "You all take this gal up on the mountain. There are some people up there who can take care of her. She might survive and she might not." This was the doctor's prescription for such as Malinda. Malinda was taken up the mountain and left with two men who had been quarantined there with smallpox.

It was said that old Ben, the first person who went up the mountain, was an ex-slave who lived on the Foster plantation. He worked for the landowner as a caretaker and acted as cook and guide during hunting season. A hunting lodge had been built on the mountain, stocked with supplies and furnished to accommodate the white hunters. Old Ben left Mobile, Alabama, because of the epidemic and came to Romulus. He had seen people in Mobile suffering from the disease and recognized the symptoms. Now he was ailing, but no one had to diagnose his condition. He left his home for he realized that he had contracted smallpox himself.

He had contact with others in the Alabama community before he knew he was sick. One was Malinda Foster. After he made his way to the cabin, he lay abed for three days, racked with fever and pain. His body was covered with pustules, and he had trouble seeing.

Ben knew of the foodstuff that had been left after the last hunting party used the cabin. Although most of the food consisted of stale bacon and molded bread, it sustained him throughout his illness.

Another Negro man stumbled into the cabin yard, the very day Ben's fever broke for the second time. Several days passed, and Ben was able to catch a rabbit and several fish from the stream. He fed the second victim and tended the victim's fever and chills.

Upon hearing a meowing sound around the cabin wall, Ben called out, "Who's there?" He heard the sound again. He followed the direction of the sound and found Malinda lying against the cabin.

Ben took Malinda into the cabin and put her in one of the beds. He now had two patients whom he treated as best he knew how. He packed quilts around them when they had chills and bathed them in cool water from the creek when their fevers rose. He did not leave the cabin because he knew that once he was healed, he was immune from catching the disease again.

Malinda's fever returned, and her rash progressed. The bumps became filled with pus. Malinda and the other occupant of the mountain cabin were helplessly ill.

The day after Malinda came up the mountain, a call was heard. "Yahoo! Yahoo!" The call was repeated over and over until Ben called back. "We brought food," the voice called from beyond the trees.

Ben drew near to the caller. There on a tree stump, in the middle of a meadow of yellow flowers, was a basket of food including vegetables, fruits, and fresh meat. The caller ran back into the woods as Ben approached the stump. "God be praised," Ben whispered.

The caller said, "I'll bring some more food in a few days." Then the caller asked, "Did anybody die yet?" Ben was glad to yell back, "No!"

As time went by, several other smallpox victims came to the mountain. Ben fed them with fish from the stream and rabbits and squirrels that he caught in traps. The fresh food also continued to be brought to the tree stump. The caller alerted Ben of his presence. "Yahoo," he would call. Then the good Samaritan would run back into the woods.

For weeks, the food continued to be brought and "Yahoo" could be heard. After the death of the first person, the question became, "Who died last night?"

When a smallpox victim died, Ben was saddened to relate the name of the victim who had died. The message was carried back to the community where the family and loved ones mourned their losses. The bodies were buried on the mountain.

Finally, when the question came, "Who died last night?" the answer came, "No one died last night." This answer was repeated for days until it was determined that the epidemic was over.

Smallpox eventually scabbed over on each survivor, leaving permanently scarred pockmarks when the scabs dropped off. These were the pockmarks that were visible on Aunt Malinda for the remainder of her life.

As time passed, Malinda gave birth to a son whose father was Hiter Wells. Her son, Sterling, bought the mountain and the land at its base. Malinda lived with her son, Sterling, and his wife, Neely. She never got married.

Although Aunt Malinda appeared ancient, she was sturdy and strong. I observed her in the 1940s still attending church. She wore slavery attire—a gray cotton dress that reached to the top of her black buttoned-up high-top shoes, a gray cap with ruffles around her face, a white starched apron, and a plaid wool shawl. Smallpox pockmarks were visible on all exposed areas of her body.

On one Sunday, near the fourth of July, boys who attended Holly Spring Missionary Baptist Church brought firecrackers to church, unbeknownst to their elders. As the congregation was getting out of their wagons, hitching their mules, and greeting each other before going inside, the boys sought out a likely victim that would be most frightened by the blasts.

The pyrotechnical boys picked old Aunt Malinda who was leaning heavily on her walking cane. The boys lit several firecrackers and tossed them under Aunt Malinda's long gray dress. She was greatly alarmed by the sound of gunshots going off under her skirt. She forgot her walking cane and jumped high off the ground several times and cried, "Shit! Shit! Shit!"

The boys were caught by their ears by every adult on the grounds. Women and men joined in the ear-grabbing. Nearly picking the boys up by their ears, the adults took the boys into the woods where they were soundly thrashed. Even those who did not have a boy in the crowd assisted in the thrashing and blessing out. That was the last time I saw Aunt Malinda at church although she lived on for many more years.

Vignette: Retracing History

In 2006, at the age of seventy-one, I took members of my family— my husband, Albert; my son, Tari; my granddaughter, Heather; and my cousin, Cleo Blackburn—up on Sterling's mountain. Cleo and I grew up in Romulus, Alabama, and we remembered people who lived around Sterling's mountain.

We trekked in from the road, through the woods, over a meadow covered with yellow daisies, up the mountain, and through a deeper forest.

After several hours of walking, we came to a creek. It was overgrown with fern and bramble. The creek water was brackish and smelled of history and days that have gone by. Trees grew around the perimeter of the creek that disappeared underneath as the stream flowed down toward the Tombigbee River.

When we reached the creek, we realized that we had gone too far. "What are we looking for?" my husband asked.

"We are looking for cousin Sterling's house," said Cleo.

"You mean to tell me that cousin Sterling's house is still up here?" I asked.

"It should be here. Cousin Sterling died over fifty years ago, but the house was still here for a long time," Cleo responded.

My husband, Albert, revealed, "I saw a house back there on the left."

We turned back with renewed energy. There, on the right of our retreat, a house could be discerned. It was not a house as one would expect a house to be. It was a four-story structure that hung juxtaposed in the trees. House beams hung at odd angles high in the utmost branches. A rafter here, a beam there, a plank hanging sideways—all the parts of the house had been stuck in the branches. As the trees grew from the floor through the roof, they carried the whole house skyward.

The wood had not rotted; instead, it had petrified into stone. The trees, from which this wood had been carved so many years ago, were from virgin trees that had grown from the beginning of time. They were bereft of pores, strong and unyielding. Without pores into which moisture could penetrate, this wood did not rot; it became stone. There, high up in the trees hung a stone house.

Only the fireplace remained on the ground as it was made of large rocks cemented together. An iron stove stood resolute in the corner. The house had consisted of one large room.

This was not a house. It was a cabin. It was a one-room cabin, such as might have been made for a hunting lodge. Had we stumbled upon the cabin in which Malinda and Jim were quarantined with smallpox over 130 years ago? It was evident that this was so.

As I stood in the cabin, the past rose around me. There, on one side of the room lay Malinda on a cot with sores all over her body. On the other side lay another victim and another. Old Ben stood by the stove cooking fish, rabbit, or squirrel. Vegetables lay on the table that no longer existed but could be imagined as part of this ancient scene.

Old Ben stopped his culinary duties long enough to put a cover on the victim with chills or to wash the other's face with cold water to reduce the fever. He bent by each and urged them to eat some of the broth or heartier food if they could. Old Ben cajoled each patient, in turn, urging them to live.

I broke from my reverie to realize that it was time to go if we were to leave the mountain before the sun went down. None of us wanted to leave, yet none of us wanted to be on the mountain in the dark. We took pictures of the area and walked away. I looked back to see the cabin hanging in the trees.

As we walked down the mountain, we grew tired and sat down beneath a pine tree, on a bed of pine needles. We were at the edge of the meadow with the yellow flowers. I must have dozed off when I heard, "Yahoo, yahoo!" coming from across the meadow. I looked in the direction of the voice and saw a stump laden with food: cabbage, tomatoes, potatoes, apples, and meat. The caller went back into the woods as a voice was heard coming from the other direction, "Yahoo, yahoo!"

"Who died last night?" I heard the first voice call from across the meadow and across the years. "No one died last night. We are coming home. We are well and won't make anyone else sick. God has spared some of us. Go spread the good news," old Ben replied from across a span of 130 years.

I awoke and dried tears that had run down my face. I could come back to the present time and know that my ancestors had survived slavery, Jim Crow, and the smallpox epidemic.

Not only did Malinda survive but her son also bought the whole mountain and we still call it cousin Sterling's mountain. Malinda and her son returned to the mountain, built a house, cleared land in the lower levels, and started a large community around the foot of the mountain. The mountain is still owned by a member of my family by the name of Hawkins.

Unconfirmed Historical Record

My grandfather, William Bailey, said that Aunt Malinda was 14 years old when he was born, two years after the slaves were freed. That would make Aunt Malinda 12 years old in 1865, the year that the slaves were freed. There is a Malinda Foster in the Holly Spring Cemetery who died in 1965. If that is Aunt Malinda's grave, she died at the age of 112.

Uncle Louis Blackburn

Uncle Louis Blackburn was the oldest child of Romeo and Lucy Blackburn who remained in Romulus, Alabama. He was my grandmother's brother. Great-Grandpa's two oldest children who were listed in the 1890 census were not seen by any living person during my lifetime. I was told that the oldest son left home early in life and moved to Georgia where two of his great-grandchildren now live. One is a doctor and one is a lawyer.

Uncle Louis grew up as the son of a wealthy Negro man, Romeo Blackburn Sr., whose wealth was acquired during the period of Reconstruction after the Civil War.

Great-Grandfather Romeo Blackburn taught his children that they were as good as anyone else. They were a proud people whose pride emanated from being a member of the Blackburn family.

Louis grew into a strong black man. Realizing that his options were limited by his race but believing in what his father taught him, he pushed the envelope of all possibilities and lived the life of a free country farmer.

Even though his father was a landowner and required little support from the white population of Romulus, Louis still experienced racial hatred and fear of being targeted by groups such as the Ku Klux Klan. He was used to segregation and institutionalized prejudices.

Uncle Louis married Sally, a girl from the community. He built a three-room house on the family farm near his mother and father. There, he and Sally set up housekeeping and farmed the acreage given to him by his father, great-grandfather Romeo Blackburn.

Louis and Sally hoped and prayed for children. Years went by and no children were born to the couple. Whether the two of them agreed to have children some other way is not known. Nevertheless, Louis begat two children by his wife's sister, Stella, who lived in their home. The son was named Fred, and the daughter was named Willie. Aunt Sally took the two babies and raised them as her own. Stella married Mr. Hood and had eight more children. One of the daughters, Annie Lee, became my stepmother whom we called Annie Lee Mama.

Stella later died of a heart attack and sunstroke while plowing a field that she and her husband had rented as sharecroppers. It was said publicly that Mr. Hood found the work too hard and left Stella and their eight children to fend for themselves. It was later revealed that he went to Tuscaloosa, Alabama, twenty-five miles away. The children never saw him again.

Many years later, Annie Lee Mama was told that her father had died. She refused to go to the funeral and damned him to hell for leaving her mother and the children, thus causing her mother to work herself to death.

After Stella's death, Aunt Sally and Uncle Louis took the remaining eight children and continued raising them until Aunt Sally died. Before she died, a baby was born to one of her nieces. This child was called Trick. When the child's mother married Uncle Ben Stewart's son, Elijah, she left the baby with Aunt Sally.

When Great-Grandpa Romeo died, Uncle Louis and Aunt Sally moved into Great-Grandpa Romeo's house and filled it to the brim with Stella's children and grandchild. Aunt Sally, who could not have children of her own, participated in the rearing of eleven children.

The two sisters, Sally and Stella, are buried in the Holly Spring Missionary Baptist Church Cemetery. I once went with my stepmother, Annie Lee Mama, to clean the weeds from her mother's grave. I remember that the grave was located in the back of the cemetery, well behind the front four rows. Aunt Sally is buried beside her husband, Uncle Louis Blackburn, inside the Blackburn plots in the first four rows of the cemetery.

The Unwanted Visitor

The male members of Holly Spring Missionary Baptist Church would gather under the pine trees and around the drinking well in the front yard of the church and tell stories that had occurred during the past week. It was a contest to be the one who could tell the most hilarious or interesting story each Sunday. The following story was told by Uncle Louis.

Uncle Louis sat under the big oak tree in his front yard, reading his Bible and dozing off during his afternoon nap. It was the previous fourth Sunday when the Holly Spring Missionary Baptist Church did not have a scheduled church meeting. He sat dozing, waiting for Aunt Sally and the oldest girls to finish cooking supper.

The front yard was shaded by a large oak tree that predated the house. The tree was there in 1870 when Great-Grandpa Romeo built his home and dominated the yard as a place for family gatherings. It was a playground for the children, providing branches for the children to climb and one strong limb from which to hang their swing. It provided shade for rest after working all day in the fields or for napping on a lazy Sunday afternoon.

Beyond the tree's shade, a large patch of cacti grew. Each year, it produced prickly pears for the making of jelly and jam. As Uncle Louis dozed off to sleep underneath the tree, a very large snake chose to slide across one of the low-hanging limbs. The snake lost its mooring and crashed down onto Uncle Lewis, who, upon awaking, found himself covered with the largest snake he had ever seen. According to Uncle Louis, the snake was over eight feet long and was as large as his upper arm.

It was conjectured that this very large snake had made its home in the hollow of the oak tree. There, the snake must have lived, year after year, eating the rats and squirrels that crawled up the tree intending to gather acorns. No one had ever seen the snake.

Both Uncle Louis and the snake were startled by the sudden contact with each other. Both became engrossed in separation from its quarry, yet each movement served to tighten their grips. They each flung themselves in a direction that became the direction of the other. Uncle Louis tried to throw the snake away from his body while the snake flung itself around Uncle Louis's neck. An attempt to remove the snake from around his neck resulted in his moving the snake around his waist. The snake appeared to grip the solid form to prevent its crashing to the ground.

For what appeared to be hours but was only a few minutes, the two struggled with each other, each trying to flee. Uncle Louis wanted to divest himself of this unwelcome visitor and to find a way to kill it.

While the struggle continued, Uncle Louis called for Aunt Sally to bring the gun. She heard his cry and came running through the dogtrot, which was an open hallway located between the two sides of the house. She saw Uncle Louis's predicament and ran for the gun. When she returned, Uncle Louis had disentangled himself from the snake, which slithered off toward the cactus garden.

Uncle Louis was crippled with rheumatoid arthritis and found it difficult to chase the snake sufficiently to overtake it. He lost sight of the snake which appeared to go into the cacti. Uncle Louis was not one given to losing in a fight. He scrambled after the snake. Leveling his double-barreled shotgun on the cactus plants, he endeavored to blow the cactus plants apart. He emptied and reloaded the gun as long as he had shells left. Finally, the cacti were reduced to rubble. Uncle Louis did not stop there; he called for the wheel barrel and the shovel with which he scooped up the cactus, shovel by shovel full, looking for the remains of the snake, which he never found.

Still not done with his enmity against the snake, Uncle Louis called for the crosscut saw. He operated one end of the saw and assigned his son, Fred, and Robert, Fred's half-brother, to man the other end. They sawed the oak tree to the ground. Aunt Sally watched the entire destruction of the family shade tree and the cactus garden. She realized that there would be no more shade and no more prickly pear jam and jelly. She sighed. Turning back into the house, Aunt Sally shook her head and said, "Louis, that snake is up in Buhl by now."

Women of Grace and Goodness

Great-Grandpa Romeo's sons were considered the most sought-after boys by eligible girls in and around Romulus. Louis married Sally, Romeo Blackburn Jr. married Hattie, Robert married Emma, and John married Etta. These girls were well-bred, proper in their demeanor, dignified in all social situations, and genteel in their spousal duties.

Aunt Sally gracefully accepted two children born to her sister and fathered by her husband, Louis, without diminishing her capacity as a human being. She later took all of her sister's children under her supervision and ultimately raised eleven children.

Aunt Hattie, who married Uncle Romeo Blackburn, was a benevolent soul who cared not only for her family but also visited the sick with such tender ministrations that she was called upon to settle family disputes and right wrongs done to women in the community. Her true strength was called into use when her brother died and left two young girls from his second marriage. Aunt Hattie's brother was a landowner and had amassed money and personal belongings that were worthy of creating a will to stipulate who would be his heirs and beneficiaries. The wealth fell to the two daughters of his second marriage.

Nothing was bequeathed to the older children from his first marriage. One of the oldest girls was determined to get hold of her father's wealth as she judged it her right as a member of the firstborn children. She entreated the two girls to come live with her and her husband and their six children. They lived on a large farm in Romulus near Aunt Hattie.

The two young girls left their father's home and farm in the hands of other relatives and went to live with their older sister, expecting to return when the oldest girl was twenty-one years old, at which time she would claim her inheritance.

The older of the two siblings was an intelligent, attractive girl of sixteen. The second was born physically deformed and mentally retarded. The youngest girl fared well with the sister's children. She was not maligned for her deformities. Instead, she presented the children with someone who was less fortunate than themselves and thus to be pitied. The older girl presented a dilemma to their oldest sister as the girl boasted of the wealth she stood to claim at the age of twenty-one.

As a symbol of her father's wealth, the girl brought fine furnishings with her when she came to live with the older sister. Among the pieces of furniture was a Murphy bed hidden in a hand-carved ebony armoire.

When the armoire was opened, the bed could be let down. The children showed us the bed, and we would play on it when we visited their home.

Handsome tables and chairs were also brought to the sister's house to upgrade her sparsely furnished home. The eldest sister wanted the remainder of the inheritance and devised a way to obtain it.

The sixteen-year-old sister ceased visiting Aunt Hattie on Saturdays and failed to attend church several weeks in a row.

When the school opened in the fall, Thero Blackburn, Aunt Hattie's son who drove the school bus, told his mother that the girl was not attending school.

Aunt Hattie asked her oldest niece about the girl's whereabouts and was given a vague answer that she was not well and that she did not feel like visiting or going to church or to school. The situation grew dire as the girl did not appear at any function and was continually described as being a little under the weather, but "all right."

Soon, Aunt Hattie became suspicious and demanded that her husband, Uncle Romeo Jr., take her to see the girl for herself.

When they arrived at the older niece's house, everyone seemed frightened and uneasy. Aunt Hattie greeted the niece, her husband,

and the children. They mumbled greetings in return and shied away from their great-aunt.

"All right now, let me see that girl," said Aunt Hattie to her niece.

"She's around somewhere. Maybe she's out back. Go outside and see if she is out back," the niece said as she encouraged her children to pretend they were looking for the young girl.

Aunt Hattie had not lived so long that she did not understand body language and winks and nods from people who were trying to hide something. She brushed past the mother and the children and went straight to the back bedroom.

As she entered, she caught her breath to prevent herself from screaming. The girl lay on a cot, on top of an uncovered mattress, lying amid dirty quilts. Aunt Hattie threw back the dirty covers and revealed a skeleton of what had once been an attractive girl. Her skin was dry and flaking off her body. Her hair had fallen out, leaving tiny tufts of fuzz here and there.

When the girl was able to discern Aunt Hattie's presence, her eyes grew wide and she began to moan. It seemed that she had ceased asking for help long ago. Now her eyes begged for mercy and relief.

Aunt Hattie called for Uncle Romeo to come and help her. He came immediately as the call seemed more urgent than Aunt Hattie was accustomed to speaking.

"Take her! Take her!" Aunt Hattie exclaimed. Uncle Romeo threw the covers around the girl, hoisted her thin frame in his arms, and headed for the door.

The older sister tried to block their exit. "Don't take her! She ain't well. You can't take her. She can't go," she said urgently. She saw her fortune slipping away after she had almost succeeded in killing the girl.

Aunt Hattie raised her hand to strike her niece. "If I wasn't a child of God, I'd strike you dead." Aunt Hattie spoke with great vehemence. When she reached the door, she allowed Uncle Romeo Jr. to take the girl to the car. Turning upon her niece, she continued, "God will deal with you. Your daddy will come back and make you sorry you ever tried to kill this child." With that, Aunt Hattie strode out the door, leaving the niece standing in a stupor.

Aunt Hattie and Uncle Romeo took the girl to Stillman Hospital where the doctors diagnosed that she had been given small doses of poison. She was within days of death. When the story was told in the community, the notion that her skin was "flaking off like a snake's skin" prompted the citizens to speculate that the older sister had ground dried cottonmouth moccasin snake remains and put that in the girl's food.

After several months, the girl began to rally and was taken home to Aunt Hattie's house. There, a slow recuperation took her two years to get well. Afterward, she returned to her father's land and lived with relatives in Green County. She never came back to Romulus again.

Meanwhile, the older sister did not fare as well. Days of wondering if Aunt Hattie had put a hex on her that would cause her father to return from the grave and constantly feeling guilty for having tried to kill her sister, the older sister went crazy. We stopped by on Sunday afternoons, after church, to play with the younger children and the mentally retarded sister. We observed the effects of the older sister's insanity.

"There's a man over there looking at me. Make him stop looking at me!" she screamed. She ran away from the area.

She frequently saw an apparition of her father. He had come back from the dead to haunt his evil daughter.

"See that man under the bed? He's looking at me. Make him stop looking at me!" she screamed.

The children would take the broom and wave it under the bed. "See, Mama. There ain't nobody under that bed," they would say.

"Now he's behind the door. There he is, standing by the fireplace. Make him go away." On and on she screamed. According to the children, she ran and screamed all day and was quiet only when she fell asleep from exhaustion.

Her husband sat in the chair and quietly observed his wife scream, run, and tear at her clothes.

One day, when we were visiting, *that man* chased her out of the house and down across the field into the woods. Only after the boys ran their mother down and dragged her back to the house did she become quiet. They seated her in a chair near her bed. There she sat, babbling and slobbering, and her eyes rolled around in her head.

We went home.

As time went by, the husband began to distance himself from the craziness that had taken hold of his wife. He struck up an acquaintance with a widow who lived along the road leading toward Coker. He would stop by each time he went to town and spend time with the widow.

One day, as the husband prepared to leave home, his crazy wife jumped into the truck and would not get out. The husband, having made a date with the widow, insisted upon going upon his errand. The wife sat in the passenger seat, immovable.

When the husband stopped at the widow's house, she came out and began talking to her suitor through the back window on the passenger side of the truck. The wife opened the passenger door slightly, and the widow placed her hand in the doorframe. The wife opened the door wider as the two talked and winked behind her head. The door was gradually opened until it was as wide as could be. As the two talked, smiled at each other, and winked their secret messages, the wife placed two hands on the lower window frame and closed the door with all her might. The widow's fingers were caught between the door and the doorframe and were nearly severed from her hand.

After suffering for two years, the wife returned to her sanity and gave birth to a baby boy. However, she was never the same again.

Craziness with Common Sense

Uncle Romeo Jr. worked at the state mental hospital as an assistant farm supervisor. The mental hospital patients who were capable of working in the fields grew the vegetables that were consumed at the hospital and at a neighboring mental hospital.

Uncle Romeo told the following story at church on a Sunday after it occurred.

When Uncle Romeo started working in the fields at the mental hospital, plowing was done with mules and plows. As years passed, the beast of burden became the John Deere tractor.

Most patients at the hospital were afraid of the John Deere mechanical machine. However, there was one patient working on the farm, who took to the tractor with great efficiency.

One day, the patient and staff farmers were clearing a new section of ground to plant additional vegetables. Trees were cut and dragged away. A large tree was cut and attached to the tractor that was being driven by the mental patient. After several unsuccessful tries at dislodging the log, the patient dismounted from the tractor and shook his head.

"What's the matter?" the white supervisor asked the patient.

"Why aren't you dragging that log out of the way?"

The patient wagged his head and refused to remount the tractor. Finally, the patient said, "It going to tip over. I ain't going to get back up there. It's going to tip over."

The supervisor yelled obscenities at the patient to intimidate him so that he would complete the job of dragging the log out of the way. The patient stood his ground. As the supervisor berated the patient, he mounted the tractor himself. He placed his foot on the gas and pressed the pedal all the way to the floor. The tractor reared up and fell backward, pinning the supervisor underneath. When he was extricated from under the machine, he was dead.

All who heard the story concluded that the mental patient had more common sense than the highly learned and trained supervisor.

It is public record that Aunt Hattie and Uncle Romeo Blackburn Jr. are buried in the Holly Spring Missionary Baptist Church Cemetery. Aunt Hattie was born in 1883 and died in 1971 at the age of eighty-eight. Uncle Romeo was born in 1875 and died in 1953 at the age of seventy-eight.

Tragedy Befalls the Family

A tragedy occurred in the Blackburn family that involved the death of a child. The child's mother and father were fighting about an alleged sexual affair between the wife and a local cab driver.

During the fight, the husband chased his wife through the house, brandishing a butcher's knife. He came to the back door and saw that the door was ajar. He discerned that someone was behind the door as it was shaking. He flung the door open, exposing his daughter, who said, "Don't kill me, Daddy." Her plea came too late as the father had already thrust the knife home. The child died from the stab wound inflicted by her father.

When the husband came to trial, he was found guilty of killing the child. The mitigating circumstances were evidence that the husband did not intend to kill the child while he did intend to kill his wife.

The trial judge allowed that the wife could state her preference whether the husband should be given a sentence of life in prison or sentenced to death. It was reported that the judge asked the wife, "Shall the prisoner be allowed to live, or shall we kill him?"

The wife was reported to have stood up and shouted, "Kill him!" The husband was put to death in the gas chamber. The wife married the cab driver. The Romulus community grieved for the child and the father.

Uncle Bob Blackburn

Uncle Robert (Bob) Blackburn married Emma. She was an educated woman who served as a substitute teacher for Romulus Colored School. This position, as a teacher, gave her high status in the community. She was a beautiful woman, very graceful, and very much in love with Uncle Bob. The couple was like newlyweds throughout their lives. I observed them holding hands, kissing, and speaking endearingly to each other when they were in their seventies. Despite their love for each other and for their children, they had a tragedy in their lives that is told in the following story.

A Short Life

One Sunday, as Uncle Bob's family was getting ready to go to church, one of the daughters revealed that she was not feeling well and wanted to be excused from attending church that day. She promised to prepare dinner while the family was away.

Everyone went to church leaving the daughter to rest and cook dinner when she felt better.

The family returned from church after several hours' absence. There on the stove were pots of cooked collard greens and black-eyed peas. There were platters of fried chicken, cornbread, and fried okra. A cake was waiting on the dining room table.

As the family entered the dining room preparing to eat dinner, screams and prayers rushed from their mouths. The daughter had prepared dinner, climbed upon the table, stood in a chair, tied a rope around her neck, and hooked it over the rafters above the table. She stood in the chair and kicked it from beneath her feet. She hanged herself.

The reason for this suicide was never revealed. The community speculated on various fronts, but nothing was confirmed. Uncle Bob and Aunt Emma mourned their daughter for the rest of their lives. They grew closer together and held onto each other to guard against the pain that the loss of their daughter caused.

According to public records, Uncle Bob died in his sleep in March of 1971. He was eighty-nine years old. Aunt Emma slipped away eight months later in October 1971 at the age of eighty-seven. They are buried in the Holly Spring Missionary Baptist Church Cemetery within the first four rows.

Uncle John Blackburn

Uncle John married Aunt Etta. She was an attractive, well-mannered person with a sweet disposition. They lived on the land given to Uncle John by Great-Grandpa Romeo after John married Etta. Uncle John built a large house to accommodate his large family.

After Uncle Louis's death, Uncle John obtained all of Great Grandpa's land east of the mountain, which included the three-room house that Uncle Louis built for himself and his bride as well as Uncle Louis's farmland. Uncle John paid Grandma Annie, his sister, one hundred and fifty dollars for her share of her father's estate. The mountain divided the land in half, leaving the western part to Uncle Romeo Jr. and his descendants.

Fred Robinson sold Great-Grandpa Romeo the one hundred and fifty acres of land. After Fred's death, his son, Ed Robinson, stole five acres of the land back. When Ed Robinson died, his son who was also named Fred drove to Uncle John's house to tell him that he owned more land than he knew. Fred, the son, revealed that his father had stolen five acres of Great-Grandpa's land.

"You see, Uncle John, my daddy, Ed Robinson, took several acres of your land." (Fred used *uncle* as a title for elderly Negro men instead of saying *mister*.)

"What land are you talking about?" asked Uncle John.

Fred continued, "You remember that pasture where my daddy kept that old bull that everyone was afraid of?"

"Yes, that bull was fenced in that pasture for many years," Uncle John remembered.

"Well, Uncle John, that land belongs to you. My daddy stole it from you, and I'm giving it back. I removed the fence. The land is yours." Uncle John could not believe what Fred Robinson had told him.

Uncle John told the story at church the following Sunday. The people shook their heads and agreed that "some white men are good men after all."

With the payoff to Grandma and the return of the acreage from Fred Robinson, Uncle John settled down on one-half of Great Grandpa's farmland east of the mountain.

Uncle John was a forward-thinking man. He used wealth, accumulated from his father and his own hard work, to live a prosperous life. He was the first Negro in Romulus, Alabama to buy one of the automobiles that Henry Ford built for the common man. He bought a Model T Ford car. He even named his second-oldest son Henry Ford Blackburn after the automaker.

When everyone in Romulus, white and Negro, were still traveling by foot, mule, horse, and wagon, Uncle John and his family rode to church and town in style. His model T Ford became a staple of the community and was called upon on many occasions when fast travel was needed.

Stories will be told describing events that include the use of this car. This was the car in which Daddy and Uncle John's son, John D., came to pick me up when my mother abandoned me and I was found at Uncle Preston's house. It was also the car that was used to take a woman named Josie Lou (Allen) Harper to Stillman Hospital in an attempt to save the lives of Josie Lou and her unborn child.

The Dare

Uncle John's boys always had the best swing in the family. It hung from the large oak tree in the front yard. A large carved seat was tied to two heavy ropes that were swung over the largest limb of the tree. The boys would swing back and forth, rising high into the air, coming down, and swinging back as far as they had swung forward. When we were present, the boys would seat us on the board and "pump" the swing to a safe level. We felt like we were flying. The youngest boy was a daredevil. He would swing so high that the swing would nearly go around in a circle.

As automobiles became more available, Uncle John bought several different vehicles. When his youngest son was a teenager, Uncle John bought an Army transport vehicle from surplus Army stock. This heavy vehicle with large tires and a large metal body was his youngest son's delight. Just as he was a daredevil on the swing, he was as reckless in the Army truck. The teenager drove his father's truck with little regard for his own safety.

One Sunday afternoon, the boy drove the Army vehicle to his friend's home. His friend had a Ford truck. They decided to race each other down the one-lane dirt road. There were some places in the road that were not wide enough for the large vehicle to pass his friend's truck. This caused one or the other vehicle to veer off the road, sending one of the trucks into a field or a ditch. Most of the time, it was the friend's truck that was sent tumbling off the road.

These events were sources of hearty laughter.

The caravan raced farther down the road until they came to a one-lane bridge over a wide creek. The two vehicles were side by side and moving fast.

As the drivers approached the bridge, they saw that one vehicle would be forced to give way. The friend's truck was traveling in the middle of the road. The boy in the transport decided that he could pass around the friend's truck and make the bridge first. He was unwilling to give way and live to fight another day. He had to win at crossing the bridge. The driver of the large transport vehicle reached the bridge and attempted to pass the truck just as the smaller truck made it safely across the bridge. The heavier Army vehicle was given just enough room on the bridge for the tires on one side of the truck to pass.

The Army vehicle flipped over into the creek. As it tumbled sideways, the boy jumped out, failing to clear the underside of the vehicle. The heavy Army transport vehicle landed on top of the boy and killed him instantly.

Years later, as the family was still mourning the loss of the youngest son, the second oldest son made a bet with several friends that he could drink a quart of white lightning whiskey. He drank the whiskey, but it flooded his heart and he died. He won the bet but lost his life.

When all their children had left home and Aunt Etta's brother-in-law had passed away, her sister Mary moved in with Aunt Etta and Uncle John. A few years later, Aunt Etta died, leaving Uncle John and Mrs. Mary in the house alone. After several months of the two living together, they decided that it was sinful for two unrelated people, male and female, to live in the same house if they were unmarried. It did not matter that they were in their late eighties or that they were brother- and sister-in-law. They decided to wed.

The Holly Spring Missionary Baptist Church members were in an uproar. To their minds, the two were related. Uncle John was a deacon of the church and should know better than to marry his sister-in-law.

Uncle John heard protestation from his children, his grandchildren, other relatives, and the church members. Mrs. Mary's family also entered the thick of the fray in an attempt to prevent the marriage.

Uncle John sat on the front porch with a loaded shotgun and challenged anyone who came to his house to tell him of the error of his ways. He threatened to shoot all comers. Reverend Holly, the pastor of the Holly Spring Missionary Baptist Church, who was out of town in California, was summoned urgently to return to Romulus to prevent the two from making this dreadful mistake. Letters and phone calls were received by Reverend Holly, entreating him to come home immediately, if not sooner.

Reverend Holly assessed the situation. Realizing that he could not tell Uncle John what to do did not return in time to prevent the marriage between Uncle John and Mrs. Mary. They were married and lived together for several years.

According to cemetery records, Uncle John died in February 1977 at the age of ninety years old. Afterward, Mrs. Mary lived with her daughter until she died in December 1978 at the age of ninety-seven. They were buried in the Holly Spring Missionary Baptist Church Cemetery.

The cemetery records show that the Holly Spring Missionary Baptist Church Cemetery corrected all errors that had been made by people in real life. Uncle John was buried beside Aunt Etta as her loving husband. Mrs. Mary Wells was buried beside her first husband, Mr. Robert Wells, as if the second marriage had not occurred.

Grandpa and Grandma William and Annie Bailey

Grandma Annie Bailey was the second oldest daughter of Romeo and Lucy Blackburn. She inherited the Blackburn's genetic height and build. She was five feet, eleven inches tall, with strong bones, a fearless demeanor, and pride of self.

Grandma was a handsome woman, who was not given to beauty, but her appearance was stunning. She had her father's facial features and his straight black hair. Grandma was outspoken and opinionated, wise with good common sense, mean-tempered, and respected by all who knew her.

On Sunday, she donned her wide-brimmed hat with flowers or ribbons on top and rode to church in a surrey drawn by two prancing horses. She wore elegant dresses with draped fronts or capes draped over her shoulders. She never went out without her hat, even during the week.

Grandma was a force to be reckoned with among the Negro and Caucasian people alike. She often said, "You got to stand for something." She planted her feet wide upon her own land and marked her territory well.

Grandma was well-educated according to the standards of her day. She could read, write, and do figures on paper and in her head. Her father, Great-Grandpa Romeo, was a wealthy Negro man, which ensured that Grandma would never know poverty or want, and she never worked in the field. It was expected that she would marry someone who could keep her in the lifestyle to which she was accustomed. She was raised with manners and style befitting a Southern lady.

A man named William Bailey, who was originally from Mississippi, settled in Romulus. He was tall and handsome and had proper manners, and he was well-read and could write with a fine hand. He possessed gentlemanly manners and fine etiquette, qualities that corresponded with the social aspects of the Blackburn family. William was welcomed into the family as a social equal and a proper mate for Annie Blackburn.

William was born to two ex-slaves who lived on a plantation in Mississippi two years after the slaves were freed. His father was killed when he was an infant. Afterward, his mother married Mr. Moss who carried her to Birmingham, Alabama.

Great-Grandmother Moss and her husband took the older daughter with them but left little William with the white ex-slave owners. The daughter grew up, married, and remained in Birmingham, Alabama.

William remained on the Mississippi plantation with the white Bailey family until he was fifteen years old, growing up as one of their children. At the age of fifteen, William Bailey left Mississippi on a freight train.

Years later, my sister Mable went with Grandpa and Daddy to visit the Mississippi home where Grandpa had grown up. Mable reported that when they arrived at the old homestead, two older white men hurried out of the house, exclaiming, "Our brother Bill has come home." This experience indicated that Grandpa's life at the Bailey home had been amicable.

When William Bailey arrived in Romulus, he brought with him enough money to buy farmland from a white landowner. The land that Grandpa William Bailey bought was swampy and overgrown with trees and brambles. Cotton and corn grew profusely in the moist, steamy canebrake that Grandpa and his boys cleared and planted.

William Bailey, called Bill Bailey by people in Romulus, was an industrious man who knew how to farm and how to manage the land, which resulted in Grandpa and Grandma becoming successful farmers. For many years, they profited from the sale of the crops they grew.

William and Annie Bailey were the style-setters for the Romulus community. They owned the first surrey in Romulus in which they rode to church and to town. They owned four horses, four mules, two oxen, a large herd of cows, and numerous goats and raised and slaughtered many hogs each year.

Grandpa built his house beside a rushing stream that flowed down the hill beside the house. The house was large by Negro standards, consisting of three bedrooms, an eat-in kitchen, and a parlor.

In the parlor was the first musical organ brought to Romulus. The chairs and couches in the parlor were covered in burgundy velvet, except for one love seat that was covered in burgundy, gold, and green brocade. Burgundy velvet swag drapes covered the windows. They puddled on the floor. A grandfather clock adorned the mantle over the fireplace. A candelabra stood on either side of the clock.

Elegantly carved tables were situated throughout the parlor, adorned with items such as the 3-D antique stereograph picture viewer that showed people working in the supply factory of Sears and Roebuck. On a personal note, I still have this item. It was owned by Great-Grandpa Romeo's first wife, who gave it to Grandma, who gave it to my daddy, and he gave it to me.

The Negro children were taught by a traveling teacher who boarded with Grandpa and Grandma as they were the most affluent citizens in the Negro community. Their children were, therefore, better educated than most other children, owing to the extra tutoring they received at home.

The Old Yellow Gal

William (Bill) Bailey was a quiet man given to sound judgment and good intentions. All of which failed him when he met a young mulatto girl of near-white complexion who lived on a farm farther over in the woods. She was taken with Grandpa because he was a successful man and the pride of the community. She flirted with him, often coming to the edge of the field where he was plowing. Grandma did not work in the field and was, therefore, not around while the flirting was taking place. Grandpa felt an urge to respond to the girl's invitation and soon found himself in the woods, culminating their mutual flirtations. The illicit courtship continued throughout the farming season.

When the crops were in, Grandpa no longer needed to leave the house to work in the fields. He found himself without an excuse to go to the woods to meet his paramour. Finally, he could no longer withhold his desire for the young woman. He began to absent himself from the house for long periods of time.

Grandma sensed that he was up to no good and decided to follow him through the woods. She took the double-barreled shotgun along for protection and just in case she found something that was not to her liking.

As she followed Grandpa through the woods, she jumped behind a tree or bush each time he looked back. He headed straight to the area in the woods where he was scheduled to meet the girl. Grandma observed his actions and saw the girl coming toward Grandpa. At that moment, Grandpa took one last look behind and saw Grandma who chose not to hide. Instead, she raised the loaded double-barreled shotgun, aimed, and fired both barrels straight at Grandpa.

When Grandpa saw Grandma and realized that she was carrying a shotgun, he dived for a ditch that was nearby. The shotgun pellets sprayed the area where Grandpa had been standing as he landed safely in the bottom of the ditch. The girl saw Grandma shoot at Grandpa and knew that she was next. Before Grandma could reload, the girl took off for home. That was the end of that liaison.

For the remainder of their lives, Grandma complained about the old yella gal over which she should have killed Grandpa.

Grandpa's Land Was Stolen

The time came when white people engaged in overturning the prosperity that Negro people had accumulated during and immediately after Reconstruction. The white people supported Jim Crow laws which included subservience of the Negro people and making sure that as many Negro people as possible, like Grandpa and Grandma, would not live better and more prosperous than whites. They sought ways to destroy the prosperity of the Negro people.

Grandpa bought his land from the Patrick family and later bought goods from the Patricks' store. He behaved as the white men did, buying throughout the winter and settling up at the end of the summer when the crops were in.

In the late spring, as Grandpa, Uncle Buddy (Daddy's brother), and Daddy were laying the crops by (plowing the crops for the last time), Mr. Patrick, the store owner, came riding on his horse. Grandpa was surprised to find this white man in his field as Grandpa's farm was a long distance off the road.

"What can I do for you, Mr. Patrick?" Grandpa asked.

"Bill, I need some money. I'm running low on cash. I'm going to collect what you owe me right now."

Grandpa could not understand why he was being asked to pay his bill at the store so early in the year as he always paid at the end of harvest time. Now, he did not have the cash to pay what he owed, and he needed additional credit until the fall came when he could pay everything from his income derived from the sale of his crops. "Mr. Patrick, you know I don't have that kind of money right now," Grandpa said. Mr. Patrick pulled out his account book showing what Grandpa had bought and signed, agreeing to pay the sum.

Mr. Patrick told Grandpa that he was calling in his debt. He indicated that if Grandpa could not pay, he would take his farm. He had the law on his side, and he was in the right to take Grandpa's farm for what was owed. In the end, Grandpa lost his farm for the price of seeds and fertilizer.

Grandpa and Grandma became sharecroppers on the Robinsons' farm. Within three years, their children moved them to a house outside the city of Tuscaloosa where my family joined them several years later. Grandma was devastated. She not only lost her home and their farm but she also lost her standing in the community. She lost her pride and dignity. She stopped going to church and grew meaner than before. She spent the remainder of her years fussing at Grandpa.

As long as Grandma could talk, she complained about the old yella gal at least three times a week. She also called Grandpa many derogatory names, such as old slavery time, old orphan. "You old black devil, you. I should have killed you about that old yella gal." She never mentioned the loss of the farm although that was the source of her anger and unhappiness.

According to cemetery records, Grandma was born in August 1871 and died (of cancer) in August 1953 at the age of eighty-two. She was buried in the Holly Spring Missionary Baptist Church Cemetery in the prestigious part of the cemetery on the front row.

Grandma Annie Bailey Died

My father and stepmother, whom we called Annie Lee Mama, lived in the same house with Grandpa and Grandma. By the time Grandma died, my four sisters and I had grown up and left home. Annie Lee Mama took care of Grandma when she became ill with cervical cancer.

Grandma Annie Bailey's daughters, Aunt Clyde and Aunt Annie, came from Detroit, Michigan, to attend their mother's funeral. After the funeral, the two visiting sisters and the two who lived in Tuscaloosa, Aunt Luella and Aunt Lucille, came to the house where Grandpa, my daddy, and Annie Lee Mama lived and collected all of Grandma's linen, silverware, quilts, and clothes. Grandpa was mourning Grandma and was unaware of what was going on around him. According to Annie Lee Mama, they left Grandpa one plate, a knife, a fork, two broken cups, and a spoon.

Annie Lee Mama came home from work and found all of Grandma's belongings piled in a sheet on the floor. In an attempt to cover their embarrassment, the daughters asked Annie Lee Mama if she wanted anything. Annie Lee Mama saw a pair of Grandma's gloves lying on top of the pile. She indicated that she would take the gloves as a remembrance of Grandma. I still have this pair of beige gloves in my keepsake drawer.

The Quilt and the Traveling Ghost

Aunt Annie, Grandma's youngest daughter, said that she was born with a *veil* over her face, which meant that she could see ghosts. Her admission to being a ghost seer was over one of Grandma's quilts that Aunt Annie took back to Detroit, Michigan.

Aunt Annie told me the following story:

When winter came, I took out the quilt I had taken from Papa after Mama died. I proudly placed it on my bed and snuggled underneath. The quilt was so warm and cozy that I immediately fell asleep. I was awakened by a sensation that felt like the quilt was moving. I awaken to find that the quilt had slid off the bed and was puddled on the floor. I thought perhaps I had slept badly and had pushed the quilt to the floor. I replaced the quilt and tucked it at the foot of the bed so that it could not slide off again.

I went back to sleep, feeling warm and cozy. As I slept, I was awakened by the movement of the quilt. I turned the light on and watched as the quilt slid to the floor and puddled beside my bed.

I folded that quilt and put it in the closet. I never tried to sleep beneath it again. I believe that Mama had traveled from Alabama to Detroit, Michigan, to prevent me, her daughter, from enjoying the quilt that I had taken away without Papa's permission. Mama showed me that she was not pleased with what I had done.

Grandma's Lively Ghost

The two years following Grandma's death, Grandpa reported to Annie Lee Mama that Grandma came back to visit him two or three times each week. Each time he told Annie Lee Mama about the visits, she tried to persuade him that it was his imagination or that he was dreaming. He insisted that "Ma came to visit me last night." He always received the same scolding from Annie Lee Mama. Why Grandpa wanted Grandma back and why he was so cheerful the morning after her visit were mysteries to us. As mean as Grandma had been, one would think that Grandpa would have been glad to finally have some peace in his old age.

Annie Lee Mama had an experience that proved that Grandpa was not dreaming and it was not his imagination. Grandma's ghost did come back.

One afternoon, Annie Lee Mama was sitting in the breezeway between the front and back doors, shelling peas. Grandma's ghost came into the room. She was humming a song as she always did when she was in idle thought. Grandma came through the door leading from the living room into the bedroom, passed by Annie Lee Mama, and continued along the fireplace mantel. She wiped the mantel with a handkerchief, checking for dust. This was something she did in real life. Annie Lee Mama was the principal caretaker of Grandma during her illness with cervical cancer. Annie Lee Mama felt that she had given Grandma the best of care and was not afraid of her ghost.

Grandma's daughters lived within walking distance. However, they rarely came to visit. When they did come, they sat and talked and did nothing to care for their mother. When the apparition moved along the fireplace, Annie Lee Mama was not afraid because she felt that she had taken good care of Grandma. Annie Lee Mama spoke, "Mama, is that you? Are you happy where you are?" Grandma did not answer but continued to wipe the mantel and hum.

"How is it over there?" Annie Lee Mama asked as Grandma disappeared.

Annie Lee Mama hurried around to Grandpa's room and told him that she had just seen Grandma. With this confirmation, Grandpa was free to tell Annie Lee Mama whenever he had a ghostly visit.

When Daddy came home, Annie Lee Mama related what she had seen. Daddy was skeptical but said little. Several months later, Daddy and Annie Lee Mama were lying in bed. The embers from a dying fire in the fireplace threw a faint light across the room. Daddy lay watching the embers spark and die, making colorful fireworks in the fireplace grate.

Suddenly, he saw Grandma walking through the room. She was humming and wiping the dust from the mantel. Daddy was not as brave as Annie Lee Mama. Perhaps he had not done all he could have done to care for his mother and was regretful of his neglect. Daddy dived under the cover and shook Annie Lee Mama until she awoke. Daddy reported from under the cover, "Mama is over there by the fireplace."

Annie Lee Mama had longed to see Grandma again as she had not gotten answers to her questions. Throwing the covers back in unison, they looked for Grandma, who had vanished. After appearing to all three household occupants, Grandma's ghost ceased its visits. Grandpa was lonesome for Grandma's presence. He missed her fussing at him about the old yella gal. He even decried the absence of her ghost.

Grandpa's Virility at Ninety Years Old

At the age of ninety, Grandpa was still a virile man. Grandma's visits had staved off his desires for the opposite sex. After the ghost visits stopped and he was convinced that Grandma's ghost would not come back again, Grandpa began to look around for companionship.

Grandpa had been a handsome man. He had been about five feet, eleven inches tall, slim but muscular from hard work. He had strong white teeth that were noticed as an attractive feature. He died with his own teeth in his mouth.

At the age of ninety, however, his height had diminished to that of a twelve-year-old boy. His erect stature that had been well proportioned and becoming was now bent at the waist to the point that he appeared to be trying to touch his toes. His walking movements took place from his waist down. The remaining torso, shoulders, and head protruded forward and went wherever his legs took them. He carried a walking stick to balance his upper body and to keep from toppling over on his head.

Grandpa was still virile and still desired the companionship of a female. He set his eyes on a middle-aged woman, Ms. Mattie, who lived on the adjoining farm. Ms. Mattie was the housekeeper for twin brothers who lived together and were raising one brother's three children.

Ms. Mattie lived in a one-room house behind the family abode. The house had seen its best days and then some. It looked like the little crooked house described in the nursery rhyme which told of the "little man, who bought a crooked cat, which caught a crooked mouse (and) they all lived together in a little crooked house."[16]

The house even had a crooked stovepipe that protruded from its roof. We were not allowed inside, but I could imagine that the inside was spotlessly clean.

Ms. Mattie was the quintessence of a spinster. She had never been married and appeared never to have had a relationship with a man. She was so straitlaced that the idea of a man touching her body would have turned her hair gray on the spot.

Ms. Mattie kept her own council and maintained her strict routine. On Friday, she left the little crooked house and walked past our house on her way to the store. She walked with such preciseness that she seemed to count each step. Counting her paces, she walked steadily up the road. If she saw Annie Lee Mama, she would bow her head curtly and say, "Good morning, Mrs. Annie Lee" to which Annie Lee Mama would attempt an expanded conversation.

"How you doing, Ms. Mattie? You on your way to the store?" Each time, Ms. Mattie would wave and continue counting her steps to the store and back.

Ms. Mattie's sojourn had not been wasted on Grandpa who watched her pass from his bedroom window. He judged that she would be ideal for his needs.

On a Friday, when Ms. Mattie approached the house, heading for the store, counting her steps as she went, Grandpa approached her from the opposite side of the house from where Annie Lee Mama could not see him.

"Psst!" he signaled to Ms. Mattie. "Ma'am, could you help me?" Everyone knew that Ms. Mattie was a Christian woman although she never went to church. Seeing an elderly man, bent double, leaning on a walking stick, calling for her to help him did not require one to be a churchgoing Christian to be willing to stop and see if she could be of assistance.

[16.] The rhyme was first recorded by James Orchard Halliwell in the 1840s and gained popularity in the early twentieth century.

"Yes, sir, Mr. Bailey," Ms. Mattie replied as she approached the trembling old man.

"Now, Ms. Mattie, you know my wife died over two years ago," he began.

"Yes, sir. I know," replied Ms. Mattie solicitously.

"Now that she's gone, I need someone to help me," he continued.

"Yes, sir, Mr. Bailey. How can I help you?"

"Well, a man has needs, you know."

Ms. Mattie did not know of which he spoke and continued to seek clarification of his meaning.

"Now I'll pay you good. I got money."

"Yes, sir. What do you need to have me do?" asked Ms. Mattie.

Grandpa was growing anxious and fearful that Annie Lee Mama would come around the corner and find out what he was doing. He had to come to the point.

"I want you to let me have some sex. I'm willing to pay you five dollars," he came to the point.

Ms. Mattie had not expected anything of this nature and was taken aback, to say the least. She felt her knees go slack. Her hair, plaited in the three braids she always wore, rose under her hat. Her eyes went back in her head. She felt as if she would faint.

She did not know how to respond as she had never been asked this question before. Even worse than asking her for sex, he had set the price higher than the going rate, which seemed appropriate as one could not imagine, as cripple as he was, how he was going to accomplish the feat of intercourse even if she had said yes.

"Mr. Bailey!" Ms. Mattie gasped. "You . . . you ought not to talk to me that way." She sputtered as she backed away from him. Clutching her grocery bag and her purse to her bosom, she sped around the house.

Grandpa knew that she was going to tell Annie Lee Mama. He hobbled to the woodpile, took the ax out of the chopping block, and sat down, waiting for the ax to fall.

Ms. Mattie went straight to Annie Lee Mama and told her every word Grandpa said. She expressed her disgust and declared herself a Christian woman who would never consort with a man outside marriage.

Annie Lee Mama, a saintly woman if ever there was one, was mortified. She flew out of the back screen door like a jack-in-the-box jumping sideways. She descended upon Grandpa, who was already sitting on the wood-chopping block, waiting for his fussing out. Annie Lee Mama attacked him with all her indignation about dirty old men and the institution of male needs.

"Pa, you ought to be ashamed of yourself. You're over ninety years old. You should have let that stuff go way back before Mama got sick. You done embarrassed Ms. Mattie to death. You need to go inside"—she pointed to the house—"get your Bible and read and pray. What would Mama say if she knew what you were up to?"

Grandpa thought about that one. Grandma would try to shoot him just like she tried to kill him over the old yella gal.

Grandpa did not lose his desire for sex nor did he bother Ms. Mattie again. He waited, hoping that someone else would come along. Someone did.

Aunt Clara, Grandpa's daughter-in-law who had run off with the traveling preacher some years earlier, came back to Tuscaloosa. She was beginning to suffer from senility. However, she could still take care of herself. She could cook and clean adequately.

During her absence, Aunt Clara's family had left the area. Her oldest daughter died. Her second daughter was living in St. Louis. She tried to go back to her husband, Uncle OG, but he had a girlfriend whom he married around the same time Clara came home. (During the era of J. P. Morgan, Grandma named three of her children with initials OG, LS, and WH, after JP.) Annie Lee Mama was having trouble with her heart and could not take care of Grandpa as she had cared for Grandma. Those who knew Aunt Clara's plight and knew that Grandpa needed someone to cook and clean for him put the two together for mutual support.

The arrangement went well until Grandpa began to feel amorous toward Clara. Having run off with the traveling preacher had given Clara the reputation of a scarlet woman. Grandpa thought that she just might agree to give him some sex.

His resolve grew until, one night, Grandpa sneaked into Aunt Clara's bed. She threw him out, packed her bags, and was ready to leave before daylight. She told Annie Lee Mama the story.

Again, Annie Lee Mama flew out of the kitchen as if propelled from a slingshot and was upon Grandpa before he woke up. Annie Lee Mama told Grandpa how he should have been ashamed of himself. She repeated all the remonstrations that she had stated on behalf of Ms. Mattie. She ended with, "Now I know why Mama said she should have killed you about the old yella gal."

When Annie Lee Mama told Daddy about these incidences, Daddy was proud of his father. He explained that with continued sexual desire, Grandpa was still a man.

Grandpa died at the age of ninety-five. Had Grandpa not burned himself while stoking the fire in the fireplace, he would have lived even longer. He had no known physical ailments. One night, Grandpa poured kerosene on the wood in the fireplace. He called this process dashing kerosene on the fire to make it catch on. He had used this method of enhancing the flame for many years. In his old age, his reflexes became slower and the kerosene drained backward onto his clothes. He was set on fire.

When Grandpa's cries were heard, Annie Lee Mama ran as fast as she could and was able to put the fire out. Grandpa's legs and thighs were burned severely. He refused to go to the hospital. He ministered to his own burns until Daddy overruled him and took him to the doctor. By that time, the burns had festered. Grandpa died from his self-inflicted burns.

According to cemetery records, Grandpa was born in September 1868. Although the death date is not on Grandpa's tomb, I attended his funeral in December 1963. He was buried beside Grandma on the front row of the Holly Spring Missionary Baptist Church Cemetery.

Ancestors, Aunts, and Uncles

Grandpa and Grandma's family members have told many of the stories that are remembered. Their lives traversed the troubled years between slavery, Reconstruction, Jim Crow, and the civil rights movement. These stories are best told through the lives of my immediate ancestors—my aunts and uncles. Grandpa and Grandma had eleven children. The first child was named Mozella. She died at the age of three months. The second child was Clelly. He married Alma. They did not have children.

Uncle Clelly was employed by the Fawcett family all his working life. Mrs. Fawcett encouraged Uncle Clelly to buy a house on Bridge Street in Northport, Alabama. In those days, Negro people could not live on Bridge Street. It was surmised by both Uncle Clelly and his benefactor that by the time the house was paid off by the rent from white people, who, for years, were the only race who could live in the house, Negro people may be allowed to live on Bridge Street. For thirty years, Uncle Clelly rented the house to white families and paid the loan off. As it occurred, the times and the neighborhood of Bridge Street did change. A Negro church was built on the street. Several houses were bought by Negro people. Bridge Street was no longer for whites only.

At long last, Uncle Clelly and Aunt Alma moved into their own home. They were old and ill when they occupied their comfortable house. Uncle Clelly had tuberculosis, and Aunt Alma suffered from heart disease and diabetes. Three years after they moved into their home, Aunt Alma died.

The following year, Aunt Alma's niece took Uncle Clelly to Ohio to care for him. When he died at the age of ninety-eight, the niece sold the house on Bridge Street for twenty-thousand dollars. Three thousand was paid in back taxes and the remainder was divided between Daddy who received seven thousand and another brother, Uncle OG, who received ten thousand.

The family agreed that the ten thousand that Uncle OG was given contributed to his death.

Uncle OG married one of the Harper girls, Clara, the one who ran away with the traveling preacher and who later lived briefly with Grandpa. Uncle OG and Aunt Clara had two daughters.

The story goes that in the fall of the year, the traveling preacher came to Romulus. He set up a large tent under which the Negro people from all over the county came to hear him preach. He was a barn burner, they said. He could hoop, meaning preach, with a loud voice and commanding words. Aunt Clara was smitten with the preacher. So much so that when he left three days later, Aunt Clara went with him to Florida, where she remained until she grew old.

Uncle OG was left to raise the two girls. The oldest girl grew up, got married, had children of her own, and lived a normal life.

The youngest daughter was a rebel. She left home and worked as a live-in maid for white employers. At the age of fifteen, she gave birth to a baby boy. The baby was given to Uncle OG who tried to raise the child as best he could but failed miserably.

The child was rebellious and troubled as he grew up. He demanded exorbitant prizes from his grandfather, including a long, yellow Cadillac car. Uncle OG could not afford the car as it was before he received an inheritance from his oldest brother, yet he tried to please his grandson by buying the car on time payments. The grandson rode away from Tuscaloosa, Alabama, in the yellow Cadillac and was not heard from for over a year. When he resurfaced, he was in Montgomery, Alabama, sick and bloated to three times his normal size. Uncle OG went to Montgomery, loaded his bloated grandson into the yellow Cadillac, and drove him home.

Uncle OG and his daughter tried to get Daddy to allow the grandson to stay with him while he recuperated so that he would be in a quiet environment. Daddy told his brother and niece, "You must be crazy. I wouldn't let that boy spend two minutes in my house."

Meanwhile, the niece was working for an insurance company where she wrote policies for old, dying people, claiming that they were healthy. When they died, she collected the premiums. She got caught and was given an ultimatum, "Leave town or go to jail." She left town.

When the grandson got well, he and his mother went to St. Louis to live with Uncle Louis, Grandma's second-oldest son. (There was a boy named Louis in four generations, beginning with the son of Great-Grandpa Romeo and ending with a Louis my children's age.)

Years later, while my family and I traveled through the Midwest, we visited Uncle Louis who told us stories about the trouble he had with both the niece and her son. According to Uncle Louis, they robbed him, tore up his house, drank whiskey, smoked, did drugs, invited riffraff into his house, and ran amuck.

He was cautious about my husband and me visiting him although we were a young couple with three small children who were only passing through and did not intend to stay the night.

When we first visited Uncle Louis, he was a stately elderly man who was restrained and cautious. Uncle Louis's wife had died before we met him. She was a school teacher in the local school district. The appearance of the house and the surrounding community showed that Uncle Louis and his wife were middle-class citizens who lived quiet, comfortable lives. Uncle Louis lived in a tall four-story house in St. Louis, Missouri. The house was gingerbread, painted in red, green, yellow, and burgundy. It had a full basement, a main floor, and two stories above the main floor. The entryway was decorated with decorative art pieces brought back from trips he and his wife had taken to the Orient. The sitting room and the dining area on the first floor were decorated in antique furniture of dark wood and satin cloth finishes.

According to Grandma, Uncle Louis left home at the age of seventeen to enlist in the Army during the First World War. After the war, he became a Pullman porter on the railroad. Even though he could have traveled on the train free of charge, he only came home to Alabama two times in the next fifty years.

He came home once when his parents lived on the Robinsons' farm in Romulus, Alabama. During that visit, Grandpa attempted to shoo a calf out of the garden. Emboldened by having all his sons at home for the first time in many years, Grandpa attempted to show off his prowess with his shotgun.

The calf had jumped over the garden fence and was eating the tender beanstalks. Grandpa took his shotgun and fired above the calf's head. As the gun roared, the calf jumped for the fence. The calf and the shotgun pellets met above the fence line, and the calf fell to the ground outside the garden. The calf was dead when it hit the ground.

Grandma, being her usual philosophical self, said, "Dah now, you done killed that calf."

Grandpa retorted, "Naw, I just sprinkled him." Daddy and his brothers butchered the calf and divided the beef among the families.

Uncle Louis came home one more time to bury his mother. He did not come to his father's funeral.

In our travels around the country every three years, we continued to stop by to see Uncle Louis. When he found out that we were not like the other family members, he tried to persuade us to remain on long visits. As years went by, Uncle Louis became friendly and very solicitous of our friendship. We exchanged Christmas cards over the years.

Although we never stayed overnight with Uncle Louis, we continued to visit him through the years. When my husband, our daughter Tamera, and I visited Uncle Lewis for the last time, she was twenty-one years old. She had been five years old when we first visited him.

When we arrived on our last visit, we found the neighborhood, that was once a beautiful community, had become a slum and was now overrun by drug dealers and criminals. Uncle Louis had been robbed and his house had been pillaged. The robbers beat him and left him bruised and barely able to walk with great difficulty.

When we last saw Uncle Louis, he was bent over at the waist with an immobile torso. He looked as if he was trying to touch his toes. His appearance was that of his father, Grandpa William Bailey, when Grandpa was in his nineties.

According to his heirs, Aunt Lucille, Aunt Clyde, and Aunt Annie, Uncle Louis died at the age of ninety-eight and willed his estate to his three living sisters. He was buried beside his wife in St. Louis, Missouri.

Enemy in the House

Uncle Louis willed his estate to his three living sisters, and Uncle Clelly, the oldest of my grandparents' children, willed his estate to his two living brothers. When Uncle OG received his inheritance from his older brother, Clelly, his daughter, came home. She put her name on the bank account and refused to allow Uncle OG to use any of his own money. When he was in his late nineties, Uncle OG rode around the neighborhood on his bicycle, picking up bottles to trade for a Coke, which he craved.

Uncle OG was a jackleg preacher who was allowed to sit on the rostrum when he attended a church. He tried preaching, but was so poorly equipped to bring the message that he was not wanted as a pastor by any congregation that could do better.

One church was so far back in the woods that it could not get anyone to come to preach or to pastor the church. It did call on Uncle OG to be its pastor. Uncle OG lived in Fayette, Alabama at the time and the church was located south of Tuscaloosa, over forty miles away.

Uncle OG was unable to afford a car. It would have been great if it had been years later and he could have driven his grandson's long, yellow Cadillac. He did have a bicycle, which he rode forty miles to the church, preached the sermon, and rode back home all in the same day. This did not last long, owing to his inability to preach, his wornout legs, and his old pieced-together bicycle. However, it did give him a pastorship on his résumé, which allowed him to sit on church rostrums with other preachers.

After Uncle OG received the ten thousand dollars from Uncle Clelly's estate, his daughter stuck to him like glue. She moved back home and would go to church with Uncle OG. Together, they would sing strange songs that they made up. No one in the congregation knew the words of the songs nor did anyone know the tunes.

Daddy told the story that on the Third Sunday in May, one year when people from all over the United States were in attendance at the Holly Spring Missionary Baptist Church, Uncle OG and his daughter sang one of their strange songs. Usually, songs that are sung in church are based on Bible stories and refrains that are common knowledge. If one part is stated, the audience knows the following lines. Uncle OG's songs included neither of these common themes.

Daddy said that none of the notes of the songs that Uncle OG sang were on the piano. He was able to confirm that notion as the musician looked for the notes and never found one. When people sang on the Third Sunday in May, the musician would find their musical key and play along with the singers. This time, she tried to find a common note of Uncle OG's song. "Ping, pang, pung, pong," she went, never finding any note that fit his tune. She finally gave up and Uncle OG sang a cappella.

Uncle OG stood near the podium and raised his voice as loudly as he could. He sang chorus after chorus of something that did not include a biblical reference, a recognizable note, a resounding tune, nor did the lines rhyme.

As he sang, he asked people to join in. "Hep me, everybody," he begged. His daughter stood up in the audience and began to "hep" him. She did not know the words of the "song" nor did she know the tune. Nevertheless, help him she tried.

The song continued until Uncle OG became so wound up in his liturgical fiasco that he leaped off the podium and landed face down on the floor beside the offering table. The distance from the top of the rostrum and the floor was about five feet, which, when added to Uncle OG's six-feet stature, the distance his head traveled was about eleven feet before it landed on the floor. The impact knocked him out cold.

The church congregation stood up en masse and strove to see where he had landed. For some time, no one came to his aid as they were so aghast that they could not move. Finally, however, two deacons rushed to pick him up from where he lay unconscious.

Daddy was in the audience. He did not move as he was already embarrassed over the song. Daddy was a favorite singer at the Third Sunday in May celebration for fifty years. Now his brother had risen to sing even though he could not carry a tune and did not have a tune to carry.

It was embarrassing. Daddy told his brother, "As long as you live, don't you ever get up in front of people and make such a fool of yourself again."

Uncle OG never sang at the Third Sunday in May celebration again. He did, however, make a fool of himself in the eyes of the family and the church members.

Uncle OG's grandson was found in a motel in Long Beach, California where he had lain dead for three days. Uncle OG allowed his daughter to bury her son in Uncle OG's free burial plot on the front row in the Holly Spring Missionary Baptist Church Cemetery. That was considered an insult to the Blackburns' ancestors as the burial plots on the fourth row with Great-Grandpa Romeo Blackburn and those going forward toward the church were available only to his children and grandchildren. This great-great-grandson should have been buried behind the ancestral line.

The daughter took her father's money, which was the subject of many angry altercations between them. Now that her son was dead and buried in his grandfather's plot, the daughter had only to get rid of Uncle OG, and she would have his money and control of her aunt's house where the two of them lived after Aunt Luella died.

One morning, the daughter called 911. Uncle OG was dead at the age of 103. He was still a virile man who had a girlfriend. He was not ill. He was in good health and still rode his bicycle to pick up cans and bottles to earn money to buy himself a Coke. Although he had ten thousand dollars in the bank, his daughter would not let him have pocket change to buy sodas.

The coroner said that the cause of death was suffocation. According to my sister, the daughter had bragged about choking her father on another occasion. It was rumored that "she done it this time." No investigation was done due to Uncle OG's race and age.

Since Uncle OG had given his own plot to his grandson, he no longer had a free plot available for his burial. His daughter would be required to buy a plot in which to bury her father.

According to Daddy who was present at the funeral, the daughter buried Uncle OG in a new section of the Holly Spring Missionary Baptist Church Cemetery that had recently been cleared and was practically free. His casket was so cheap that the corpse started falling out of the bottom when the pallbearers were taking it to the gravesite. They were forced to hold the bottom of the casket together by hand until they arrived at the grave opening. The grave was not marked.

The following Third Sunday in May, when flowers were placed on the graves, the daughter could not find her father's resting place. I saw her throw a handful of flowers into the bushes.

According to cousin Latham Blackburn Harris, the church members felt so badly about one of the families being buried thus that they had Latham Harris, the great-grandson of Romeo Blackburn, to whom the grave-digging position had passed, exhume Uncle OG's body. He was buried on the fourth row with his grandfather, Romeo Blackburn Sr. An attractive gravestone was purchased by the church and placed above his grave. Now, he lies in sweet repose amid his ancestors.

Several years later, Uncle OG's daughter was found dead in Aunt Luella's house. She had been dead for three days, just like her son.

She was buried behind the fourth row in the Holly Spring Missionary Baptist Church Cemetery. My husband, Albert, attended the funeral. She was buried in a beautiful casket with a white lining, and an imposing gravestone was placed above her grave. It was said that she spent her father's inheritance of ten thousand dollars on herself and on her own funeral.

Black Beauty

To be born a Blackburn in Romulus, Alabama was to know that you were Negro high society, that you were highly prized for marriage, and that you could get away with just about anything you did. To be a Blackburn also meant that you were likely a very beautiful female or a handsome man.

Two of the granddaughters were rare beauties. The beauty of these two cousins was legendary. Caucasian and Negro people stared at them as they passed by. People spoke of their beauty in hushed reverent tones. (There have been Blackburn beauties like these two in every generation.)

The two girls were cousins who had inherited their grandfather's features. They embodied the facial appearance of the ancient Moors. The cousins were black with skin the color of onyx. Their faces were similar in description; their noses, not flared and wide, seemed to harken back to an African nasal structure that was Arabic and northern African. Both were tall, stately, poised, and graceful.

The first cousin's beauty was her crime as her husband imprisoned her for being so beautiful. He did not allow her to go out alone, nor did he allow her to talk to other men. On occasions, when she came home to see her mother and father, her husband flew into a jealous rage when he saw her talking to her male cousins.

At the beginning of their courtship and marriage, she loved her husband because he was so attentive and appeared to love her totally. After months of being married to him, she became aware that his jealousy outweighed the tenderness he portrayed when they were alone.

She tried to leave him, but he would always find her and force her to return home. Afterward, he would resume his tenderness in private and his jealousness in public.

The pressure of being married to such a beautiful wife and his fear that someone would take her away from him worried her husband until he began to drink heavily. When he was intoxicated, he would physically abuse his wife and threaten to kill her.

She was so afraid that she began to lose weight. Her beauty did not wane, however. She became more beautiful; thin, lithe, and winsome was she.

One day, she decided, come what may, she was going to church. She dressed in her best clothes, curled her long black hair, painted her lips, and put on high-heeled shoes. She headed for the door. As she reached to turn the doorknob, a shot rang out. A bullet pierced her neck, next to her carotid artery. She fell to the floor as if dead. Her husband saw her fall, assumed that he had killed her, and turned the gun upon himself. He placed the gun into his mouth and pulled the trigger.

A neighbor heard the two gunshots and called the police. The wife was rushed to the hospital where the doctor revealed that the distance between the gunshot wound and her carotid artery was the distance of the thickness of a sheet of paper. Her husband was pronounced dead at the scene of the crime.

The wife lived. For the remainder of her life, a knot could be seen on her otherwise beautiful neck. She died at the age of forty-seven and was buried in the Holly Spring Missionary Baptist Church Cemetery. Her name was Snow.

The second cousin was as beautiful as the first but had a fiery personality. She acknowledged her beauty and flaunted her looks for all to see. Even in her early teens, she realized she was beautiful and that other people stared at her. She gave others a full view of her beauty, her charm, and her vivaciousness. She caught the eye of every boy in the community. Unfortunately, the one that was most taken with her was one of her first cousins.

The father of the girl was Romeo Blackburn Sr.'s son. The mother of the male suitor was Romeo Blackburn Sr.'s daughter.

Romeo's daughter married into the Harper family whose patriarch was nearly white. The patriarch's parents were a mulatto woman who was partly white and a well-known white man, who was one of the community leaders. This couple bore a son that was as white as any other white person in Romulus, except he had one drop of Negro blood.

The Harper patriarch's bloodline was confirmed when his Caucasian sister asked him to come to her bedside where she lay dying. As a deathbed confession, she acknowledged him as her brother. It was too late for him to turn white as he had married a Negro woman and had children. Perhaps, it was never possible for him to live as a white man in the Southern states as one was considered black if he had one drop of Negro blood in his veins.

The male cousin, who was the grandson of Mr. Harper, had light-colored skin and curly hair. He was considered very handsome.

As the two first cousins became aware of their own attractiveness, they ascertained that they were equal in beauty and deserved each other. They fell madly in love.

The two sets of parents forbade them to see each other. They explained the nature of cousins and the incest that would occur if they were lovers. The church pastor talked with them. He prayed with them. Nothing and no one could stop them from loving each other. They were headstrong and wanted their way.

The boy's parents bought him a car as a bribe to leave his cousin alone. The car only enabled him to meet his cousin in the woods or to take her away from home on long drives.

Months went by while relatives and church members prayed that the two lovers would come to their senses. They did not. Instead, the girl became pregnant.

When the female cousin's condition became apparent, the whole community knew that the two cousins had conceived. There was much gossiping, wagging of tongues, and saying that it served them right as they thought they were better than everyone else.

The parents of the two cousins conspired to save the two children from ridicule and ex-communication from the church. The mother of the boy took the girl on a trip to Ohio where another sister lived. There, they remained until a baby boy was delivered. The aunt came home telling everyone she had adopted a child. Everyone knew that the baby was her grandchild. The child's father was sent to live elsewhere, and the girl came home a month later. The male cousin's mother raised the child as her own son.

The two lovers went free of any responsibility for the child, and the child was forever marked by the close genetic relationship of his parents. He was mentally deficient. When both of his grandparents died, he nearly lost the farm he had inherited from them.

His grandfather had purchased fertilizer from a white man's store. For several sacks of fertilizer, the store owner's sister took the farm and began to rent it to sharecroppers. The boy's uncle paid for the fertilizer and redeemed the farm. Then he bought it so that it would remain in the family. This was the same store owner that took Grandpa William Bailey's farm for the price of seeds and fertilizer.

A few years later, the beautiful female cousin married the son of a wealthy Negro widow. The widow's family was not an attractive group of people. The son was not in the least handsome and did not fit the image that the cousin had preferred for a mate. However, any marriage was a feather in her cap, as she had a baby out of wedlock, which would have marked her for scandal and ex-communication from the church had she not been a Blackburn. Her marriage was greatly appreciated by her parents.

The widow's son and new daughter-in-law came to church and were admired by the congregation for the loving couple they appeared to be. Everything was not as it seemed in the family, however. The beautiful cousin, now the spouse and daughter-in-law, did not show love and affection to her husband at home. The widow encouraged her daughter-in-law to be happy. She bought her fine clothing and gifts, and she made sure that her son treated her with care.

The female cousin had not forgotten her male cousin, the love of her life. She was still beautiful, and her beauty was observed by men of all races. She was prepared to seek her need for sexual fulfillment elsewhere.

It was the practice for the insurance man to come by the house to collect premiums for the death policies the widow kept on her family and herself. One day, the widow left the money for the premiums with her daughter-in-law while she went to town to check on the nightclub she and her sons owned. The beautiful daughter-in-law was home alone.

The insurance man knocked on the door.

"Who's there?" inquired the daughter-in-law.

The insurance man announced himself and she opened the door. Standing in the doorway was the most beautiful woman the insurance man had ever seen. There on the doorstep was a handsome white man. He was six feet, two inches tall with coal-black curly hair. His eyes were blue. When he saw her, he gasped. Her beauty took his breath away. The daughter-in-law had a similar reaction when she saw the insurance man. She invited the insurance man inside the house. Before he left, they had committed the oldest sin known to man. She fell madly in love, and the feeling appeared to be mutual.

Afterward, the two lovers found each other in the woods, under the house, in the barn, just anywhere they could hide from her family. Every Saturday, when the family went to work at the nightclub, she was free to meet her lover. She feigned illness many Sundays when he came to call.

She was radiant with love, so much so that her cousin Willie (Uncle Louis and Stella's daughter) asked her why she suddenly looked so happy. She had to tell someone. She told Willie everything about her lover. Willie scolded her about an extramarital affair with a white man, especially about getting impregnated by him.

"If you have a child by him, everybody will know. Your husband is jet-black. The baby will be half white. You can't get away with it. Don't forget, you already had a baby out of wedlock." Willie talked until she could not say anything more. As usual, the beautiful cousin did not listen.

When it was obvious that she was with a child, her mother-in-law told the church congregation that she was going to be a grandmother. She was ecstatic with happiness. The daughter-in-law was worried even though she had allowed her husband to have sex with her as a precaution for this very inevitability. She hoped that the baby would be born dark enough to make her husband believe that it was his child. Even better, there was a small chance that it was his child.

When the child was born, it was completely white. The child's mother was frightened until she saw how her mother-in-law did not question the child's whiteness but was just as affectionate with the child and her daughter-in-law as she could be. The husband did not seem to notice either.

The child grew up as the grandchild of the wealthy widower and the daughter of her son. There was never a question from the grandparent and the father. The community and the church congregation knew that the little girl was half white. The community just shook their heads and kept their own counsel.

The beautiful cousin eventually divorced her husband. Still, her daughter was well provided for by the husband's family. When the child graduated from high school, the widow and her son paid her tuition to Alabama State College. There, she met a young man whose parents owned a mortuary. After the first year in college, she married the young man who was drafted into the US Army shortly thereafter.

For the next four years, she completed her college degree and returned home to Tuscaloosa where she lived near her mother.

By the time the daughter's husband was discharged from the Army, three children had been born. The family lived in Tuscaloosa for several more years, where rumors were heard about the tumultuous relationship between the daughter and her husband.

One day, as the daughter sat in a rocking chair facing the window, she was shot in the back of her head. The husband was charged with his wife's death. The husband went to trial and was found not guilty based on the contention that one of the small children was playing with a handgun and accidentally shot his mother dead. It was said that the husband took the children and left Tuscaloosa, Alabama. This information was never confirmed.

Tongues wagged in Romulus, Alabama when church members met at the Holly Spring Missionary Baptist Church. Everyone said if the grandmother had been alive, someone would have been brought to justice for killing her beloved granddaughter.

After the death of her daughter, the beautiful cousin continued to live alone. Her sister's brother-in-law asked her to marry him after his wife of many years passed away. The cousin never lost her beauty. When she died, she was still a very beautiful woman. According to in the rose bushes below. My naked body was scratched and bleeding as I lay amid the thorns, completely naked.

I could hear the woman cooing to her husband, trying to distract him as she retrieved my clothes and was about to throw them out of the window. I could tell that she had my clothes in her arms when her husband asked, "What's that you got? What you doing with men's clothes?"

This woman was not slow on the uptake. "Look at what I bought for you yesterday, honey. I bought you a suit, hat, and some shoes," she said to her husband.

The man liked my clothes because he had been unable to buy clothes like these for himself.

Damn, I thought. When the clothes were accepted by the man, I wondered how I was going to get home buck naked.

After the man went into the bathroom, the woman threw an old pair of pants out the window with my underwear and car keys on the top.

The following night, I eased into the nightclub and sat in the shadows. I no longer had a suit to wear. I didn't have a good hat and shoes. What I was wearing was old and torn up.

As I sat in the dark, the woman from the night before and her husband came into the room all hugged up. He wore my brown wool suit. The coat fell below his knees and had a rolled collar. The pants were pleated with a rolled cuff at the ankles. He wore my Stacy Adam shoes, turned up at the toe. He also wore my brown fedora hat, broken down over his right eye.

A murmur went up in the joint. "Them is Mr. Louis's clothes" could be heard whispered around, the room when they saw that man in my clothes.

That man had on every stitch of clothes that I wore to his woman's house. He would have had on my drawers, except the woman threw them out the window with some old pants and my car keys.

The man started imitating me, trying to dance into the room the same way I did when I got everyone's attention. He stood in the middle of the floor and snapped his fingers above his head, and his woman clung to him like she was glued on his body.

As the man went through his attention-getting gyrations, it was evident that he knew about me making love to his wife. His wife must have known what was good for her because she never left her husband's side.

I remember the night the juke joint died. We had had our share of partying, fighting, f——ing, and dancing in that joint. We never thought it would stop. Like I always say, "Everything that is that good for colored people, white folk always take it away."

There were two women who had controlled what went on in the nightclub. One was named Daisy and the other one was called Stack-O-Dollars.

Now Daisy and Stack were the ones who came every night to satisfy the sexual needs of the town fellows and those country boys who came up on Friday and Saturday nights.

Daisy was a short, dark woman with large hips and big breasts. She was not considered pretty but was cute and had great sex appeal. She knew how to persuade a man to go outside behind the building and get what he wanted after he paid her a dollar.

Stack-O-Dollars, on the other hand, never tried to entice a man; she just walked into the room and the men flocked to her like flies to honey.

Stack was six feet, two inches tall. She had a small waistline and big hips. She looked like a honeybee in heat. Her legs were so long that men wanted her to wrap them around their necks and have her standing against the back of the building. Stack was in control and made sure that every man who got any sex paid her a dollar, which she pushed down her blouse between her two big breasts that looked like the end of two torpedoes.

One night, all hell broke loose. Daisy started undercutting Stack-O-Dollar's price. They both had been charging one dollar. Now Daisy began to charge seventy-five cents or even a half dollar to the farm boys who didn't have a dollar. They just had change.

Stack saw Daisy coming back inside after having left with a man with whom Stack had haggled over the price of sex. He didn't have a dollar, just seventy-five cents. Yet he had been with Daisy.

Stack confronted Daisy, asking her how much the man had paid her. Daisy revealed that she had "picked him clean," meaning that she had accommodated the man for the change he had in his pocket.

Upon finding that Daisy was giving sex for less than one dollar, Stack went wild. She grabbed Daisy by the front of her blouse, ripping her blouse and her bra from her body. Dollar bills and coins flew everywhere.

Daisy was quick to respond. She kicked Stack in the groin, and the fight was on. They tore each other's clothes off and were soon naked, except for their shoes. Naked and bleeding, they fought on.

The patrons in the nightclub hooted and urged the women to fight. The sound of the patrons, rooting the fighters on, disturbed the neighborhood. One citizen called the police.

The patrons took sides and bet on who would be left standing. What they did not bet on was that the toughest police officer in town would answer the citizen's call. The colored people called this infamous officer "Papa Frank."

Papa Frank was a white police officer whose claim to fame was that he could quell any disturbance that occurred in the colored community. He was known for his ability to intimidate colored people.

He was big and tall with a large belly that fell over the top of his pants. He wore a black leather flap jacket with a large shiny police officer's badge affixed to his left chest. The jacket fit snugly over his belly, on top of khaki pants, encased in tall black boots. On his right side, he wore a very large gun in a large black button-down holster. His attire was topped off with a tan cap with a black bib. Even at night, Papa Frank wore black sunglasses, which added to the scary effect that made colored people cower whenever Papa Frank showed up.

Papa Frank rode up to the west end nightclub on his motorcycle. Behind him was his sidekick, another officer, on a motorcycle. Their sirens were blaring. At the sound of the motorcycles and the sirens, the whole colored neighborhood ran for cover.

When Papa Frank stepped into that joint, the colored people broke out through every opening in the place. They broke down doors and leaped out of windows. Everybody made themselves scarce. I wanted to see what would happen, so I hid under a table.

Papa Frank's eyes focused on Stack and Daisy fighting and rolling around on the floor. They were so busy fighting they didn't even know that the police were there.

Papa Frank reached down and raised Daisy up off the floor by her throat. He hit her in the head with his gloved fist. The blow was so hard that Daisy flew through the air and landed on the other side of the room.

Stack stood up, looking around to see where Daisy had gone. She was in such a daze that she didn't know that the police were there. Papa Frank turned on Stack. He hit her under her chin, like Joe Louis hit Max Schmeling. "Voop!" Stack squealed like a stuck pig.[18] She flew through the air backward and landed under the bar, out cold. Neither woman moved for an hour.

That was the night the juke joint died. Papa Frank told the club owner to close the place down and never open it again. The nightclub owner did as he was told and closed the place down for good. That was when colored people left the South, heading for northern cities. They went to Buffalo, Cleveland, Detroit, Flint, and other places in New York, Ohio, and Michigan.

That was not the night Papa Frank died though. I heard that his death took place some years later.

Here ends Louis's stories.

[18.] blog.detroitathletic.com/2012/.../the-brown-bomber-was-no-average-joe//
Cached

Louis Bailey's Life Continued

Louis's stories were numerous. He had new material for every family gathering. His life continued to create new stories.

Louis left Tuscaloosa, Alabama after the nightlife ceased to satisfy his need to live on the wild side. He went to Detroit, Michigan where he lived for the remainder of his life and continued his lifestyle of debauchery and violence. He beat a man to death with a chair for touching his girlfriend's thigh, for which he spent only six months in jail.

He dragged another man into his apartment when the man was caught looking into his window. Louis shot the man, then called the police and explained that he found the man in his house and shot him in self-defense. Once the Peeping Tom found out whom he had tried to rob and who had shot him, he told the police, "No, Mr. Louis didn't shoot me, no, suh. I got shot in a drive-by." The man was more afraid of Louis than he was of the police.

An altercation between Louis and his nephew, Daddy's sister, Aunt Annie's son, ended in Louis throwing the nephew out of his own kitchen window into the snow. Louis also threw Aunt Annie's husband out of his own house onto the paved sidewalk and cracked his skull. This duo, son and father, had an altercation that resulted in the father killing the son with a butcher's knife in the same kitchen.

At the age of seventy-five, Louis got religion. He got married to a decent woman, started going to church, became a church deacon, and settled down to family life. He did not leave his entire nature behind, nor did he divest himself of his gun.

Louis's stepson sassed him one night as he lay in bed beside his wife. He heard an argument between his stepson and stepdaughter.

Louis told the young man to be quiet and to leave his sister alone, whereupon the young man said, "You shut up, old man, or I'll go upside your head." Louis reached behind his head with both hands and brought out his .38 caliber pistol from underneath his pillow and shot the young man in the mouth. The bullet went through the young man's lips, knocking out all his front teeth and lodging in his jaw. Louis went back to sleep.

The mother who knew of Louis's past cautioned her son, "You had better do what Mr. Louis tells you to do." The stepson never sassed Louis again.

The stepson was so afraid of Louis that when he went to the hospital, he told the doctor that he had been in a car crash and that was how he lost his teeth. Neither the doctor nor the victim suspected that a bullet lay in the young man's jaw where the bullet remained.

The young man died a year later of complications associated with a head injury. At the autopsy, a bullet was found in the young man's jaw. Neither the bullet nor the head trauma was associated with Louis who was not charged with the young man's death.

Louis Bailey grew old and sick. He had rheumatoid arthritis, diabetes, and high blood pressure. Louis lost one leg to diabetes. Then another leg was taken off. He was placed in a nursing home for the aged and disabled. Before he died in his late eighties, he also lost both his arms.

The nurses reported that Louis lay in bed, just a torso and head, and flirted with the nurses until the end of his life. He would say to the nurses as they came to tend him, "Girl, you so fine. Look at you. Umph, umph, umph. Them's some hips you got on you. Lord ham mussy. Makes me wanna get up from this bed and take you for a spin. Mussy Lord."

The nurses would laugh and say, "You go on, Mr. Louis."

Louis's spouse heard him tell the story about working at a mortuary where he would take the new underwear intended for the dead and bury the dead in his dirty underwear. Even though Louis was buried without his arms and without his legs, his wife made sure that Louis was buried in new clean underwear.

Stack-O-Dollars

Stack-O-Dollars found herself unemployed. The only skill she had was prostitution. This skill was useful to her in finding someone who would take care of her. She found a young man who was addicted to sex. He was Otis Bailey, my cousin. He had been raised by Grandma along with my other cousin, Louis Bailey. His mother was Daddy's sister, Aunt Lucille.

Stack was just what Otis needed. As long as he would pay her, she would perform. He paid Stack-O-Dollar for sex, sometimes two or three times in one night. If he worked hard, he could pay her five dollars each night and he could have sex five times.

Otis was a country boy with no sophistication and was so enamored with Stack that he asked her to marry him.

Early one Saturday morning, Otis came to our house, where we lived with our grandparents, to introduce his new bride to his family. He walked in the door, followed by a giant of a woman.

She was much taller than he, about six feet, two inches to his five feet, eleven inches. Adding another three inches to her height were the high-heeled black patent leather sandals she wore. She wore a matching black patent leather belt cinched very tightly around her wasplike waist. Her skirt was short, barely reaching below the curve of her hips. Her blouse was tight-fitting, allowing each breast to protrude to a point of its own. Her hair was cut short and plastered to her head. She wore heavy makeup with long eyelashes and full red lips. Her earrings dangled to her shoulders. Stack was sex personified.

As the duo entered the house, we all ran to see Otis's new wife.

Uncle Buddy, who was a minister and was visiting his parents that day, looked on and exclaimed, "That's Stack-O-Dollars!"

Daddy's eyes bulged out. You could almost see his eyes shoot out on a string and say, "Boing!" and then snap back into their sockets.

Annie Lee Mama was unmoved by Stack's looks but was concerned about morality. She said, "Otis ought to be ashamed of himself, bringing that woman in here over these children." She protected us like a mama bear.

Although I was not near enough to hear what Grandma said, when Otis introduced his new spouse to her, I can imagine it was something like, "Da now, you done gone and messed yo self up with some good-for-nothing, piece-o-trash nobody." I did hear Grandma say to Otis as he left, "Y'all git on up the road. No need to bring that sort a thing 'round here." Stack was not welcome in Grandma's house.

Grandpa most likely reacted like Daddy but said nothing. He did not wish to remind Grandma of the ol yella gal. Otis and Stack went to Detroit, Michigan where Otis lived and womanized until he died at the age of eighty-five. Stack-O-Dollars died mysteriously within a few years of arriving in Detroit.

The Black Hand of Death

A soldier, who came to Tuscaloosa to visit his mother, went to the Stardust Club to get a beer. Clubs were no longer called juke joints.

The Stardust was the new nightclub down on Thirty-Second Avenue. This soldier was standing at the bar, drinking his beer, when Papa Frank and his sidekick entered the barroom.

This soldier did not live in Tuscaloosa and didn't know the fear that the local citizens held for these two police officers. In addition, this soldier had experienced trauma in the war and was said to be suffering from a little shell-shock. The meeting of the two forces was a deadly combination.

The police officers accosted the soldier by saying, "What you doing here, boy?" The soldier did not respond. The officers continued to harangue the soldier, calling him nigger over and over until Papa Frank's sidekick observed that the soldier had a gun in the front of his belt.

"He got a gun. He got a gun!" yelled the deputy.

Papa Frank and the deputy reached for their guns. Papa Frank and his deputy had been accustomed to intimidating colored people by their appearances, their loud voices, and the use of their fists. They had enjoyed a reputation of being "badder than the baddest nigger in town." They probably never had to pull their guns from their button-down holsters before this incident. They were slow on the draw.

The soldier saw himself being harassed after he had gone to war and risked his life to fight for a country that still considered him a second-class citizen. He saw the enemy preparing to shoot him. He had been trained to kill the enemy before the enemy killed him. Also, he was a little shell shocked. He turned and fired, killing both officers before their guns cleared their holsters.

Papa Frank and his deputy, who had been feared by every colored person in Tuscaloosa, Alabama, now lay dead on the Stardust Club barroom floor, having been killed by a colored man.

The news traveled like wildfire. "A colored man done kilt them two badass police officers." There was pride in the voices of every colored man, woman, and child who passed the word along. Colored men and boys were told to stay indoors and off the streets. The colored community went underground.

After the soldier killed Papa Frank and his deputy, colored people were extremely cautious about anyone coming to their front doors. When knocks were heard at the door, the person inside would say, "Who dat?"

The person outside would try to ascertain to whom they were speaking. They would ask, "Who dat?" This method of ensuring that the person inside the house and the one outside were known to each other was made into a comic skit that went like this:

Outside: *Knock. Knock. Knock.*
Inside: Who dat?
Outside: Who dat?
Inside: Who dat?
Outside: Who dat?
Inside: Who dat sez who dat, evy time I sez who dat?

Colored people waited for the Ku Klux Klan to ride through the colored neighborhood in retaliation for the killing of the two white police officers by a colored man. The KKK was afraid to come into the community with the bad-colored soldier still on the loose.

The shooter ran. He went to Moody Swamp where he lived off the land for a week. Of course, the soldier did not have his camping gear, canteen, K rations, or bedroll. All he had was his gun and a few bullets left. When the bullets were gone, the soldier could no longer protect himself.

After a week, the soldier came out of Moody Swamp, surrendered to the police, and was placed in jail. Owing to the killing of two famous white police officers by a colored man and that the jury was all white, the case seemed to be open-and-shut for a death penalty decision.

A trial was held for the colored soldier who had killed two upstanding white policemen. He was judged insane as the reason he shot the lawmen. White folk said, "That nigger must be crazy."

No, he was not crazy. The soldier saw the two officers as the enemy. He killed the two officers before they could kill him, just as he was trained to do in the Army.

Nevertheless, he was placed in an insane asylum for several months. After which, he was released and allowed to leave Alabama.

The soldier went to a northern state and disappeared.

Moody Swamp

According to historical records, Moody Swamp is an antediluvian swamp fed by the Black Warrior River. The swampy basin once covered a vast portion of Tuscaloosa County. Over the years, the water receded into the riverbanks during the dry season and flooded back to cover some of its original territories during the rainy season.

It was not until the Tennessee Valley Authority provided dams and flood control that the once-flooded areas dried up and farmers cleared some of the fertile lands for homesteading and farming. (On a personal note, my husband and I own a farmland that is part of the Moody Swamp basin. We have created a subdivision of one hundred homes on this land.)

When my grandpa, William Bailey, lived with us on the farm in the Moody Swamp basin, he would go hunting in the swamp. He would hunt coon, opossum, rabbit, and deer. There were other more dangerous animals in the swamp that he did not hunt although these animals probably hunted him. There were bobcats and several species of venomous snakes known to inhabit Moody Swamp.

One night, as Grandpa was hunting in Moody Swamp with his three hounds, he became separated from his hunting dogs. He called to them and whistled, yet they did not return to his side. The dogs went home and went to sleep in their doghouse.

When Grandpa tried to return home, with no help from his dogs, he realized that the moon was not visible and the forest was pitch-black. He could not tell which way to go home, and the more he tried to determine the directions home, the more he got confused and lost. He was afraid of the snakes and even the bobcats. He could shoot the bobcat, but the snakes were another matter. His greatest fear was that in the dark, he might step on a snake and get bitten.

Instead of moving around and creating more opportunities for a snake to present itself, Grandpa decided to wait until the sun came up to give light and point the direction home. Meanwhile, he relied on an old folks' tale that if you make a circle with a rope and lie down inside the circle, snakes will not crawl over the rope and bite you. Grandpa had brought along a length of rope for such an inevitable need.

Early the next morning, Grandma realized that Grandpa's dogs had returned home without him. She told Daddy who went to find Grandpa. Daddy took the lead dog, put a cord around his neck, and followed him back to where Grandpa lay sleeping, unbitten, inside his rope circle.

Acts of Criminal Mischief?

In spite of the contributions that Negro people have made to society, scientific and literary analysis of the comparisons of Negro and Caucasian intelligence postulate that the Negro is inferior to the Caucasian race. The classification of cranial capacity and the bell-shaped curve theory on IQ differences have supported the thinking of many Southern whites. It was believed by some that the Negro people did not have the intelligence to perform acts of great magnitude.

In the Southern states, an act of criminal mischief by a Negro would be considered punishable as the Negro person would be judged low-functioning like all Negro people were believed to be, and it would be considered that the person would have done the act not because he was crazy and didn't know any better but because he just wanted to get into mischief.

On the other hand, if a Negro person did a purposeful act of extreme violence, the Negro person would be considered insane as Negro people were incapable of performing great feats of any kind on purpose.

An example of this way of thinking occurred when Neelie Abner Foster, a thirty-year-old psychotic colored woman, committed an act of criminal mischief when she burnt Uncle John Wells's barn down. She did the deed because Uncle John told her to go home where she belonged. She wanted to stay with Uncle John and play with his children. Being denied this privilege meant that Uncle John had rejected her personally. It never occurred to Neely Abner that Uncle John did not want Neely around his little children. Her response was to burn his barn down on her way home. She was sent to jail for three years for having done an act of arson.

Even as children, we knew that Neely Abner Foster was crazy. We could not understand how a judge and a jury could conclude that she was in her right mind when she burnt Uncle John's barn down.

My sisters and I saw Neely Abner one day when we were coming home from school. We had separated ourselves from the other children walking home and were hurrying because Daddy had told us to get home as fast as we could. He had work for us to do.

As we passed the farm of Grandma's brother, Uncle Bob, we heard the motor of the white children's school bus coming behind us. (In 1940, white children had bus transportation to school and back home; Negro children walked to and from school.)

The dirt road upon which we all traveled ran down a hill into a dip in the road and went up a steep incline to reach the level surface beyond. The bus was coming fast as the driver seemed to accelerate down the hill to climb the oncoming hill without changing gears. We were caught in the dip in the road and were forced to climb up on the embankment to escape the dust and rocks that the bus spewed on us and the words, spit, and crumpled paper wads that the white children directed at us.

We made it safely to the field above the embankment and came face-to-face with Neely Abner. She was alone, hoeing out Uncle Bob's sweet potato patch. She looked at us as if we were manna from heaven, and we looked at her like she was the crazy cousin we had heard so much about. We looked back into the concave road where the bus was rumbling by. We could not retreat in that direction. We stood there, being caught between a rock and a hard place.

Neely Abner looked to us like the old witch who captured Hansel and Gretel in the children's story. She wore several layers of rags that hung loosely from her torso. A gray bandana covered her head where sprigs of hair stuck out above and below. Her eyes were swollen and runny. Snuff dripped from her loose lips. She popped her toothless mouth several times before she spoke.

"Hey," she croaked. "I know y'all. You cutin [cousin] LS's putty [pretty] chulluns [children], ain't ya? Yea, y'all so putty. Load [Lord], ham' mussy [have mercy]. Y'all 'bout the puttyst thang dese old eyes dun seed in a long time. Come over heah [here] and giv' yo cutin Nel'abner some tsugar [sugar]."

She advanced toward us with the raised hoe as she spoke. We knew she was not threatening us with the hoe, just following the practice of placing the hoe on one's shoulder when not in use. However, we were scared of her because we knew that she was crazy and that she had been in prison. Also, we had no intention of kissing her.

We backed off. Sister Mable said, "Let's run." Mable was an exceptionally fast runner. Sister Gladys was almost as fast. Our oldest sister, Lois, never ran. She just walked fast. Sister Gloria was not fast at running, and I was too small to cover much ground.

Lois took charge and responded to cousin Neely Abner, "Maybe some other time. We have to go now. Daddy is waiting for us." We eased down the side of the embankment, back into the road, whereupon Mable took off running, nearly catching the white children's school bus. Gladys followed. As we eased out of her presence, cousin Neely Abner was heard saying to herself, "Dem sho is sum putty chilluns. De jus don wanna giv no body no tsugar."

Even we children knew that Neely Abner was crazy. Yet she was adjudged sane by an all-white jury and was sent to prison for three years.

Because of the ways in which Southern whites judged colored people, Neeley, who was insane, was treated more harshly for burning down a barn than the sane soldier that killed the two policemen.

Concern for Fair Treatment for Black People in the United States

The colored soldier and others who fought in American wars epitomized concerns that black people had for their service and subsequent ill-treatment when they returned to the states. In January 1991, I wrote a letter to a member of Congress to address my concerns for the issue of the black and Latino soldiers fighting in foreign wars. The letter reads as follows:

At a time when we have been encouraged by the remembrance of Dr. Martin Luther King Jr. to dream of peace and success as citizens in a country that has for so long denied us chances for total success, we find our members being inordinately represented in the armed forces that are poised to fight for a people we do not know, we do not share in their riches, and from whom we will receive no compensation for the lives that will surely be lost.

The black race has been first in battle and last in employment. We have been first in poverty and last in colleges. We have been snatched from our homeland and made a part of the history of a people who have dehumanized us, ostracized us, and denied us the rights of passage into the mainstream of employment and high socioeconomic standing. Why then should we be required to fight for this country to ensure the safety of those who have perpetrated such atrocities against us?

As a black person, I am decidedly against fighting a war that will kill so many black young people that our numbers will be diminished for generations to come.

Just as America has taken forty years to negotiate a peaceful settlement with Russia, a peaceful settlement must be negotiated in the Middle East. Only in a world without war can black people hope to reach the mountaintop envisioned by Dr. King.

Let us, on January 15, in honor of Dr. King, make a decision not to go to war and remove our young people from the battlefield.

When black soldiers return home from war, do not forget their willingness to sacrifice their lives for a country that has not been supportive to them and their kind. Reaffirm your commitment to affirmative actions for employment for black and Hispanic people and support college scholarships and education for people who have, for so long, been denied an equal share in the prosperity of this nation.

For the blood we have already shed, we demand the right to dream and to have the opportunity to live out the creed that all men are created equal.

Black Is Beautiful

During the journey of my ancestors, the name of our race changed many times. Because our ancestors had been taken from the continent of Africa and brought to America by slave profiteers, the first name designations were Africans and blacks. When we were enslaved, we were called slaves. After we were freed from slavery, we were called Negroes or niggers. As time went by, we became colored. During the 1960s, we decided that we were black. We further declared that black is beautiful. Later, we adopted a new name that showed pride in Africa, our homeland, and at the same time, it showed pride in being citizens of America. Our name became African Americans.

The death of Papa Frank and his deputy ushered in the hiring of a black police officer. His name was Ape Skin. He was hired to police the black community now that the remaining white officers were afraid to do so.

Ape Skin was given a car to ride in by himself. He could only arrest black people. If he came across a white person committing a crime, he was required to call a white officer to make the arrest.

As time went by, other average-looking black men were hired as police officers. The fear of the white police was no longer pervasive in the black or African American community in Tuscaloosa, Alabama.

The white police force selected Ape Skin because he had the appearance of an ape. This act was supposed to be an affront to the black community. Ape Skin got his name because he was shaped like a gorilla, with long arms, broad shoulders, and a slim lower body. His face was round, with small bead-like eyes that peered out from under a heavy protruding bone structure, situated where his eyebrows should have been. We did not mind that he looked like an ape. We were so proud to have one of our own as a police officer. Yes, Ape Skin was black and he looked like an ape, but he was not an affront to our sensibilities; we thought that Ape Skin was beautiful.

Howard Bailey

Aunt Luella, Louis Bailey's mother, was Daddy's oldest sister. Her second son, Howard, left home when he was seventeen years old to join the US Navy. He was a quiet gentleman who, as far as everyone knew, was successful in the armed forces. He served thirty-two years and retired with honors.

According to Aunt Luella, somewhere in Howard's career, drug dealers placed drugs in his duffel bag and, thereafter, bribed him to bring drugs back from abroad. They threatened to expose him to the US Navy personnel. Even after he retired, the drug dealers threatened to kill him if he did not continue to help them.

About three o'clock one morning, Howard arrived in Tuscaloosa, Alabama having driven nonstop from Long Beach, California.

Years before, he had married Thirsey Mae Reed, my cousin on my birth mother's side, who lived the nightlife and did not take care of the children. Howard brought the children to his mother, Aunt Luella, and asked her to keep and raise his two small boys and the three-month-old baby girl.

He told her about his troubles and let her know that he would be murdered and he wanted his children to be safe. Aunt Luella raised Howard's three children. They grew up to be outstanding adults who made contributions to their communities and were highly respected.

During the time the children were growing up, Aunt Luella became the founder of a church that flourished and became one of the largest African American churches in Tuscaloosa, Alabama. Her picture, along with the three children and Aunt Lucille, is displayed at the entrance of the church with the inscription Founder.

Sadly, Howard's prediction of his violent death came true for he was murdered. He was hanged in Long Beach, California.

Aunt Luella told the following story after she returned from Long Beach where she went to retrieve Howard's body. Unbeknownst to Howard, the woman who became his girlfriend was connected to the drug cartel. After distracting his mind from his troubles and assuring him that he was imagining things, he began to relax and live a normal life.

One day, the girlfriend went to the store to get beer and cigarettes. While she was gone, two men came into their apartment, subdued Howard, and hung him behind the door with his own belt. They tightened the belt loop around his neck, pulled the remaining end of the belt over the door, and closed the door on the belt. As the door closed, they pulled the belt through on the other side until Howard was lifted off the floor. He died hanging behind the door. The girlfriend never came back home.

Aunt Luella, Howard's mother, gave up her free burial plot in the Holly Spring Missionary Baptist Church Cemetery and interred Howard on the front row. The Blackburn/Bailey family did not disparage Howard's burial on the front row even though he was a great-grandson because he was buried with military honors.

Aunt Luella Bailey had a tumor in her side for thirty years. She was afraid to submit to an operation that would have removed the tumor early in her life. After a long time, the tumor became cancerous. Aunt Luella died in her eighties. Since she had given Howard, her son, her free burial plot, she was not buried in the Holly Spring Missionary Baptist Church Cemetery.

The Second Herman Bailey

Aunt Luella's third son, Herman, was one of the nicest people in our family. His mother named him after her brother, Uncle Herman Bailey. The second Herman was a minister and the pastor of a church in Cincinnati, Ohio, for many years. Public records show that Herman died at the age of eighty-two and was buried in Ohio.

Shakespeare was right in the case of the three brothers. "The evil that men do lives after them; the good is oft interred with their bones."[19] So it was with these three brothers. We all remember Louis's exploits and often laugh at some of his stories. We rarely speak of Howard and Herman.

[19.] Act 3, scene ii of *Julius Caesar* by William Shakespeare (spoken by Mark Antony)

The First Herman Bailey

The first Herman was Uncle Herman Bailey, Grandpa and Grandma's third son. The first Herman Bailey was a rascal. He was born when his parents were wealthy and able to provide a life of plenty for their children.

The two oldest boys, Clelly and Louis, had been raised differently before the family gained prominence as wealthy Negroes. Clelly was a quiet man who married Aunt Alma and lived a subdued life. Louis left home when he was seventeen to join the Army. When he retired from the armed service, he moved to St. Louis, Missouri.

The first Herman seemed to have had a Jekyll and Hyde[20] personality. On the one hand, he was charming and lovable. On the other hand, he was evil and dangerous.

Herman did as he pleased around his parents' home. If he wanted to help his father in the field, he did so. If he did not want to work on any given day, he went hunting or sought a loose woman or a gambling game in which to get involved. When he was eighteen years old, he married a handsome girl named Bama, who was not attractive but was a lot of a woman. She was pleasant to look at. She was slightly plump, with large breasts and rounded hips. She had curly hair, which she wore sleeked back in water waves. She had large dark eyes with long eyelashes, which she knew how to flutter when she was being seductive and charming. It was said that she was most satisfying in bed. Yet she was saintly in her discourse and

---

[20]. *Strange Case of Dr. Jekyll and Mr. Hyde*, written by Scottish author Robert Louis Stevenson, published in 1886

well-liked by everyone she met. Herman loved Bama with both his personalities.

After they were married, Herman moved Bama into the house with his parents. For many months, Herman worked with his father on the farm and remained at home with Bama on the weekends.

Finally, his Mr. Hyde personality got the best of him, and he began to leave home on the weekends and not return until Sunday night. Bama did not complain. She remained faithful to him and waited until he returned. She never scolded him for leaving home no matter how long he stayed away. Herman, on the other hand, never explained where he had been or with whom he had stayed. In reality, he would frequent the honkey-tonks in the woods where he would drink, gamble, dance, and lay with the foulest of women and fornicate the time away.

One Sunday night, he arrived home dirty and smelling of swill and women. He sauntered into the bedroom he and Bama shared and thought that she would have changed in her demeanor toward him for the way he was treating her. Instead, Bama was her usual sweet self. She had water-waved her hair, bathed and perfumed her body, and dressed in her sheerest nightgown. She had cooked all his favorite foods and placed them on a table by the fireplace.

When Herman saw that Bama was being more solicitous toward him after all he had done to her, he could not stand it anymore. He picked up each dish of food and threw it into the fire. He even threw the cake into the flames. All the while, as he threw item after item into the fire, he rebuked her for loving him, for her kindness, and for her trying to entrap him. Bama fled from the room. The following morning, she packed her belongings and went home to her mother.

Herman continued his split life, first being charming and good and then being evil. After many months of living without Bama, he went to her and entreated her to return home with him. She refused.

Finally, he went to Pizitz Store in Tuscaloosa where only the finest clothes were sold, usually to rich white people. Herman bought Bama a full-length fur coat. When he presented the coat to Bama, she could not refuse to return home as she wanted the coat more than anything.

Herman moved Bama up to Tuscaloosa in a small house where they set up housekeeping for just the two of them. Herman kept his Mr. Hyde personality at bay, and they were very happy.

Herman went to work as an odd jobber who could make all kinds of home repairs and work on construction projects. He was congenial and well-liked by all with whom he worked. Every month, Herman made a payment on Bama's fur coat at Pizitz. Finally, Herman finished paying for the coat, but Pizitz refused to admit that the coat was paid off and continued to bill him. He went to the store and proved that he had paid off every cent of the coat. He refused to pay Pizitz another penny. Pizitz sent the city police to arrest Herman for nonpayment of the coat.

When Herman heard that the police were looking for him, he hid out. He did not go to work. He sent Bama to Ohio to live with her sister.

She never came back, and he never remarried.

The manhunt for Herman grew intense. The Ku Klux Klan, who were members of the police force, became involved in the search for Herman. His relatives and friends were hounded to reveal his whereabouts.

One night, as the search for Herman intensified, the Mr. Hyde side of his personality came out. He decided to hide in plain sight. Herman borrowed a wagon and a mule. He dressed in ragged clothes and a floppy straw hat. He drove the wagon uptown in full view of the police. He even drove by the police station where he was stopped by several policemen. Herman, who was normally well-spoken, asked, "Who's ya'll looking fur?"

A policeman said, "We're looking for an old lazy, slew-foot nigger named Herman Bailey. Do you know him?"

To which Uncle Herman replied, "No, suh, I don' know no slew-foot nigger dat's named no Herman Bailey." Then Uncle Herman asked, "What's he looks lak?" To which the police gave their stereotypical description of a colored man.

Now Herman was a handsome man, about five feet, eleven inches tall. He had brown skin and soft, thick hair. His face was well-shaped, with sparkling (some said devilish) eyes, and he sported a neatly trimmed mustache. He was muscularly built and was fit from working in construction. He was normally a dandy who dressed to show off his looks. The description he was given of himself truly did not describe the real Herman Bailey.

Herman said, "Boss, I ain't seed nobody looking lak dat. If'n I does see sich a nigger, I be telling you rat soon."

Herman clicked to the old mule, "Giddy up thar' mule." Whereupon he continued to ride around town all night. The following day, Uncle Herman went to Montgomery, Alabama where he lived until he died. For fifty years, whenever he came to Tuscaloosa to visit his family, his visit was kept a secret for fear that the city police would apprehend him for the nonpayment of the fur coat he bought for Bama, his beloved wife.

When Uncle Herman died, Daddy went to Montgomery, Alabama and brought his body home. For the first time in fifty years, no one had to remain silent when Uncle Herman came to Tuscaloosa. He was buried in the Holly Spring Missionary Baptist Church Cemetery, albeit in an unmarked grave.

Aunt Lucille

The second oldest daughter of William and Annie Bailey was named Lucille. She was highly intelligent and was sent to Stillman College to continue her education after she completed her grammar schooling in Romulus. The family was proud to have a daughter in college.

One day, Lucille came home and announced that she was with a child. After the child was born, Grandma kept the boy and raised him. They named him O. P. Bailey, which was later changed to Otis. He was the cousin who married a woman named Stack-O-Dollars.

Members of the Holly Spring Missionary Baptist Church who had babies out of wedlock were excommunicated from the church. They were considered loose women and outcasts. Since Lucille was a descendant of Romeo Blackburn Sr., she was not considered a loose woman. Although Lucille was not excommunicated from the church, she was not able to marry a man in her age range.

Aunt Lucille married an elderly man named Herbert who had children older than her. One of the older daughters told me that their father was a mean man. Their mother died young and his children ran away from home the moment they could "hop a train, marry a man, or go live with relatives."

Aunt Lucille and Uncle Herbert had eight children. He beat the boys with chains and whips and beat Aunt Lucille for the least infraction.

When Aunt Lucille was ready to deliver their eighth child, Uncle Herbert sat upon her and beat her with a whip. Even though it was raining, sleeting, and extremely cold, Aunt Lucille, wearing only a gown and a robe, ran from her house to the house of a midwife, Aunt Icey Belle Stewart, some three miles away.

Daddy learned of the situation and came home to get his gun to kill Uncle Herbert. He told Annie Lee Mama that Uncle Herbert had beaten Aunt Lucille as she ran three miles in the sleet and rain until she reached the home of Uncle Ben and Aunt Icey Belle. Annie Lee Mama tried to talk Daddy out of shooting Uncle Herbert. Daddy left home and met cousin Willard Blackburn who drove Daddy back home after convincing him that his family needed him more than Uncle Herbert needed killing.

Even though Aunt Icey Belle was the best midwife in the area, she knew that she could not save Aunt Lucille for she had been beaten too badly. Aunt Lucille was taken to Stillman Hospital where she had gone to college years earlier.

The lives of the baby and Aunt Lucille were saved by the doctors at Stillman Hospital. Grandma and Grandpa had left their sharecropping farm and had moved to Tuscaloosa near Stillman College. Aunt Lucille remained in the hospital and at Grandma's house for nearly a year. She recovered, except for her knee which was inflamed for the rest of her life. After age eighty, one of her legs was amputated.

According to public records, Uncle Herbert died in the 1950s. Aunt Lucille (née Bailey) lived on for sixty more years.

Personally, my husband, Albert, and I visited Aunt Lucille when she was 103 years old. She recited the twenty-third Psalm, and she also recited poetry. She sang two songs with me—"Precious Lord" and "His Eye Is on the Sparrow." She knew the verses of both songs.

My family and I attended Aunt Lucille's funeral when she died in 2011 at the ripe old age of 107. She was buried in a mausoleum crypt in the Inglewood Memorial Cemetery in Inglewood, California.

As a point of information, Aunt Icey Belle was the midwife for the Romulus community. She was married to Uncle Ben Stewart.

Uncle Ben Stewart was my grandmother Rebecca's half-brother on my birth mother's side. Their mother, Great-Grandma Antietam, was racially mixed with Negro, Caucasian, and Indian ancestry. She had straight hair and gray eyes. Uncle Ben's father was reported to have been a Pygmy slave brought from the Congo in Africa. Uncle

Ben was four feet, five inches tall. He had black skin, straight hair, and gray eyes. Uncle Ben married Aunt Icey Belle, who was five feet, ten inches tall.

Sister Mable remembered seeing the couple come to church, walking through the cemetery path that was a shortcut from their house. According to Mable, the couple appeared to be a woman coming to church with her twelve-year-old son. Nevertheless, Uncle Ben was a strong man who owned and farmed his own land. He was gentle, kind, well-loved by his family, and respected by the community.

Uncle Ben and Aunt Icey Belle had three boys who were all Pygmy size—four feet, four inches to four feet, seven inches tall. The genetic code to be short-statured still exists in the family. Uncle Ben's great-great-grandson who lives in Tuscaloosa is about four feet, eleven inches tall.

Grandma Rebecca Reed

I heard this story being told by the adults who talked when they thought we children were not listening or that we did not know what they were talking about.

Grandma Rebecca Reed was the mother of my birth mother. One day, Grandma Rebecca and Mrs. Tooson met down by the creek that ran at the foot of what later became known as Sterling's Mountain. It was rumored that a child, or maybe two, had been born to the liaison between Mr. Tooson and Grandma Rebecca Reed. Mrs. Tooson wanted to put a stop to the goings-on.

Grandma Rebecca was crossing over the creek on the footbridge made of felled trees, split into halves, that spanned the water. As Grandma reached the middle of the bridge, Mrs. Tooson jumped out of the bushes alongside the creek and inquired, "Why are you still messing with my husband? He said he was through with you after you had that last child, Louridell."

Grandma Rebecca turned to go back the way she had come, trying to elude Mrs. Tooson who was armed with a club. As Grandma Rebecca retreated, Mrs. Tooson started rocking the logs that comprised the footbridge. Back and forth, she rocked the logs on their round side until Grandma Rebecca fell into the creek.

Nothing Mrs. Tooson could have said or done would have angered Grandma Rebecca more than drenching her in the creek. Falling into the creek was demoralizing and dangerous as Grandma could not swim. She screamed and beat the water until she was able to catch a large fern that grew along the bank of the creek. By this time, Mrs. Tooson was upon her with the club. "I told you to leave my husband alone. You think 'cause you were married to that white man you are better than everyone else. That don't give you the right to take other folks' husbands," she repeated with every blow.

Now, Grandma Rebecca was no pushover and, upon getting her footing on the creek bank, started to return the blows upon Mrs. Tooson.

Mrs. Tooson was right about Grandma's marriage to a white man. She married Mr. Reed who came to America from Ireland during the potato famine in 1850[21] when he was a young man. He traveled throughout the Southern states during slavery and the Civil War. His occupations were digging wells and fashioning ax handles. He did not accumulate wealth in America; he barely kept his body and soul together. For reasons unknown to the family, he spent his time with the Negro people, the downtrodden, and the poor.

Grandpa Reed arrived in Romulus a tired old man. He sought lodging with my great-grandmother, Antietam Stewart. Although Antietam was a Negress, she had a fair complexion.

She was racially mixed, mostly Indian and African, but she also had Caucasian ancestry. Rebecca, Antietam's daughter, a girl of fifteen, caught Mr. Reed's eye. They were married. Their three oldest children appeared Caucasian. As the family grew, the remaining children were born with darker complexions designated as mulatto.

Grandpa Reed died in his nineties after digging a well for a white family on a cold wintry day when the temperature was in subzero degrees. Before leaving for home, he begged the woman who owned the well to allow him to change into dry clothes behind the cookstove in the kitchen. The woman refused. He walked home in his wet clothes that became frozen stiff from the cold. When he arrived home, the family heard his approach as his frozen coat was scraping the ground. He was put to bed and died of pneumonia three days later.

Rebecca had married the old man, Mr. Reed, when she was fifteen. After his death, she was still a young woman who had needs.

She had many affairs but settled on Mr. Tooson as her main love. She was now in the creek, fighting for that love.

---

[21]. en.wikipedia.org/wiki/Irish_Potato_Famine

After the fight was concluded, without any declaration of victory, Grandma Rebecca went home, had a heart attack, and died.

Grandpa and Grandma Reed were buried in the Holly Spring Missionary Baptist Church Cemetery beside a large oak tree. The tree has long since been removed. Although the tree is gone and there are no headstones to mark their graves, the spot where they are buried is undisturbed. There is a slight indentation in the ground, revealing that bodies are buried underneath.

Eula Reed, Our Birth Mother

Daddy married Eula Reed, our birth mother, when she was fourteen years old. She was a beautiful young mulatto girl with light olive skin, long black curly hair, light brown eyes, and a stunningly beautiful face. It was said that she was the most beautiful girl outside the Blackburn family that ever lived in Romulus, Alabama. Grandma Rebecca encouraged Daddy to marry Eula so she would have someone to take care of her.

Unfortunately, Daddy and Eula Mama lived with his mother, who was a strong, overbearing person, and took an instant dislike to Eula. First, she was more beautiful than Grandma's girls who were jealous of Eula. Second, she was too young to be married. As a child, she still needed rearing.

Grandma took on the task and required Daddy to whip Eula Mama when Grandma thought she had misbehaved. This treatment led to many fights between Daddy and Eula Mama. Even after they moved into a house of their own, the fights continued. Daddy tried to raise Eula and to curtail her activities as if she were a child. She rebelled and fought for the freedom to be a grown-up.

They moved to Mrs. Ora Miller's farm. One day, while Daddy was beating Eula, she ran into Mrs. Miller's house for protection. Daddy continued to chase her and attempted to enter the house, whereupon Mrs. Miller drew her pistol and said, "LS, if you come another step toward this child, I'll blow your brains out."

Daddy was very jealous of Eula Mama's beauty, which caused him to accuse her of looking at other men even when she might not have been guilty. Daddy, on the other hand, was a handsome man who received many invitations from women and was not entirely free of his own guilt.

Daddy and Eula Mama had five children within six years by the time Moody spirited her away.

Her first foray into the world occurred when Eula Mama begged Daddy to allow her to go to the Foot Washing at Weeping Mary Baptist Church in Coker, Alabama with Uncle Preston, her oldest brother. Daddy trusted Uncle Preston as the honest, kind person he was and allowed Mama to go. She wore a pink dress with a large pink bow tied around her hair, which fell down her back.

Late in the night, Uncle Preston returned without Mama. He sat on the porch and cried while telling Daddy that Eula would not come home with him. He stayed late pleading and trying to get her to come back with him. Instead, she went to Northport with Uncle Moody.

Daddy went to Northport and brought Eula home. She remained for a short time and left again. One cold, rainy night, when Daddy was away, Eula Mama left four children in bed, bundled me up in a blanket, and rode away with Uncle Moody. I had to be taken along because I was a nursing baby.

Lois, the oldest child, told the story. When Eula Mama left, Lois was six years old and was the oldest of the four children left alone in the house down in the country. She suffered from earaches and was in severe pain when Eula Mama left. Lois said a car came up the road and stopped at the house and that the last thing she heard was Eula Mama's heels clicking on the wooden floor. She was gone.

After Eula Mama left, Lois became the caretaker of the other three children even though she was only six years old. Daddy would bank the fire, putting large logs in the rear of the fireplace and piling coals in the front so that it would burn slowly. He would put peas on the stove to boil. He showed Lois how to stand in a chair and stir the peas to ensure that they did not burn. Although Lois was very intelligent, she could not attend school the year Eula Mama left.

After many days of leaving the four small children in the house to fend for themselves during the winter, Daddy took them to Eula Mama who was living with her sister, Aunt Estelle, in Northport, Alabama. Eula Mama got a job working at the Birchfield Hotel in downtown Tuscaloosa. She worked all week and went out on the town with Uncle Moody and her friends every weekend.

Mable, the second oldest sister, remembers the last time they saw Eula Mama. She told me this story. It was a Friday night and Eula Mama was getting dressed to go out. Aunt Estelle said to her, "Eula, you got to stay home with these chaps on the weekend. I take care of them all week, and I get tired. They are your children."

Mabel heard Eula reply, "I'm not going to stay home. I'm going out and have me some fun. We're going to Mobile. In the morning, you take them children over to OG's house. LS comes to town every Saturday." (Uncle O. G. Bailey was my father's brother and L. S. Bailey was my father.) "Leave them there. LS will pick them up." With that, Mabel said, she heard Mama's heels clicking across the floor and Eula was gone.

The following morning, Aunt Estelle took the four girls—Lois, Mabel, Gladys, and Gloria—to Uncle OG's house. Again, I remained with Eula because I was still a baby. When they arrived at Uncle OG's house, they found Aunt Clyde visiting. Daddy permitted his sister, Aunt Clyde, to take Gladys, the third child, with her to Kentucky. Daddy took the other three girls home to Romulus, Alabama.

Daddy filed for divorce. The judge gave Daddy the four oldest children. The judge declared my fate by decreeing that if the mother puts the baby down and the father picks her up, the baby will belong to the father.

Our birth mother, Eula, let nothing interfere with her going out and having fun with Uncle Moody and a man named Mr. West. When she could not find a babysitter, she took me along. One night, she left me in a truck, alone, for hours.

Moody, Eula's youngest brother, would not rest until Eula had divested herself of her children. He insisted that Eula get rid of me and my brother, who was born after the divorce. Uncle Moody took Eula, my baby brother, and me to a house in the woods where I was abandoned. Daddy found me and took me home to live with my four sisters and his new spouse, Annie Lee. Our new mother taught us to remember our birth mother by calling her Eula Mama. We called our new mother Annie Lee Mama.

The last time I saw my four sisters together, I was nine months old. Nevertheless, I remembered that there were four girls. When I came home, at nineteen months old, I asked, "Wher' d' utter wun?" (Where's the other one?) I was so young that my words were not clear.

Daddy spoke of this incident well into his nineties as he was amazed that I could remember all four of my sisters from the age of nine months and recognize that one was missing when I came home at nineteen months old.

The baby that was born after the divorce, who later proved to be Daddy's child, was given to Mr. and Mrs. Dunnigan. Mrs. Dunnigan was a childless woman who raised the child as her own. His original name was L. A. Bailey. Mrs. Dunnigan renamed him James.

James tells of the years he waited for Eula to return to take him home with her. He told how he cried when the children born to his foster father and another woman teased him, telling him that his mother did not love him and that she was not coming to get him. At age seven, he gave up expecting Eula to come and take him home.

Years later, James grew up to be the spitting image of Daddy, with voice and mannerisms just like his birth father. When James was eighteen, he came to California where Lois and I were living. James and us five sisters have been united as true brother and sisters since he was 21 years old.

Uncle Moody

After Grandma Rebecca died, Uncle Moody and Aunt Dorothy, her youngest son, and the next to the youngest daughter, went to live with their oldest brother, Uncle Preston, who lived on a part of the family land. Louridell, the youngest daughter, was taken by her older sister, Estelle, who lived in Northport, Alabama. Uncle Preston and Aunt Estelle took their young siblings to live with him because they were too young to live on their own.

Moody was mulatto with cocoa-brown skin and black curly hair. He was short for a man, about five feet, seven inches tall. His physique was not notably attractive, and he did not dress particularly well. Yet his personality drew people to him as lovers, friends, and acquaintances. People said, "You can't help liking the guy."

The first indication that Moody was going to live the life of Pan, the god of debauchery, came when his brother's daughter became pregnant with Moody's child. She was fifteen and her uncle Moody was eighteen. Uncle Preston ran Moody out of his house. Having fathered a child by his niece did not daunt Moody. Instead, this was his passage into manhood.

Moody went to Northport where he frequented the Bloody Bucket nightclub and honed his skills as a debaucher and a lout. Moody was equal to the patrons at the Bloody Bucket where someone died from a knife or gunshot wound every week. It was said that after every weekend, buckets of blood covered the rooms and grounds. To wit, the name the Bloody Bucket.

Moody did not work. He lived off women whom he met at nightclubs and parties. He became an alcoholic and was a gambler and a brawler. His fights were legendary. He fought with men and women and took on all comers. He carried a knife and a gun and used both in his altercations.

Uncle Moody's first convert was our birth mother. We called her Eula Mama. It was he who spirited Eula Mama away from home the first time when she did not come home with Uncle Preston. It was Moody who accompanied Eula Mama and her friends on their nights and weekends out the town.

Aunt Pladelle

After Eula had divested herself of her two remaining children, Moody and Eula decided to free Aunt Pladelle from her husband, Uncle John.

Pladelle was the sister born between Eula and Moody. She was fourteen when she married Uncle John, who was forty years her senior. When Uncle John's spouse died, he fulfilled his dream to have Pladelle for his own.

Pladelle was attractive, not beautiful like Eula, but cute and cuddly. She was short-statured and plump. Her legs were bowed, a feature that the old wife's tales declared supportive of sexual prowess.

Daddy told us the story that Uncle John could not chance some other man seeing Pladelle, so he imprisoned her inside the house. When he went to the field, he nailed the windows and doors shut from the outside.

Three children were born to the couple. The children grew up imprisoned inside the house. Pladelle became so accustomed to being inside the house that she sent the children behind the stove to defecate and to urinate. When Daddy saw what was behind the stove, he said that he was unable to eat the fried rabbit that Pladelle cooked for dinner the day he and Eula visited her home.

Zeke the Man

Perhaps it was a benevolent act to free Pladelle. What happened next was pure Moody.

Moody had a friend named Zeke. He was a tall, good-looking man with a light complexion and dark curly hair. Even though Zeke was married, he was a womanizer from his heart. He had sex with many of the women he met working as the traveling milkman. Every morning, Zeke toured the countryside, picking up fresh milk from farmers who had more milk than they needed for their families and wooed their women when the men were not around.

One day, Moody accompanied Zeke to pick up milk and purposefully went by Pladelle's house. The two visitors chatted with Uncle John out in the field and ascertained whether he could spare some milk for which he would be handsomely paid.

Several days went by when milk was picked up from Uncle John and he was paid in cash. Finally, Zeke came by on Saturday when Uncle John was not in the field but was sitting on the front porch. He had not nailed Pladelle up that day. Moody engineered this event to allow Zeke and Pladelle to meet. They met and fell in love on the spot.

Later, Moody came by with Zeke and negotiated a release for Pladelle, allowing her to leave the house with her brother. From that time on, Pladelle took trips with Moody and Zeke which began a relationship that lasted for over twenty years. Pladelle and Zeke had several children together, the last of whom was born dead. The infant was buried in the casket at the feet of Uncle John, who died the week the child was born.

Moody Leaves Town

By the time Moody reached his twenty-fifth birthday, he had behaved so badly that the police in Northport and Tuscaloosa posted him out of town. He could not return home to his brother's house due to their estrangement over the birth of a child with his niece. As luck would have it, his second oldest brother, Spergin, came to the rescue.

One bright spring day, a tall white man came to our school with our cousin, Thirsey May, Uncle Preston's youngest daughter. The man was our uncle Spergin from Mississippi.

Although he looked white, he was our birth mother's second-oldest brother. Uncle Spergin was recruiting families to work on a plantation in the Mississippi Delta.

When Thirsey May told us he was our uncle, the whole school population gathered around to dismiss the assertion that a man as white as he could be related to us and to our cousins. One of our cousins, Minnie Ora, looked on with interest. We all went home and told our parents that our uncle wanted us to go to Mississippi. Uncle Spergin and Uncle Parker came to the house to discuss our going to Mississippi to work on the plantation in the Delta. Daddy enlightened us that to live on the Mississippi Delta was to become slaves. He told us that our uncles should have been ashamed of themselves for trying to enslave their relatives.

Uncle Spergin did recruit two candidates. One was cousin Minnie Ora, the daughter of Mama's brother, Parker, and the other was Uncle Moody.

Minnie Ora had argued with Mr. Patrick while she was working in his cotton field. Mr. Patrick was the white man who took

Grandpa William Bailey's farm. Uncle Parker, Minnie Ora's father, was sharecropping the farm that was taken from Grandpa.

The farmer hit Minnie Ora in the head with a hammer, which left her with brain damage and with a constant ringing in her ears. Moody had been posted out of town. Uncle Spergin's invitation had come at an opportune moment for both victims.

Without Uncle Moody, her mentor and guide, Eula Mama got remarried. She had five more children whom she loved and cared for during the remainder of her life.

Sold into Slavery in 1943

The day came for Spergin, Moody, and Minnie Ora to leave for Mississippi. Moody sat in the front seat of the car with his brother in whose company he was proud to be. He was heading for a new start in Mississippi. There, he expected to find new adventures and to exploit his relationship with his very important brother.

Minnie Ora sat quietly in the back seat. She did not have sense enough to envision a future; she was content to leave Romulus no matter her destination. She did have enough foresight to fry herself a chicken, bake herself a cake, and roast herself some sweet potatoes.

As the car traveled west, Minnie Ora pulled a chicken leg out of her bag. She munched on chicken. Moody smelled the food and inquired why she had not offered any to them. Minnie Ora was not prone to speaking to men or offering them any chicken. Moody reached back and took the bag and began to eat his fill. Minnie Ora began to cry aloud and to wipe her nose on her sleeve. Spergin told Moody to give the girl back her food. Minnie Ora was quiet for the remainder of the trip.

They traveled through the state of Mississippi and crossed the Mississippi River. The Delta Plantation on which Spergin worked was located on the western side of the river, on the Arkansas side.

At long last, the car stopped at a gate that was staffed by a guard carrying a rifle. The trio had reached the Mississippi Delta Plantation. The guard knew Spergin and waved them through. Spergin stopped the car before reaching the large house that could be seen from the gate.

Spergin turned to Uncle Moody and said, "In here, you can't tell anyone that you are my brother. Here, I am a white man. Any trouble from you will get you killed." He turned to Minnie Ora and said, "You will work hard and will not give us any trouble if you know what is good for you."

Next, he told the two that they would live together as husband and wife as only one house would be available to them. It did not matter that Moody was Minnie Ora's uncle. The two were told that they would work in the fields six days each week. They would be allowed to rest on Sunday and when it rained. Furthermore, they would buy everything they needed from the company store and would never be allowed to leave the plantation grounds.

This was the first indication that Moody and Minnie Ora had been sold into slavery in 1943.

The uncle and niece lived together as husband and wife and had two children in the three years that they lived on the Delta Plantation. They tried to work enough to end the year without debt. No matter how hard they worked or how little they bought from the company store, they ended the year in debt with the company. During these three years, they tried, unsuccessfully, to escape.

Finally, the couple and the two children did escape. One Sunday, they joined the cows that grazed in the meadow and moved with them toward the front fence. Each adult took a child; bending over, they matched their strides with the rear legs of a cow. As the cows reached the fence, the couple climbed through the fence and escaped. They were not seen by the guards that were posted around the perimeter of the plantation.

The four escapees caught the Arkansas bus to Tuscaloosa. The bus traveled back through Mississippi. The Arkansas bus was not searched by guards from the plantation who were looking for Moody and Minnie Ora as a childless couple on the Mississippi bus.

Moody Returns

Moody returned to Northport and Tuscaloosa where he had been forgotten by the police but not by the women in Northport and Tuscaloosa nightclubs. He returned to his old haunts and to the women who took him home, fed him, and loved him.

Moody's women were usually attractive and sexy until he met Lucy. Now Lucy was ugly by all accounts. She was built like a man with muscles and a square jaw. Her face was marked with numerous scratches and knife wounds. She was nearly bald.

Lucy had a male companion who knew what made her desirable even though it was not obvious to anyone else. Moody decided that there must be something about Lucy that was not visible but was worth investigating. Whatever it was, he wanted some of it.

Moody began his pursuit of Lucy, which angered her male companion. Before long, the man challenged Moody to a duel. It was mid-1900s in Tuscaloosa, Alabama where duels had never been fought even before the 1800s when they were popular elsewhere. The weapons of choice for both dualists were shotguns.

The day of the duel came. The two dualists stood back-to-back, with guns held at the ready. The count of ten was begun. On the count of one, Lucy's male companion stepped off, walked ten paces, and turned. However, on the count of one, Moody started running for a ditch that he had gauged as being near enough for him to reach and jump into by the count of ten. As Moody lunged for the ditch, the man turned and pulled the trigger on both barrels of his shotgun. Moody was unable to make the descent into the ditch and was caught on the upward swing of his flight. He was blasted in his rear from his head to his heels. He even had shotgun pellets in the bottom of his feet.

The ambulance carried Moody to Druid City Hospital where our brother-in-law, Wimberly Dantzler, worked. He reported that the doctors and nurses picked shotgun pellets out of Moody and deposited each in a metal bedpan. Wimberly reported that the doctor, nurses, and nurse aides stood by watching the extraction of each pellet. Moody was not given an anesthetic and yelped at each extraction. The sound went *ouch, ping, ouch, ping* for hours.

When Moody recovered, he pursued Lucy with gusto. He had to find out what made her so highly regarded in spite of her appearance. His pursuit of Lucy ran up against Lucy herself. A fight between Moody and Lucy ensued. Lucy was his match in a fistfight and was, at times, out fighting Moody. As he was losing the fight, he bit into her ear. She continued to whip him. He did not let go of her ear. Finally, the ear came off in his mouth. Moody had bitten two-thirds of Lucy's ear off her head.

Moody had found his match in a fight. He had also gotten Lucy's attention. Without delay, the couple mated. Moody found out what made Lucy desirable and why the man had been willing to fight to the death for her love.

Moody and Lucy were married. They both stopped drinking and going to nightclubs. They went to church. Moody got a job. They had a son whom they raised to be a good citizen. The two lovers lived together until Uncle Moody died in his late eighties.

The Deacon

One of the deacons at Holly Spring Missionary Baptist Church was a womanizer from his heart. Every attractive adult female parishioner was fair game for the deacon. He had been married for years, yet he could not refrain from chasing after every woman who would acquiesce to his advances. The deacon and his twin brother married two sisters. The deacon was five feet, ten inches tall. His twin brother was six feet, two inches tall. The sisters were of similar height as the men; one was tall and the other was short. The short-statured deacon married the tall girl, and his tall brother married the short sister.

People said that the deacon was overmatched with a wife that was much taller and tougher than him. It may have been true as far as size and strength went, but the deacon, being a virile man, needed a great deal of female companionship, not someone with size and strength. Sadly, his wife did not offer him comfort to the degree that he needed, and anyway, it was his nature to desire that which was just out of his reach.

An apple on the topmost bough was sweeter than one at hand. Meat was tastier if he had to hunt it or catch it. He liked deer, rabbit, and fish much better than chicken and pork. He needed the challenge to fully appreciate anything in life. So it was with women.

An escapade where the deacon sought love and was nearly exposed dealt with the wife of Harvey Stewart.

Harvey was the son of Aunt Icey Belle and Uncle Ben Stewart. Uncle Ben was four feet, five inches tall. Harvey was slightly shorter at four feet, four inches tall. Harvey's wife, Arlina, was five feet, ten inches in her stocking feet. The deacon felt that this woman was easy pickings since she had to be longing for some sizable companionship and little Harvey couldn't do much to deter him even if he found out.

What the deacon didn't know was that Harvey had one special skill, which had been developed during his youth out of the need to protect himself from the larger, stronger boys. Harvey could throw a rock farther, faster, and harder than anyone else. My daddy told me that Harvey could throw rocks around corners. Daddy said he saw Harvey do it.

A rock incident happened one day when Harvey and the bigger regular-sized boys were playing and wrestling each other. Each time someone took on Harvey, they subdued him. After losing a match, Harvey became angry, picked up a rock, and hit his adversary at close range. For fear that Harvey would hit him again, the boy ran around the corner of the house, out of sight of everyone, and hid where he thought he was safe.

Harvey never left his position. He picked up another even larger rock, reared back, threw up his little left leg, cocked his little right arm, and let the rock fly. The rock whistled as it flew toward the side of the house, then rounded the corner and hit the boy in the head. From then on, Harvey was well respected by his fellow playmates, who no longer regarded him as less tall than them.

The deacon sparked Arlina for several weeks. She used a ruse to fool Harvey that she learned from the older women. If you leave your undergarments, preferably your drawers, that had been worn all day on the pillow at night, your husband will think you are still lying beside him. It worked for some time as she placed the underwear that she had worn all day upon her pillow and quietly crept from the bed. She tiptoed out of the house and ran eagerly into the bushes below the house. The deacon was waiting there.

One fateful night, Harvey awoke with an urgent need to go to the outhouse. He lit the coal oil lamp beside the bed, leaned over to tell Arlina that he was going out, and found only her underwear on the pillow.

Harvey searched the house and decided that Arlina had removed her underwear because she needed to go outside as well, but she was not in the outhouse or any place nearby. "Oh! The old drawers on the pillow thing." He remembered hearing about that old wives' tale. "I'll just wait here on the woodpile until she shows up," he said to himself.

In about an hour, Arlina came out of the bushes and began to climb the hill to the house. Harvey waited until she came near the woodpile. He rose to his tallest four feet, four inches and whacked her up beside her head with a piece of stovewood. She was surprised by the teeth-shattering blow that came out of the darkness and realized that Harvey was on the other end of the piece of wood that struck her. Startled and hurt, Arlina fell to the ground. As she tried to rise, Harvey struck her again and again until she confessed where she had been and with whom.

When she was able to get up, Harvey allowed her to go into the house. He dressed her wounds and sent her to bed without her drawers. On Sunday, Harvey insisted that Arlina accompany him to Holly Spring Missionary Baptist Church, bandaged head and all. When asked what had happened to her, Arlina and Harvey told the truth, except the identity of the third party. When asked for the name of his spouse's lover, Harvey would only say, "Watch and you will know."

The first Sunday after the event, the deacon came to church as if nothing was amiss. He showed interest in the battered Arlina but offered no words of comfort. He could not be implicated. He had his reputation to uphold.

On the following Sunday, however, the deacon did not attend church. He had never missed attending church before as far back as anyone could remember. His absence was noted by the pastor who asked Mrs. Minnie, the deacon's spouse, to rise and give an account of the deacon's absence.

Mrs. Minnie was a proud woman and saw her duty to make a good impression in front of the congregation. She rose to her feet, held herself as tall as her six-foot frame could muster, adjusted her large brimmed hat just so, straightened her dress, turned her belt so that the buckle was positioned just above her navel, dabbed her cheeks with her lace handkerchief, and said, "Ahem. Giving honor, Reverend Pastor, I rise to give an account of Deacon's absence as much as my humble self can do." Here, she smacked her lips, lowered her eyes, and clutched her fingers, interlocking both hands in the proper speaking form when presenting before a group of her social peers.

Smack came the lips. Lower went the eyes as she presented the facts to her greatest ability. "Your Reverend, sir. We found Deacon lying in the field. He was out cold. Somehow, Reverend, we don't know how it happened, but he had been hit in the head by a rock." When Daddy and other men who had grown up with Harvey heard Mrs. Minnie's description of the deacon's injury, they knew who had been the third party with Arlina and Harvey.

"Watch and you will know," Harvey had prophesied, knowing that his rock-throwing skill would even the score with the deacon for trifling with his wife.

The Day of the County Fair

The source of one of the longest-running stories occurred on a farm that was adjacent to where we lived when we worked on the Graham farm. The event occurred on the day of the county fair.

Nearly everyone in Tuscaloosa County, Alabama was going to the county fair. The fair was an event held every year at the end of harvest time when the hay and corn were in the barn, the cotton was sold, and the fruits and vegetables were preserved in Mason jars. Hogs and cows were fattened for the winter—hogs to be killed and salted down and cows to be brought to the barn to be sheltered from the frost and coming winter storms.

Pumpkins were big and ripe. Farmers brought their largest pumpkin to the fair where the owner of the largest pumpkin received bragging rights for the year. Every pumpkin was sold to the city people who saved them until Thanksgiving when pumpkin pies were on the menu.

The fairgrounds were separated into two sections, one for white only and one for colored only. On the white-only side, many events took place that were not duplicated on the other side. There were entertaining events such as clowns, organ grinders, horse races, 4-H club prizes for livestock, and more. There were cotton candy and popcorn machines dispensing treats to the children. They had ice cream and candy bars.

The colored people had a small area on the southern side of the fairgrounds where they set up their curb market. This was the main attraction where they sold vegetables, meat, eggs, butter, canned fruits and vegetables, quilts, and sundry goods to the colored people who lived in Northport and Tuscaloosa. Colored families refrained from eating eggs and butter for two weeks. Eggs were stored in a cool place, and the butter was hung down the water well on a rope so that it remained fresh. Jars of peach and fig preserves were sacrificed. Red and white potatoes, sugarcane, and sorghum stalks were added. Collard greens were cut and bundled late the evening before to ensure their freshness. These items were placed on sale at the curb market.

On the colored-only side, the churchgoers sang spirituals to entertain themselves. After the vendors set up their wares, there was time for harmonizing. A soprano voice would start a well-known hymn. The altos and tenors would join in, and the deep voices would add the bass. If Ms. Polly Knox was present, an operatic soprano voice could be heard. The melodious harmony usually floated over the racial dividing line, and visitors from across the fence came near to listen. Sometimes, they came around to the colored side where they not only listened, but they also bought cakes and pies baked by women who, until recently, had been the purveyors of all things delicious in the white folks' kitchens.

Colored and white people alike traveled by wagons or rode in the few cars and trucks that the well-to-do possessed. This event signaled the end of the year's field labor for the Southern farmers.

The roosters were still asleep in the barnyard, their heads tucked under their wings, dreaming of the time when they would chase the hens around the yard, seeking procreation activities. It was too early for them to crow, too early to provide the farmers' wake-up call.

On the day of the fair, the reverend rose from his bed without the benefit of his rooster's cock-a-doodle-do. The excitement of going to the fair propelled him out of the bed at four in the morning while it was still dark.

The reverend wanted to get an early start so he could get one of the hitching posts near the curb market.

"Get up, y'all," the reverend called. "We got to beat the crowd."

His wife stirred, moaned softly, and said, "I don't feel good this morning. I been feeling poorly for some days now. I don't feel like going to the fair."

The reverend was highly surprised as well as distressed. What would he do without his wife to help him sell the goods he had loaded on the wagon?

No amount of persuasion changed his wife's mind. "Well, he'd just have to make do," he said to himself. Too bad his wife hadn't come along. Yet there were good sides to that too. He could talk more freely to the women and could spin bigger yarns with the men. His wife would not know how much money he made at the curb market, which would allow him to keep a few dollars without her knowing.

At last, he called Money, his oldest son, to tell him that he would have to stay at home. "Money," he said, "you got to stay here with your Mama today. She's feeling poorly and can't go to the fair."

Money was very disappointed. He wanted to go to the fair and run amok around the grounds. He was prone to getting into mischief wherever he went. This new arena was calling him to explore and find new ways to get himself into trouble. He had planned a foray into the white-only section of the fairgrounds. He wanted to see the big prize bulls the white boys raised. He knew the white folk had more stuff than the colored folk. Money was determined to see what they had. Now he had to stay home with his mama.

Reverend was glad to leave his son behind. On the farm, he was likely to be contained to known troubles. However, he knew his son had his heart set on going to the fair. It occurred to the reverend that if he gave Money the use of the shotgun for the day, something he had always wanted, it would make up for his not going to town.

"Now, Money, I want you to guard the house and the farm. Don't let nobody come onto the place. You take the shotgun, load it with buckshot. You shoot anything that comes 'round here that ought not to be here." The reverend thought he had given clear instructions.

Money had never been allowed to have the shotgun to himself. "What good was the old fair compared to having the shotgun to himself for a whole day?" He grinned.

Money envisioned all the wonderful things he could shoot. He could shoot that old limb that's been hanging over the well. Why, he could blast it down. He would go hunting and bring a rabbit, maybe two rabbits, back for supper. He would . . . His mind could not fathom all the things he could do with that shotgun if he had it for a whole day. Now, he would be in charge of saving his mama and the farm from any intruders.

The fair dwindled in its importance, and Money rose to the occasion. He was in charge and had his shotgun to prove it. Reverend hitched the mules to the wagon and left the house on the run. He took the road, heading for Booth Town, that would take him through Coker and Northport, to the drawbridge that provided passage over the Black Warrior River, and into Tuscaloosa. He continued to urge the mules to trot until he reached Booth Town. There, he slowed the mules to a walk. When it was light enough to see the road, he was pleased to see there were no fresh wagon tracks. He was ahead of the crowd. He settled down for a pleasant ride.

From the looks of it, this would be a fine day. The sun rose over the forest, revealing a clear blue sky. This was the time of year when the leaves were turning from green to yellow, gold, orange, red, purple, and brown. The symphony of colors interspersed with the green pine needles presented such a cacophony of hues that the reverend was prompted to cry out, "I serve a mighty God. Look at His works." Yes, this was going to be a good day.

Reverend was a pious man in his own way. He attended Holly Spring Missionary Baptist Church every Sunday where he sat on the rostrum with the pastor. Although he truly believed that the Lord had called him to preach, everyone came to realize the Lord had not given him the ability to carry the Word to the people. He was not gifted with a silver tongue. Truth be known, his tongue was one of his biggest problems. He stuttered and he didn't have a good command of the English language. Although on a one-on-one basis he was intelligible and conversant despite the stutter, it was difficult to understand anything he said when he was standing before the congregation. In front of an audience, one word could take minutes to emerge as something intelligible.

The other problem Reverend had might have mitigated the first if it too had not existed. Reverend was not hideous or anything like that. He was just plain homely.

He was tall and lanky with extremely long arms, so much so that his sleeves were never adequate to cover his wrists. His hands were large and long, causing his arms to appear even longer. His facial features seemed to be the result of a mule's kick which flattened his nose against his face. Had Reverend been an attractive man, women may have tolerated his inability to speak as Baptist women seemed to have been fonder of preachers than they were of regular men.

Reverend sat on the dais at Holly Spring Missionary Baptist Church for years without being asked to bring the message. Finally, the day came when Reverend was permitted to preach a sermon. This occurred when the pastor of Holly Spring Missionary Baptist Church was in the hospital. On this Sunday, Reverend preached his first and last sermon. No one ever figured out the text of his sermon nor did they ever discern the message he intended to convey. He stuttered and sputtered for thirty minutes by the clock, which seemed several hours by the embarrassment and emotional agony the congregation endured. This sermon left the older women in the amen corner in tears, the deacons in the deacon's corner on pins and needles for him to finish, and the teens and younger children rolling around on their seats with laughter. It was a disaster never to be repeated. Nevertheless, Reverend continued to sit on the rostrum with the pastor year after year. He assisted the pastor with activities, such as burials and baptisms.

During the ceremony of baptism, Reverend's long arms and big hands were assets that ensured the safety of the converts as each sinner was dipped under the water, then raised out of the water, saved from sin and from drowning. All of which would not have been possible without Reverend's assistance as the pastor only had one good arm. Reverend's wife got over the effects of her husband's disastrous sermon and even began to take pride in being a preacher's wife.

As unattractive as the reverend was, his spouse, on the other hand, was a handsome woman. She had comely features with thick, slightly curly hair, very large hips, and large protruding breasts.

One deacon, in particular, took notice of the reverend's wife's female attributes as she switched her hips down the church aisle going and coming to her seat in the women's amen corner. On several occasions, when they were entering or leaving the church, he whispered complimentary comments to her. This deacon was able to elude his own spouse and the reverend while a warm feeling grew between the two admirers.

Words were passed between the deacon and the reverend's wife after church the Sunday before the day of the fair. A tryst was planned. Each would allow their own spouse to go to the fair—alone.

The two would-be lovers had not counted on the reverend's son, Money, and the double-barreled shotgun loaded with buckshot.

The reverend's wife grew highly agitated as the hour for the rendezvous grew near.

"Money, you go sit on the front porch and watch up the road. Make sure nobody comes in the yard. I'm going to the bushes to use the toilet. You know that old outhouse is falling down. It ain't safe to go in there. I'll be right back." She said these words to Money, hoping that such an explicit command would ensure that he remained in the front of the house for a long time.

"Yes, Mama," Money replied, not paying much attention to what his mother had just told him. His mind was on the shotgun and finding something to shoot.

After a while, Money remembered that he had planned to shoot two rabbits for supper. "That's what I'll do right now," said he to himself.

Off he went.

Around the house, he ran.

Into the woods, he dashed.

Soon, he realized that if he was going to catch a rabbit, he had to be quiet.

Stealthily, he skulked through the tall sagebrush into the low bushes where rabbits were likely to hide. Suddenly, he saw a bush move. He thought he had found his first rabbit. Yes, he had checked the buckshot. The gun was fully loaded.

Slowly, he crept toward the bush. He raised his gun, readied it for firing.

It was not a rabbit behind the bush. Those were his mama's legs. There were two other pairs of legs visible under the bush. Money crept closer.

His mama was lying on her back and someone was on top of her trying to "kill" her. She was naked. Her dress had been pulled above her breast. His mother was moaning and crying out intermittently.

The person moving up and down on top of her was also naked from the waist down. It was the deacon who loved women.

It took Money no more than a second to decide that he had to save his mama and he had the weapon in his hands.

Money raised the shotgun. As the man raised his rear end upward, Money fired both barrels into his buttocks. Buckshot spewed from the gun like bees from a beehive. The pellets tore into the two victims as the *boom* of the gun was heard. His mother espied Money aiming and firing the gun only an instant before the buckshot came toward her exposed face, arms, and legs. Instantly, she tried to shield her face behind the deacon's head with limited success. Her body, legs, and arms were pinioned beneath his heavy body. She froze. The remnants of the pellets entered the exposed side of her face and the upturned portions of her arms and legs.

The deacon didn't see anything, save his lover's mouth gaping open and her eyes bulging out. He felt an unusual twist of her body. Had he not, at that instant, felt a thousand bees biting into his backsides, he would have responded to his lover's behavior as an orgasmic consequence of his lovemaking.

When he heard the *boom* of the gun, he knew he had been shot. The searing pain that overtook his rear assuaged his sexual fervor as his emotions changed instantly—from sexual desire to a will to live.

Due to the pain, he could tell that he was still alive. His lover appeared to be dead. In actuality, she had fainted, dead away.

All the deacon could think of was to escape. There was no time to tend his lover or to ascertain the identity of the assassin. He could not go back because the shooter was back there. He had to escape forward. His lover lay in his path. He pulled himself over her "dead" bleeding body, strewing a trail of semen and his blood over her. He went forward without regard for her safety. He hurried on until he found a low-lying bush under which he hid.

Throughout his retreat, he cried out in a loud voice, "Oh my god." Over and over, he screamed this mantra interlaced with, "Jesus Christ, I been shot."

As he called on supreme beings and considered his condition, he realized his social position was in jeopardy. He was a deacon of the Holly Spring Missionary Baptist Church and the son of one of the church's founders. He had been caught having sex with the reverend's wife.

His own wife, who was much taller and bigger than he and of whom he was physically afraid, would exact a terrible price for his indiscretion. She had made his life miserable for months after hearing of another suspected liaison where he had been hit in the head with a rock for trifling with another man's wife. This time, he had been caught red-handed, or red butted, if you will. If he did not die from the buckshot, she would surely kill him later.

Mrs. Minnie, the deacon's wife, was a pillar of the church and, like himself, was related to one of the church's founders. In deference to Mrs. Minnie's social status and his own miscreant behavior, he would be ridiculed and thrown out of the church. His life as a well-respected deacon was over. Upon these reflections, he added to his diatribe, "She's going to kill me."

Money stood wide-eyed and openmouthed, staring at his mother's visage. She lay exposed with her dress wrapped around her neck. Since he had never seen his mother's unclothed body, he misunderstood the opening between her legs, the flattened reclining breast, and the act of her fainting. To him, she had been split open, her breast had been punctured, and she was dead.

Money dropped the gun, backed away from the scene, turned, and ran. He ran indiscriminately for some time. Looking up, he saw he had run to the grocery store down the road from his house. Into the store, he stumbled. "My mama dead. My mama dead." He repeated his message over and over.

Luckily, the store owner had not gone to the fair. This was a day of business for him. The money made at the curb markets would be exchanged for dry goods that the farmers did not produce.

"What you say, boy?" The white store owner repeated until Money added to his outcry, "I shot my mama. She dead."

The store owner grabbed Money by the arm. "Show me, boy," he said.

They ran across the road. Money led the grocer through the sagebrush into the bushes. A fruitless search ensued. His mother was gone.

After Money ran away, his mother came to herself, sat up, realized what had occurred, and scurried to the house where she hid in the root cellar.

"Here, boy," the grocer said. "Your mama done gone home. Take this gun home and put it away. Your daddy ought not to let you have no gun. You ain't got enough sense to be given a gun."

Money ran to the house and called his mother over and over, but she did not answer.

Meanwhile, the grocer heard a male voice in the nearby bushes, "Oh my god. Jesus Christ, I been shot. My wife, she's going to kill me," the deacon lamented.

The grocer cautiously drew near to the trembling bush from which emanated the mournful lament. He called out, "Who's there?"

The deacon recognized the grocer's voice. Not wanting a white person to find him disrobed and shot, he hushed his voice into a low moan. The grocer drew near.

"Deacon?" the grocer questioned. "What happened?" The deacon moaned louder. "Did Money shoot you?" the grocer asked.

"Um, aou . . . don't know." The deacon moaned louder still. Not having seen who fired the gun, he really didn't know who had shot him. He suspected that the reverend had come home, found him with his wife having sex, and shot them both.

The deacon lay on his stomach, bleeding profusely from the holes dug into his skin by the buckshot pellets. His backside—from his heels to his head, except for the space around his shoulder blades that was covered by his undershirt—looked like a million beetles had curled up on his back.

"Deacon, we got to get you some help. I'll go get the truck. You wait here!" shouted the grocer. Of course, the deacon had no choice but to wait. He couldn't go any further without generating excruciating pain with every attempted move. He lay immobile and waited for deliverance.

The deacon had time to reflect not only on his present state but also on his recent escapade that had resulted in his head being nearly crushed by a rock. He believed that his affiliation with another *pretty lady* from the congregation had been the cause of his headache.

Now the deacon had been caught red-handed. There would be no guessing who was with the reverend's wife. He would be banished from the church. He would lose his standing in the community. His wife would surely kill him. He began to cry and pray.

Meanwhile, Money's mother had emerged from the root cellar to comfort Money when she heard him howling loudly about her death and that the angels had taken her straight to heaven because he couldn't find her.

His mother had picked out the shotgun pellets with tweezers. Her bleeding face, arms, and legs frightened Money all the more. She quieted him by telling him, "It don't hurt, son. I'll be all right. Now you go help the grocery storeman. Tell him I'm all right, I ain't dead. Run along now. Take this quilt. He might need it."

After much persuasion and assurance that she was all right, Money went back to where he had left the grocer and told him that his mother was alright. She was alive and she was at the house. His mother was not alright. Money's mother stopped talking that day. She went about her chores and took care of the family without saying a word. As time went by, she became more and more depressed.

Money assisted the grocer to hoist the deacon into the back of the truck. They wrapped him in the quilt to cover his wounds and to cushion him from the rough ride into town. "Boy," said the grocer, "you go back to the house and tell your mama I'm going to take the deacon to town to see the doctor. He won't last long if they don't get this buckshot out of him and stop the bleeding."

"Yes, sir," Money responded. He was very glad to get away from the deacon and the evidence of his deed. The grocer eased the truck out of the bushes, across the straw field, and onto the big road in front of the house.

The house was located at the fork of the road where the big road went straight ahead or turned either right or left. This road was called the big road as it was the main thoroughfare. Other lesser roads ran back into the woods where single families lived or where several houses constituted a community.

People in Romulus had long realized that by using a clock face to simulate travel routes, one would determine his location and the quickest road to take to the city. The grocer decided which road to take immediately. His choices, which lay between going left or straight ahead, had been decided by his location along the big road as all locations along the circular route were designated by their corresponding hour. Clockwise was to the left while counterclockwise was straight ahead. Tuscaloosa City is located at twelve o'clock. Romulus is located south of Tuscaloosa and Northport cities, Coker, and Booth Town. It is west of Fosters and Dry Creek and southwest of Stillman College, once known as Stillman Institute. The Negro hospital was located at Stillman.

Booth Town is at nine, Cocker at ten, and Northport at eleven. The fairground was located at one o'clock and Stillman Institute Colored Hospital was located at three. The grocer and the deacon were located in the truck at seven o'clock. Their destination was at three o'clock. The quickest route lay counterclockwise, which meant they must take the road straight ahead.

The truck rumbled along the dirt road, made passable by the road repairs President Franklin D. Roosevelt provided through the Work Progress Administration (WPA) workers who repaired the county roads, covered them with gravel, and made the roads smooth.

They passed the school for white children. On the right, they passed cousin Cleo Blackburn's house where his wife, Lilly Mae, and the children were in the yard. They rounded the curve in the road and passed the homes of Uncle Bob, Aunt Leanna, and Uncle Ben, and finally, they passed Holly Spring Missionary Baptist Church.

A view of the church spire gave the deacon a feeling that "the devil is going to get me!"

The deacon glimpsed Aunt Susanna, whom we called Aunt Babe, sweeping her yard at her house across the church. Around the bend, they rambled past Mrs. Ora Miller's farm. At five o'clock on the map clock, they came to Fosters, Alabama. They passed the overflowing well that spewed water from an underground river, never ceasing since time began. The deacon could tell when they turned north on Highway 11. His pain was eased dramatically by the smoother road surface.

Highway 11 ran north and south and was the main highway for folk who traveled throughout the eastern part of the United States. Highway 11 began in Picayune, Mississippi, at the Pearl River border with Louisiana and went all the way to its northern terminus at the United States-Canadian border.

Not only was it heavily traveled, it was also maintained by convict laborers who gave their lives to keep the dirt packed hard and the ditches repaired and cleared. Convicts are immortalized as ghosts who are said to haunt stretches of Highway 11 in Alabama.

It was not until the WPA under the New Deal with President Franklin D. Roosevelt that Highway 11 was finally made into a proper gravel road. It was paved many years later. The truck in which the deacon lay crossed over the Black Warrior River on the Fosters Bridge at four o'clock on the map clock. The bridge was made of lumber. Massive beams supported the structure, crossties were laid crosswise, and slabs of lumber ran the length of the bridge.

Had this event occurred years earlier, the pair would have had to traverse the Black Warrior River by Foster's Ferry. Even earlier, they would have had to go over the river by skiff. The earliest settlers, the American Indians, crossed the Black Warrior River by canoe.

My grandmother, Annie (Blackburn) Bailey, and her cousin crossed the Black Warrior River at the same location in her youth when skiffs were used. Grandma told the story that she and her cousin had visited relatives in Liberty, a Negro community on the eastern side of the river. They boarded a skiff to go home on the western side. As they paddled across the river, the skiff sprang a leak. Grandma began to bail with a bucket that was left in the skiff for this purpose, and her cousin began to stroke the paddle faster, trying to reach the other side before they sank. Grandma expressed how frightened the two were. They urged each other on by shouting, "Bail, sister, bail!" The other responded, "Stroke, sister, stroke." The two repeated these commands over and over to bolster their courage and efforts. The skiff went down as they reached the shallow side of the river. They waded ashore.

The wounded deacon was aware that, at about three-thirty on the map clock, the grocer's truck in which the deacon lay passed Liberty, the settlement that was founded by freed slaves. Throughout his travels, the deacon prayed that no one would see him and guess that he was bundled up in the bed of the truck, fleeing his own disaster and heading toward the city where his wife, the reverend, and everyone he knew would be present at the county fair.

The time had not been lost on the grocer. He was concerned about maintaining Reverend on his farm as a sharecropper. He had to make sure that this incident did not cause the reverend to leave him. He had done his best to ensure that the reverend could not leave. When it came time to settle up, that is, to see if the reverend had raised enough cotton and corn to pay for his credit at the store and his rental of the land, the landowner had made sure that the reverend would be in his debt. In this way, the family had to remain on the farm one more year and try again to get out of debt. With the landowner doing the figuring, they would be required to remain.

While the truck rumbled along toward its destination, the fair-going crowd was enjoying a festive day of selling, eating, and singing, oblivious to the trouble that was about to descend upon them.

At three o'clock on the map clock, the truck driver drove up to the emergency room entrance of Stillman Institute Colored Hospital.

Thanks to the Presbyterian Church and Dr. Charles Allen Stillman, the colored people throughout Tuscaloosa County received medical care by certified doctors and nurses trained on the Stillman campus.

While the Stillman medical staff extracted the shotgun pellets from the deacon's rear, the grocer hurried to the county fair.

He quickly found the reverend and Mrs. Minnie and told them what had happened. They knew something terrible had happened when they saw the white man coming to greet them. Others crowded around as the two were told about the shooting of their loved ones. Upon hearing the story, an "oh my god" went up all over the curb market. Some cried; others laughed. Nearly everyone said they were not surprised.

Reverend and Mrs. Minnie quickly harnessed their mules to their respective wagons and retrieved their unsold goods. They drove to Highway 11 and headed south.

The day at the fair was ruined for everyone who abandoned the curb market and followed the wronged pair to Stillman Institute Hospital.

Neither Mrs. Minnie nor the reverend committed murder that day. Mrs. Minnie dealt with the deacon when he was well enough to return home. Reverend did the same with his wife who he found sitting in the dark house, staring into nothingness. She continued to stare, thusly, for the rest of her life.

Reverend made her go to Holly Spring Missionary Baptist Church the following Sunday. The deacon did not come. Mrs. Minnie did not need to rise to give an account of her husband as everyone knew why he was not present.

Holly Spring Missionary Baptist Church had strict rules against immorality and sin. If a member of the church committed adultery, gave birth to a child out of wedlock, or backslid after getting religion, they were required to come before the congregation and ask for forgiveness. The deacon and his lover fell into this category big-time. Each of the sinners was to come before the church and ask forgiveness upon their return.

The reverend's spouse stood silently and did her penance on the Sunday following the incident. The deacon was unable to return to church for some time as he required several weeks to recuperate.

The Saturday night before, the deacon was to return to church and the church members were to hear the deacon's confession, members of his family, including his brothers and their spouses, met at Holly Spring Missionary Baptist Church to execute the forgiveness ceremony.

The men carried their guns and placed the weapons on the seats beside where they sat. If anyone who was not a member of the family came, the men would use their weapons to dissuade the outsider's attendance. The women carried sheets to cover the windows of the church. These precautions were taken to prevent anyone from seeing the light in the church.

While the forgiveness meeting was in full swing, a member of Holly Spring Missionary Baptist Church named Willie James Robinson came down the big road in front of the church and saw a glimmer of light in the church windows. Willie James was a truck driver for the logging camp and often took his last load home at night to save driving time in the morning as he lived closer to the sawmill. Whenever Willie James passed the church and the cemetery, he looked in that direction to see if ghosts were visible in the graveyard. Upon seeing the light in the church's window, Willie James parked his truck down the road and crept up to the church.

He was afraid to enter as he could not imagine who might be inside and what they could possibly be doing there at such a late hour. He even imagined that some of the souls buried in the cemetery may have decided to hold a church meeting one more time.

The church was not lit by electricity in those days. It was used at night only for revival meetings. During revival, lamps were situated throughout the church, especially on the pulpit and around the sinners on the mourners' bench. Since it was not revival time, Willie James knew whatever was going on in the church should not be taking place.

Willie James heard the voices inside the church and recognized those of the deacon and his relatives. He circled the church until he was able to find an opening under a sheet that did not fully cover one window. To his dismay, the deacon, his brothers, cousins, and their spouses were holding a confession and forgiveness ceremony for the deacon. Willie James crept away from the church without being detected.

The following Sunday morning, people came from near and far to witness the confession of the deacon. People who had not been in attendance at church since last Easter, Third Sunday in May homecoming, or Christmas came to Holly Spring Missionary Baptist Church that day.

The Sunday church meeting went on as usual and was nearly concluded when a member rose and addressed the pastor, deacons, and congregation. The inquisitor asked when the congregation would hear the deacon's confession and request for forgiveness. The deacon's family members who had been in attendance the night before rose and admonished the inquirer, telling him that the deacon had asked for and had been granted forgiveness. The matter was closed, and there would not be any more discussion regarding the deacon and his sins. That was the way it would stand. That was to be the end of the story.

That was not exactly the way it stood nor was it the end of the story. Willie James Robinson told everyone to whom he spoke about the night he found the deacon's family forgiving him without the church members being involved. From then on, for years to come, people in Romulus told the story about the deacon and the reverend's wife and what Willie James had seen the night the deacon's family forgave him in a private ceremony.

The church people shook their heads and decried the unfairness of the treatment of the two victims. They indicated their disgust by a form of "Tsk, tsk, tsk." For our people, this sound is made with closed jaws and a grunting sound from the throat that is "Umph, umph, umph." These sounds accompanied a great outcry about the secret meeting and failure of the pastor to have a public vote on whether to forgive the deacon or to remove him from membership in the church. "Umph, umph, umph." The people saw that the power of the church founders was alive and well, allowing their children to escape punishment and public ridicule while exacting shame on others more lowly born.

To the pastor's credit, he did preach a strong sermon about fornication and lust on both Sundays. He invoked the name of Jezebel several times on behalf of the reverend's wife. He mentioned King David and Bathsheba, suggesting that the deacon would be punished for his sins of fornicating with someone else's wife.

The pastor stopped short of excommunicating the woman since he knew he would run up against the founder's family if he did the same for the deacon.

The reverend's wife came to church the Sunday after the incident. Her last day of attendance was the Sunday that the deacon came back to church. She observed that nothing happened to the deacon during the service. He was not admonished, voted on, nor did he stand before the congregation to beg its pardon. She was distressed by the unfairness of her treatment. The deacon said nothing to his past lover who never came to church again. "Umph, umph, umph."

When the reverend wife's absence was noticed, Aunt Hattie and a few good souls asked about her and were told that her health was failing. Within six weeks, she died without uttering another word after the day of the shooting. It was said that she died of shame. "Umph, umph, umph."

She was buried in the Holly Spring Missionary Baptist Church Cemetery.

This was not the end of the story. This story became one of the principal stories of my people and has been told and retold ever since it happened.

Third Sunday in May Homecoming

The Third Sunday in May homecoming at the Holly Spring Missionary Baptist Church was started in 1885 to celebrate the first anniversary of the church. This celebration has continued, to date, since 1885.

Family members come back from all over the country to attend this celebration. Every Third Sunday in May, members of the Blackburn, Bailey, Thomas, Wells, Foster, Reed, Harper, Knox, McKinney, and other long-standing families return to place flowers on the graves of their ancestors, to participate in the singing and praying, and finally, to eat dinner on the ground. Back in the day, the women of the Holly Spring Missionary Baptist Church prepared the dinner at home and brought boxes of food to church. They would bring fried chicken, ham, roast beef, greens, beans, black-eyed peas, fried corn, potato salad, rice pudding, sweet potato pie, peach cobbler, cake, and sweet tea. In recent years, a kitchen has been built in the basement of the church in which dinner is prepared and served.

In the olden days, each woman placed her food box in order of her relationship to the founding fathers of the church. The Blackburns were first in line. They placed their boxes along the shaded side of the church building. Next came the Baileys, the Wells, and the Fosters. Those members who were not related to the founders had to place their boxes under the trees in the yard. Those who were newcomers to the community were relegated to a place near the drinking well, the farthest distance from the church building.

The week before the Third Sunday in May Homecoming was replete with preparation for dressing each member of the family in the finest clothing that could be purchased. Everyone had to have new shoes, dresses, and suits. The women wore new spring outfits. They wore bigger, more colorful hats on the Third Sunday in May than any other Sunday, except Easter. Their dresses were of the newest styles and the brightest colors they could find.

Daddy was the first man to wear a white suit and white shoes to the Third Sunday in May celebration. This wardrobe choice became a staple of good grooming as white suits and white shoes are still the choice of the best-dressed men attending this celebration.

In 2010, my cousin Latham Blackburn Harris wore a white suit to the Holly Spring Third Sunday in May celebration. He had a matching shirt, tie, handkerchief, and white shoes with gold tips on the toes. I remarked that he was so sharp that if he died right there in the church, when he reached heaven, God would not make him change his clothes.

We buried Daddy in a white silk suit with a matching shirt, tie, handkerchief, and a white stingy brim hat. Latham could have joined Daddy in setting the dress code in heaven.

For the Third Sunday in May homecoming, the children wore new clothes. Dresses included wide skirts that were held high with crinoline underskirts. Shoes were mostly white or black patent leather. The girls had their hair pressed, curled, and adorned with ribbons.

I knew that Daddy never had enough money to outfit all five girls, himself, and Annie Lee Mama. Since I was the youngest child, I went unnoticed as part of the parade. On two occasions, I deferred to the other family members.

When I was eight years old, I informed Daddy that I could wear my old shoes and I would polish them adequately. He agreed and did not buy me any shoes. In preparation to polishing my shoes better than ever before, I took a wet cloth and scrubbed them clean. Then I applied the polish as liberally as I could manage. After the wet application, my shoes did not shine. Daddy was angry with the result as my shoes appeared dull and old.

The second time I deferred to the family occurred when we lived in Tuscaloosa. Since I was old enough to join the dress parade, I determined that I would remain home with Grandma and Grandpa and permit Daddy to spend money on the other members of the family.

My sisters wore the newest styles. Mable and Gladys wore draped dresses in lavender and blue with red high-heeled shoes and purses. Gloria wore a lavender dress with tiers of ruffles that had white lace between the tiers. She wore white shoes.

I asked that they bring me a plate of food from the Blackburn family food boxes. I asked them to bring me some fried chicken, potato salad, greens, cake, and pie. I remained home and looked forward to eating fried chicken, potato salad, greens, cake, and pie. When the family returned, I was devastated to find that the family had forgotten to bring me a plate of food.

Mrs. Laney Kelly was a newcomer to Romulus. It was never explained why she wore a green outfit every year. She wore a green dress, a green hat, green shoes, and green stockings. She carried a green purse. She was never seen in any other color, except green. It was later in life that we learned that there was such a thing as Kelly green. Perhaps Mrs. Laney Kelly knew that her name meant green.

Even though Mrs. Kelly wore green, she was capable of using other colors, such as yellow, pink, red, and brown. These colors were displayed in the cake she brought to the Third Sunday in May homecoming celebration. The first year Mrs. Kelly brought food, her multicolored cake caused a stir throughout the church grounds.

Usually, the Holly Spring Missionary Baptist Church family only ate the food their spouses or family members prepared. The families were very particular about who prepared their food. They would not eat foods if they did not know whether the preparer was clean and if the food was prepared under clean conditions. Mrs. Kelly was an unknown entity. No one knew if her food was clean and so refused to eat from her box. She was relegated to feeding visitors from out of town.

Daddy was prone to pulling jokes on his favorite cousin, Cleo Blackburn. When they were in the town of Tuscaloosa, Daddy played a joke on Cleo over a new pair of shoes. Daddy had seen a pair of shoes that he liked so well that he had to have a pair. The store owner could not fit him exactly, which resulted in Daddy taking a pair one-half size too small.

He was delighted with the shoes and threw his old pair away to wear the new shoes around town. As he strutted in his new shoes, the one-half inch began to matter and the shoes began to hurt his bunions. Soon, he was in terrible pain from the rubbing of the shoes. He spied Cleo.

"Hey, bud," the name he called Cleo. "Do you like these shoes?" asked Daddy.

"Yes, those are some good-looking shoes!" Cleo exclaimed.

"You want to wear them for a while, see how they fit?" asked Daddy.

"Yes, man. I'll wear them," said Cleo as he and Daddy exchanged shoes.

When Daddy put on Cleo's old, comfortable shoes, he sped up the street and around the corner. He remained out of Cleo's sight for the remainder of the day. Sometimes, he would be around the corner, listening to Cleo ask, "Has anybody seen LS?" No one had seen Daddy as he made sure that he stayed out of sight.

When it was time to go home, Daddy showed up. "Hay, bud, how did you like those shoes?" he asked.

Cleo said, "Man, take these shoes. They sure hurt my feet."

Daddy took his shoes back and only wore them after he took his knife and made sandals out of them.

Now Mrs. Laney Kelly's colorful cake presented another opportunity for Daddy to play a joke on his best friend, Cleo. Daddy asked Mrs. Laney Kelly for a plate of food. "I'll take a big piece of that colored cake please," he said.

Mrs. Kelly was so delighted that Mr. LS had asked for her food. He was welcome to get food from every box on the grounds. Women, old and young, were glad to serve Mr. LS. He was a handsome man who was well-dressed and was highly regarded by everyone at the church. Furthermore, he was the grandson of Romeo Blackburn Sr.

Mrs. Kelly piled the plate high with food and placed a large piece of multicolored cake on top of the pile. Daddy walked over to his cousin Cleo. "Man, you ought to taste this food," he cajoled.

"Who cooked that cake?" Cleo asked.

"Oh, somebody over there." Daddy pointed in the direction of the church members' food boxes.

Cleo took the plate and marveled over the cake. He had never eaten colored cake. The yellow, brown, green, red, and pink cake was quickly devoured.

"Man, that was good cake!" Cleo exclaimed.

Daddy began to laugh and slap his knees with his hat. When Cleo found out why Daddy was laughing, Cleo took off his hat and chased Daddy around the grounds, hitting him with his hat every time he caught up with him.

Daddy and Cleo were closer than brothers. They truly loved each other. They were friends all their lives, and Daddy spoke of how much he missed Cleo after he passed away.

Daddy sang a solo at the Third Sunday in May celebration for fifty years. He became the most celebrated performer. He continued to sing long after he was ninety years old. Even after he became so old that he could not attend church, people asked if he would be present and if he would sing.

Mrs. Laney Kelly came back to the Third Sunday in May homecoming for many years. Eventually, she moved away from Romulus.

The Naked Churchgoer

Joseph Foster, the great-grandson of Jack Foster, is now the caretaker of the Holly Spring Missionary Baptist Church Cemetery. Joseph told me the story of going to church naked when he was a small boy. I met him while he was mowing the cemetery lawn and asked if I could tell his story. He laughed and told me that he would be honored to have his story in this book.

"We come naked into the world and naked we leave this world. In between, we must wear clothes." If Annie Dora, his mother, said those words once, she said them a thousand times. Little Joseph Foster heard his mother every time she said it. Yet he took off his clothes every time he got out of her sight. There was something about being naked. There was a freedom of movement, and the wind felt good upon his skin. He also liked to feel the warm sun on his shoulders. Clothes constricted his movement and held him back when he tried to run or climb the low branches on the walnut trees that grew in his yard.

Joseph was three years old and had not learned the purpose of clothing as covering one's nakedness. He saw no problem with others seeing him without clothes as long as Annie Dora did not catch him. She spanked him as she put his clothes back on his body. He tried to keep away from her for fear of being spanked, not for fear of being seen naked.

The Foster family lived across the road from Holly Spring Missionary Baptist Church. There were Uncle One-Arm Jack, Aunt Susanna (Babe), Jack Junior, and Annie Dora (their son and daughter-in-law). Little Joseph was the apple of everyone's eye. He was spoiled and headstrong. At three years old, he had a mind of his own and demonstrated such with great determination. He kept Annie Dora on her toes.

On one Sunday, Annie Dora dressed Joseph in his Sunday clothes, his little blue and white sailor suit, his white socks, and his Buster Brown shoes. She left him with his grandparents who always took the children to church when services began. Annie Dora taught Sunday school which started one hour earlier.

When his mother left for church, she admonished Joseph as sternly as she could and promised him a hard spanking if he took his clothes off or if he got them dirty. He was to be on his best behavior for his grandparents, and he was to come to church with them unchanged. Annie Dora repeated her mantra, "We come naked into the world and naked we leave this world. In between, we must wear clothes."

Joseph remained clothed for about ten minutes. Then his sailor suit became constrictive and he felt the call of the wild. He also grew tired of waiting for his grandparents to get dressed. He quickly stripped himself of the suit, socks, and shoes and ran outdoors.

From across the road, beautiful music reached his ears. Sunday school was in session. He liked singing, especially when his mother's voice was included. Before he knew what was happening, he was walking across the road, onto the church grounds, and up to the church steps. The steps halted his progress as he was too small to walk up the four tall steps leading to the sanctuary. He bent over and crawled up the steps one at a time.

Joseph pushed the door open, allowing the music to spill out. He walked into the church and headed down the aisle, looking for his mother. He did not realize that he was naked; he was just the way he wanted to be. He forgot his mother's warning.

The Sunday school class nearest his point of entry consisted of children and teenagers. When they saw Joseph, they began to laugh with gusto, disturbing the other classes grouped in the church. The children laughed and pointed at the little brown naked boy walking down the aisle. He was so short that the others could not see him and wondered what the children were laughing about. The adults shushed the children who continued to laugh and point down the aisle.

Finally, Joseph came into view of the men who were seated in the amen corner at the end of the aisle down which Joseph came. The deacons and elders harrumphed and tried not to laugh. They whispered among themselves—why Annie Dora had not dressed the baby before coming to church. "She should be ashamed," they whispered.

Joseph continued in pursuit of his mother, turned the corner in front of the pulpit, and headed for the last class which included the grownup females. Annie Dora was there. He saw her about the same time she saw him. The women gasped. He ran to his mother's side. Annie Dora never stopped explaining the lesson. She reached down, picked Joseph up, and used the Sunday school lesson leaflet to provide Joseph a fig leaf.

Aunt Susanna had looked everywhere for little Joseph. She found his clothes in a pile on the porch. The only thing she could imagine, though just barely, was that he had gone to church naked.

His grandmother ran as fast as she could to catch him before he was seen. It was too late. She found Joseph sitting in his mother's lap, fig leaf and all.

They spanked him soundly and put his clothes back on. Annie Dora changed her mantra, "You came naked into this world and naked you will leave this world. If you are not careful, you will leave this world sooner than you think."

At this writing, Joseph is still alive. He is an elder at Holly Spring Missionary Baptist Church and the caretaker of the cemetery.

The Nearly Naked Churchgoer

Uncle Parker, my birth mother's brother, shares Joseph's title as the other person who went to church in the nearly nude. Uncle Parker awoke from a drunken stupor on Easter Sunday and found that his entire family had gone to church. Uncle Parker never went to church. Every Sunday, he spent his day drinking the corn liquor he made in his whiskey still. He made his brew from an old recipe that had been given to him by other brewers. He combined ground cornmeal, malt, yeast, barley, hops, and water. Sometimes, he added his own special seasoning to the brew. He would throw a piece of fat hog meat into the mix and let it rot. He placed his still near the stream that ran by his house. It was well under the trees so no one could see the smoke from his fire. He knew how to brew and proof his liquor. He drank nearly as much corn liquor as he sold.

Parker was a brute of a man. He was six feet, seven inches tall and was as broad as a horse across the chest. He was as shaggy as a sheepdog with black curly hair on his head, face, and chest. He had an oversized belly that jiggled up and down when he laughed. He laughed often and very loudly. When he determined that everyone had gone to church, he decided he should go as well.

The family spent weeks buying cloth and ribbons to sew dresses for every girl, and they bought pants, shirts, and ties for the boys. Every family member had new shoes. Uncle Parker had shown little or no interest in the Easter preparation. Therefore, Aunt Lurley assumed that he was not going and made no preparation for him to do so. As he mused about the family at church without him, he became determined to join them on this bright Easter morning. He completed his toilet, which included rubbing his forefinger over his teeth, gargling water, and spitting it out. He ran his fingers through his hair, beard, and chest hairs, dislodging kinks and food particles that were stuck to his tresses.

Now for his wardrobe—he had to find something to wear. The clothes he owned consisted of two pairs of overalls, two plaid lumberjack shirts, and a pair of brogan shoes. These items were not appropriate to wear to church on Easter Sunday. He had to find something dressier.

On the floor in the rag closet, he found a pair of pants. They were not his pants, but they were wide enough for his legs to fit into. He searched for a belt to secure the pants over his buttocks and under his belly. There was no belt in the house that would reach around his girth. He found a rope. This he laced through the loops of the pants and tied it in front in a slipknot to accommodate duty's call.

Now he searched for a shirt. There was no shirt in the house that he could get his arms inside. During his search, he found a coat. He liked the color of the coat, a nut-brown, but he couldn't tell whether it was a man's coat or a woman's coat. He tried the coat on. It fit over his arms, but the lapels did not meet in front. Nevertheless, he liked the coat and decided to wear it.

Still without a shirt, he happened upon a very colorful tie. He liked the colors in the tie since they matched the color of the coat. Notwithstanding that he never found a shirt, he wrapped his tie around his neck and let it hang down his naked hairy chest. After many attempts to fashion his tie properly, he gave up and tied it in a double knot.

Now for the shoes. He tried to get his feet into every shoe he found around the house. Nothing fit. The weather was warm enough for him to go barefoot, and so he did. When Parker had donned all his wardrobe, he stood in front of the mirror and admired himself. *What a fine-looking man I am*, thought he. His hair and beard glistened in the light.

Several wardrobe malfunctions would have been obvious to a more sober person. However, Uncle Parker did not disparage the juxtapositions of his wardrobe elements. He had on a nut-brown coat although it covered only his shoulders. Being bereft of a shirt was not deleterious as his tie was very colorful. His pants were admittedly a little short, but since he was not wearing shoes, no one could tell just how short his pants were from the shoe tops.

It was getting late. He hurried along the wooded path that went past the creek where church baptism took place and approached the church from the rear. He saw no one on his journey from home to church. As he approached the corner of the church, he heard the choir singing: "I come to the garden, alone. While the dew is still on the roses." The hymn should have ended with "None other has ever known."

The choir loft at Holly Spring Missionary Baptist Church is located beside the pulpit, facing the congregation and the door through which Parker entered. He stepped into the church just as the choir was ending the hymn. When the choir members saw him, they forgot to sing the last line of the song, "None other has ever known." Their collective knees buckled, and they fell into their chairs.

The church was filled to capacity as it always was on Christmas and Easter. All the members were present, and visitors from other churches and family members who traveled from other states to be home for Easter were there.

The church ushers usually found seats for visitors and seated them ceremoniously. Parker didn't know the protocol nor did he wait for the ushers to get over being stunned by this spectacle standing before them. Parker saw an opening on a nearby row and headed for the spot. He pushed his way across the people sitting in the row and found his seat. There he sat, wondering what joke had been told just before he entered the church.

As the congregation began to focus on Uncle Parker and his attire, they gradually reacted in waves. The choir director had already lost control of her members. Various forms of laughter emerged. Some members fell out of their seats, others doubled over and cried with laughter, others just held their stomachs and rolled from side to side.

The children and teenagers were next to see this strangely attired giant enter the church. They began to laugh loudly, catching the attention of their parents and other adults who were wondering what the matter was with the choir and the children.

Soon, the entire church, including the visiting preachers on the rostrum, began to react. The general population found no need to withhold their laughter. They let go with such hilarity that they not only laughed uproariously, but they stomped their feet and laid on one another's shoulders and laps. The visiting pastors held their hands before their faces and pretended to wipe their faces as they cried into their handkerchiefs. The men in the amen corner tried to hold themselves together as they were the pillars of the church and needed to set the standards of behavior for everyone. They lost their collective composure and hooted and howled.

The women in the women's amen corner reacted in various fashions. Some appeared to faint; others ducked under the backs of the pews; others sat there and cried. The church ushers noticed the women who seemed to have fainted and rushed to their sides as fast as they could. They too were immobilized by the looks of Uncle Parker's shirtless, hairy stomach and chest, his female coat, his short pants tied with a rope, his bare feet, and especially his shirtless tie.

The ushers opened the front of the blouses and fanned down the bosoms of the fainting women. Then they pulled the women's dresses backward and fanned down their backs. The ushers did their best to rouse the fainting women but lost their resolve intermittently when they could no longer refrain from laughing and hitting their own knees with their fans. The picture was comical: fan the fainting person's front, fan her back, hit your knees with your fan, and laugh or cry for a while. When the usher was able to start the routine again, the tableau was repeated.

Aunt Lurley, Uncle Parker's wife, sat in the women's amen corner and stared at her husband. *What could he be thinking? He knew he didn't have clothes to wear to church. Why did he come to church looking like that?* she thought. Finally, she shook her head and acknowledged that if anyone would do something like this, it would be Parker. She rose from her seat, excused herself from her pew, and started across in front of the congregation. She was a stalwart woman, having lived with Parker for many years; nothing could faze her or make her lose her composure.

Aunt Lurley was a study in contrast to Uncle Parker. Where he was a large man, she was small-statured and petite. Uncle Parker looked white with curly hair. Aunt Lurley was dark-skinned and had short kinky hair. Where he was loud and uncontrolled, she was quiet and thoughtful. While he controlled others with his loud voice, Aunt Lurley quietly controlled Uncle Parker. He lived in fear of her. She was the perfect woman for him.

Now there is a procedure by which women in southern country churches excuse themselves when they are leaving the church during church services. First, they bow their heads, place their left hands upon their bosoms, tiptoe to the altar, and genuflect. They peer at the pastor from an upward, sideways glance to see if they are going to be excused. While all this is going on, the parting sisters raise their right hands and stick their forefingers up in the air. Sometimes, for the best effect, the finger is twisted from side to side to denote serious intent.

Aunt Lurley knew this procedure and acted it with perfect precision. As she went through her exit protocol, the congregation laughed, cried, and fainted worse than ever. Aunt Lurley did not seem to notice. She went down the aisle in which Uncle Parker was sitting, reached over those sitting nearest the aisle, and grabbed Uncle Parker by his singular tie. It, being tied in a hard knot, held fast. She pulled at the tether until he arose from his seat, stumbled over the feet and legs of those in between, and fell into the aisle behind Aunt Lurley. She pulled the tie over her shoulder with two hands as if she was pulling a load of hay and headed for the door.

As the pair exited the church, the pastor tried to restore decorum. Being a principal of a high school during the week, the pastor thought of calling a recess but had no precedent for such a maneuver in church. Instead, he began his sermon. The pastor gave the introduction to his sermon and stated the subject of his text. "Today, the subject of my text will be: He arose." Where upon, the congregation, still thinking of Parker arising from his seat, being yanked by Aunt Lurley, fell to laughing again. The pastor had to laugh a little himself as he hoped God had a sense of humor. He stated the subject of his text again, this time giving a description of who was being referenced. Then he said, "Let us pray."

These stories of Joseph Foster and Uncle Parker happened in the 1930s. They would be told over and over for years. I heard both stories being retold as late as 2009.

L. S. Bailey (Daddy) as a young man.

Daddy and friends
L to R: Uncle Clelly Bailey, cousin Cleo Blackburn
(Bud, Daddy's best friend), L.S. Bailey (Daddy),
and cousin Willard Blackburn.

Daddy as a middle-aged man.
He is standing in the park.

ANNIE LEE BAILEY
Annie Lee Mama was our stepmother.
"Her love made her beautiful."

Daddy and his children.
L to R: Joice, Gladys, James, Mable, Lois, Gloria, and Daddy.

Eula Curry
Eula Mama was our birth mother.

SISTERS
Sitting L to R: Glady's, Mable, Lois, Gloria,
(standing) Joice.

"Those two little devils."
L to R: Joice, Gloria.

DR. JOICE CHRISTINE BAILEY LEWIS

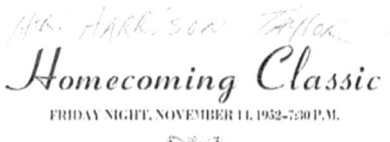

Albert Lewis, running back.

The Lewis family at daughter's wedding.
L to R: Tari, Joice, Tamera, Terry Pettigrew (son-in-law), Albert, Al Deric, Sheralyn Lewis (daughter-in-law).

Mr. L. S. Bailey.
Daddy as an elderly man.

The mansion home of Mr. Albert Lewis Jr.
and Dr. Joice C. Bailey Lewis.

Arthur Prince from New Orleans

This story was retold by Negro and Caucasian people alike as it reflected upon the lives of people of both races. Romulus was a closed community. Whenever a stranger came to Romulus, everyone took notice. White people and Negro people wanted to know who the person was, why he was in the area, and how he would conduct himself as a citizen. It was a warm, sunny fall day when Arthur Prince came to Romulus, Alabama.

A man-sized black bird came flapping down the road. Its wings flew back and forth with grace and purpose, catching the morning breeze. The bird's head glistened in the sunlight and darted from side to side as it flew down the road. In spite of its fluid winged movements, it never left the ground.

"Jessie," Mrs. Emma Patrick called to her Negro servant. "What's that big black bird doing walking down the road? He's as big as a man. I ain't never seen no black bird that big in my life." Mrs. Emma was Emma Strickland from Greensborough whose family had owned Jessie's mother and father.

Jessie heard Mrs. Emma calling and rushed to her side. Jessie was born on the Strickland plantation, and she and her parents had stayed on after the slaves were freed. When Emma got married, Jessie came to Romulus, Alabama as Emma's personal servant.

Fifty years had gone by while the two women remained together.

After Mrs. Emma's children became adults and her husband died, she and Jessie were the only two people living in the house on Romulus Road in Romulus, Alabama. Jessie knew how flustered Mrs. Emma could get over the least little thing. As they grew older, now in their middle seventies, Jessie was the one who kept a level head in times of confusion.

Jessie looked up the road and saw a lone black figure walking toward them. It was a man wearing a black cloak and a tall hat. He did look like a black bird. Yet anyone could see that it was a man who resembled a large black crow.

"Miz Emma, that's a man in an ol' black coat. That ain't no bird," Jessie spoke as she emerged from the kitchen and approached Mrs. Emma on the screened-in front porch.

The caped man drew nearer to the front yard. Not only did he wear a black gentleman's cape and a black shiny top hat but he also carried a black shiny cane with a gold-painted knob. He measured his steps with a tap of his cane for every three steps he took. Upon closer inspection, the women could see that he wore a white dress shirt with ruffles down the front finished with a black bow tie. He was dressed in evening attire. As he passed, he tipped his hat in a good morning salute. Jessie dipped her head and bent slightly at her knees. Mrs. Emma stared at the man, uncertain whether she should acknowledge his greeting as she was not sure the man was colored or white.

"Is that a white man?" she asked Jessie.

"Can't you see, Miz Emma? That's one of them Creole men, like we saw in New Orleans." The two women had accompanied Mrs. Emma's husband to New Orleans on several occasions over the years. During every visit, Jessie had admired the men and women with olive complexions who spoke French, dressed in elegant clothes, strutted down the street, and sat in the street cafés. Jessie was impressed with these people who were neither colored nor white. They were not someone's servants. They were respected and treated like first-class citizens.

"What is he doing in Romulus?" Jessie wondered as she knew that in Romulus, he would be treated like a colored man. Romulus was a closed community even though it was racially split between the Negro and Caucasian people. Each group was closely knitted together, either in blood relationships or by marriage.

There was a familiarity that existed among all members of the community which ensured that each person was known to the other.

When a stranger came into the community, it was considered news at best and a downright intrusion at its worst. The person had to take his place among one race or the other and behave like the race he ascribed to, or he had to leave the area.

Occasionally, the two racial groups merged when a Negro child was born White. There were times when a white child, born to a white woman, may have had Negro blood, but if he was white enough, his mother never revealed his parentage. Deacon Harper was born to a Negro woman, and he was as white as any white man ever was. He looked like the man who, in later years, would sell chicken all over the world. He had a goatee shaped like a V and a mustache that swooped across his lips and turned up at the ends. He wore round wire-rimmed glasses. He wore a white suit, black shiny shoes, a white shirt with a black string bow tie, and a white straw hat, and he carried a black walking cane. His attire was exactly like his future doppelganger.

Deacon Harper's granddaughter told the story about the merging of the two races when Deacon Harper's white sister called him to her bedside as she lay dying. "I want you to know that you are my brother," she said. "I have always known that my daddy was your daddy, and I watched over you all your life. Although I wanted to tell you that you and I were brother and sister and that I loved you, I could not tell you before now." She died shortly thereafter.

Grandpa Reed, my mother's father, was a white man from Ireland. His marriage to Grandma who was part Indian, Negro, and Caucasian, required that he live as a Negro man. Whites treated him with the same disrespect and requirements of subservience afforded all Negroes in Alabama.

Mrs. Emma and Jessie watched as the man in the black coat turned into the Patrick Store. Mrs. Emma's spouse had built the store next door to their home many years earlier. The women knew that the present store owner, Cas Patrick, Mrs. Emma's son, would be able to tell them all about the man. Cas ran the family store and was a source of information for the entire community. His store was located at the northern end of Romulus, and everyone traveling down the road stopped at the store to buy a cold drink or other goods. Cas never failed to extract information from every traveler.

When people in the community came to the store to shop, they obtained the news of the day or the week and carried the message back to their family and to people along their routes home. Cas Patrick's store was the center of communication for the Romulus community.

Mrs. Emma bade Jessie to kill a chicken and fry it. She called Cas on the telephone and invited him to lunch. The stage was set for the two women to find out who this man was and where he was going.

The great inquisition began the minute Cas stepped on the front porch.

"Who was that man in the black coat? Is he colored or white? Where is he going? Why is he in Romulus?" Mrs. Emma asked questions nonstop.

Jessie had a list of questions of her own, but she busied herself with lunch preparations and pretended not to be listening to the answers Cas gave.

Cas pretended he did not know which man Mrs. Emma was talking about. "What man are you talking about, Mama?" he asked.

"You know what man I'm talking about, and you know you do," Mrs. Emma scolded.

"Well, first, he's not a white man. He's one of those gens de couleur libres, the free people of color, from New Orleans." Cas was intelligent and well-traveled even though he was considered by some to be just a farmer and a country store owner.

Cas started to reveal what he knew about the man in the black coat. "That man had some problems in New Orleans. He's looking for work. I told him the only work around here is farming. I offered him that vacant farm if he wants to share crops with me. He can stay and work there. He's going over to the farm and will come back and let me know what he decides to do."

Mrs. Emma and Jessie would have to wait to hear what the man with the black coat had decided. Now that he was not white, Mrs. Emma wanted to know more so she would have something to gossip about when she went to church on Sunday. Jessie wanted him to stay and take over the work of the farm. Although she was too old to interest the man, she would be satisfied to know that he was in the neighborhood and that she could dream of what might have been.

Mrs. Emma asked that which was laying heavily on Jessie's mind. "What's his name?" Jessie stopped moving about and listened intently for the answer.

"His name is Arthur Prince," said Cas. "Arthur Prince from New Orleans."

Jessie was satisfied to continue placing the fried chicken, turnip greens, boiled corn, and cornbread on the table. She could wait to find out what Mr. Arthur Prince decided to do. Later in the afternoon, Cas called his mother and told her that Arthur Prince had decided to take the house and farm and share crops for a year.

Cas was disturbed that the man paid for his supplies with cash. Cas needed to establish credit at his store for the man so Cas could dupe the man into staying longer to pay off his debts.

This ongoing debt was the method by which white farm owners took advantage of Negro sharecroppers. No matter how much the Negro farmer's crops were worth, the Negro owed so much at the store that he could never pay it off. Year after year, he was required to recommit to another year of sharecropping to try again to get out of debt. Cas wondered if he would be able to play such a trick on Arthur Prince.

The word that a man named Arthur Prince had moved into the vacant house on the Patrick farm spread over Romulus like wildfire. The Negroes knew that the man was not white and that they were free to be on familiar terms with him. Negro farmers went by to meet Mr. Prince and to see if they could assist him in any way. They invited him to Holly Spring Missionary Baptist Church. Several weeks later, he attended church and was introduced to the congregation. The unmarried women of the church took notice that he was unmarried and that he was handsome. He was a bit old for most of the girls. There was one girl who was much older than most of the unmarried girls in the community. She had been passed over by the local boys and did not have a boyfriend. She was not attractive, not very bright, and had big slew feet. Her name was Mary.

When Mr. Prince inquired where he could find a girl who would move in with him, take care of the house, and help him on the farm, Mary was suggested. It was said that they got married, but no one ever knew for sure.

Mary was afraid of Mr. Prince. She found him foreign and different. It was difficult for her to address him as an equal because of the differences in their ages. She did not know whether to answer yes or yes, sir. For an answer, she rephrased the question in a positive way. She settled on a mixture of *Mr.* and *Arthur* which came out as *Me'Artha* and a restatement of each question he asked her.

He would ask, "Has the coffee boiled yet, Mary?" She would reply, "Coffee done boiled, Me'Artha."

Mr. Prince gave Mary one bedroom, and he took the other. He did not make sexual advances toward her for several weeks. Mary did not have a boyfriend, but she was not a virgin.

She met a young man from Mantua who had taken her virginity and had sex with her as often as he could meet her in the woods near her home. They had a rendezvous spot in a culvert beyond her father's fields.

There, they would meet and engage in sex that did not include lovemaking. The young man had seen animals on his farm copulating. It was this behavior that he mimicked when having sex. Mary also knew nothing about foreplay and gentle touching. All she knew was that the young man jumped on top of her, entered her body, and climaxed shortly thereafter. She enjoyed the sex act as she understood it as it was the only contact her body had with another person since she was born.

After several weeks of living with Mr. Prince, he slipped into her bed one night just as she was falling asleep. Mr. Arthur Prince was a man who knew how to make love. He touched Mary's body with gentle, slow movements. He undressed her slowly and caressed her hips, thighs, breasts, and her face. He kissed her lips and whispered gentle words to her as he explored her body with his hands and his lips. When he began to make gentle love to her, she experienced an orgasm.

Finally, after he had roused her to a fevered pitch, he entered her body. This was a familiar sex act, and she responded with such force that he was surprised and delighted. Soon, they climaxed together.

This night was repeated several times each week until Mr. Prince was smitten with Mary. He had thoughts of settling down and staying in Romulus.

Mary, on the other hand, enjoyed the lovemaking events but still wanted the activities with her young lover to continue. He, too, wanted Mary and came by one day when Arthur Prince was in the field.

The moment he entered the house, he slammed Mary against the door, entered her body, and thrust her against the door with such force that she felt she was being split asunder. Before her lover left, he and Mary made a date to meet in the culvert beyond her father's field on Sunday afternoon.

When they reached the culvert, the young man grabbed Mary and prepared to throw her to the ground. She resisted. Instead, she sat down on the ground and invited him to do the same. She began to undress him and asked him to undress her. As they undressed each other, she led him into touching her body and gently caressing her hips, thighs, and breast. Then she showed him how to kiss her lips and her nipples and how to touch her in private places. Mary caressed the young man. Soon, he was carried away and began to enjoy the lovemaking that she was teaching him.

Mary continued to participate in sexual contact with both Arthur Prince and her young lover.

After many episodes of making love between Mary and her young man, they both found themselves very much in love. Toward the end of the year, when the crops were in and it was time for Arthur Prince to decide whether he would remain for another year, Mary told him that she planned to leave with her young lover.

On Sunday, the young man came to Mary's parents' home to fetch Mary. She went to Mantua and married the young man. They had six children and became leading citizens in their community.

Arthur Prince lost all interest in remaining in Romulus, Alabama. He gave his personal possessions to Mary's parents, locked the door of the house in which he and Mary had lived for one year, and donned the wardrobe he wore when he arrived.

Mrs. Emma sat on the screened-in front porch and called out, "Jessie, come here!" Jessie came forward and looked outside.

There, passing the house was a man in a black cloak with a tall black hat. He wore a dress shirt with ruffles down the front, a bow tie, and he carried a walking cane. He stepped lively past the house as he walked quietly out of Romulus. He tipped his hat and said, "Good morning."

This time, Mrs. Emma felt obliged to respond. "Morning," she said.

Jessie, on the other hand, spoke out, "Good morning, Mr. Arthur Prince. We're sorry you are leaving us." She bowed her head in reverence and bent her knees in a curtsy.

Mr. Prince doffed his hat and continued up the road. As he walked with a three-part cadence, his cloak flew rhythmically in the wind and his top hat glistened in the sun. He did resemble a large black bird heading away from Romulus, Alabama. It was said that Mr. Arthur Prince returned to New Orleans.

Jessie continued to work in the house, slower now that her body was aging. Her knees hurt and her back ached. Yet she cleaned the house and cooked food for Mrs. Emma. On the second Sunday in every month, she cooked dinner for Cas and his family, who came to eat the Sunday meal with Mrs. Emma.

On a second Sunday in October, as Jessie prepared the table for dinner and Mrs. Emma sat on the screened-in front porch waiting for her family to come from church and eat dinner with her, Jessie heard her cry out, "Jessie, Jess, Je . . ."

Something was wrong. Jessie hurried as fast as she could to the front porch. When she reached Mrs. Emma, she found her holding her chest and slumped over the arm of the swing.

Jessie hurried to her side. Mrs. Emma slid out of the swing onto the floor. Jessie tried to catch her but failed as Mrs. Emma was too heavy for Jessie to support her weight. The two old friends slid to the floor together. Jessie knew that Mrs. Emma was dead when they hit the floor.

Cas and his family came for dinner. As Cas hurried ahead of his family eager to see his mother, he found Jessie sitting on the porch, holding Mrs. Emma in her lap.

"She's gone," Jessie said, tears streaming down her cheeks as she looked up at Cas. "She's gone."

Cas ran to his mother and checked her vitals. She was dead.

The family did not sit down to eat dinner. Neighbors came to see the family as soon as they heard the news of Mrs. Emma's death. The food Jessie had cooked was consumed by neighbors and hungry children. The table that Jessie had set with plates and glasses turned down to keep flies off their surfaces, silverware rolled inside napkins, and a centerpiece of cut flowers in the middle of the table remained on the table. Jessie moved from the house on Romulus Road for the first time since she arrived fifty-four years earlier. She lived with her niece until she died at the age of ninety-three. She was buried in the Holly Spring Missionary Baptist Church Cemetery in an unmarked grave.

Years later, Cas died and his family moved away. The store and the house were abandoned.

On a personal note: One day, when we were going to visit our cousin who lived nearby, my sister Mable took us to the back of the house on Romulus Road. We looked through the windows where we could see the dining room. The plates, glasses, napkins, and centerpieces were still on the table. The centerpiece had dried up to resemble dead grass. Spider webs and dust covered everything.

Daddy told us that it was said that the house was haunted by Mrs. Emma's ghost. According to sightings, Mrs. Emma's ghost was known to make infrequent visits to the house in time for dinner on the second Sunday of the month.

Daddy's First Girlfriend

Eula, our birth mother, and Annie Lee were not the only women in Daddy's life. When he was twenty years old, Daddy decided to marry a girl from Mantua. He met her at the Third Sunday in May family reunion that took place at Holly Spring Missionary Baptist Church.

Daddy continued telling this story when he was well into his nineties.

"I was twenty years old when I met this young woman whom I thought was cute. Her face was pleasant. Her figure, though short, was well-developed with large busts. She had bow legs, which was a sexual attraction in those days. She did have some unattractive features, which included very short hair and slew feet, and she was built low to the ground, weighed down with big hips.

"I decided that it was time for me to marry, and so far, I hadn't found anyone that I liked any better than I liked her. I went to visit my girlfriend at her church several weeks in a row. Then I started courting her in her house. We kept company for several months. After a while, we began to have an understanding that she was my girl.

"I discussed marriage with my mama, who agreed that it was time for me to get married. Once the decision was made, I began to feel a little sorry that I would lose the freedom to like other girls. So, I decided to wait a while to see if that feeling went away. I didn't go to see my girlfriend for nearly a month. Finally, I made up my mind to go through with the marriage. I borrowed my cousin's car and drove to Mantua with the intent to ask her to marry me.

"When I arrived at the church, I expected her to be glad to see me. Instead, she confronted me with such anger that I was shocked. She wrung my tie up into her hand and twirled it round and round her wrist until she cut off my air. As she choked me, she spoke between clenched teeth, telling me how bad I was for not coming during the past month. I tried to tell her why I had delayed my visit, and I tried to tell her that I wanted her to marry me. She wouldn't let up nor would she allow me to explain.

"After a while, I wanted to hit her and make her release my necktie, but I didn't hit her because we were on the church grounds. I was glad I hadn't done more than try to release her grip because when I looked up, I saw her sisters moving into a circle around us. One of the sisters was big and muscular like a boy and had a face with ridges like a washing rubboard.

"When I was able to get loose from my girl, I ran to the car and took off. I didn't look back."

Daddy told my husband this story many times. Each time he told the story, he would say to my husband, "You had better be glad I married Eula instead of my first girlfriend. Had I married her, your wife would be short, built low to the ground with a big butt, have slew feet and hair about this long." He would hold his pointing finger and his thumb about an inch apart.

Each time, my husband would say, "Thank you, Daddy."

Daddy Marries Eula Reed

The year following Daddy's courtship with his first girlfriend, Grandma Rebecca, the mother of Eula, my birth mother, asked Daddy to marry Eula and to take care of her. Eula was fourteen years old that year. She was fair-skinned with dark curly hair. She was considered the prettiest girl the people in Romulus had ever seen. Both Negro and white people marveled at her beauty. The whites considered her too beautiful for a Negro man to marry.

Daddy, on the other hand, was brave enough to marry Eula but was jealous of her beauty and tried to prevent her from being admired by other men. Even when Eula did nothing to encourage the looks of other men, Daddy took offense and beat Eula for any looks she received.

Daddy and Mama lived with Daddy's mother and father. Eula was subjected to the harsh treatment of Grandma who disliked Eula for her beauty and for her brash behavior toward her elders. Often, Grandma would have words with Eula during the day when Daddy was out working and would report the events to Daddy in the evening. Grandma would tell Daddy to whip Eula for sassing her. This abusive behavior on Daddy's part hardened Eula's heart and made her rebellious.

Daddy and Eula lived together for seven troubled years. During that time, Eula Mama gave birth to five girls named Lois, Mable, Gladys, Gloria, and Christine. She was secretly pregnant with the sixth child when she left Daddy for the first time. She told people that Daddy was not the father of our brother who was born after the divorce. This misinformation denied Daddy the chance to find our brother and to bring him home to live with us.

The first time Eula left home, she left with Uncle Preston to attend the foot washing at Weeping Mary Church in Coker, Alabama. Daddy agreed to her going with Uncle Preston as he trusted him and felt that he would bring Eula home safely. She would not return with her brother, Preston, however.

Daddy went to Northport and brought Eula back home. She remained for a short period of time and left for the last time. Daddy took the children to live with her. She later sent the four oldest girls home to live with Daddy. Gladys went to live with Daddy's sister, Clyde, who lived in Kentucky. I, Christine, remained with Mama because I was a nursing baby. I was left with strangers by Eula one year later. Gladys came home several months later than I.

Even though she lived only twenty miles away, we saw Eula Mama, the name we now called our birth mother, only three times and I saw her briefly one more time in between the time she left us and when I was ten years old. She visited us once at our home.

Once, Eula Mama came to Holly Spring Missionary Baptist Church for the Third Sunday in May celebration. She was dressed in a flowing blue and pink flowered dress and a matching hat. She was very beautiful. We wanted to acknowledge her as our mother, but we were conflicted as we did not wish to offend Annie Lee Mama, our new stepmother.

True to her way of handling our conflicts, Annie Lee Mama made us embrace our birth mother.

Eula Mama bought us an ice-cream cone from a woman who made homemade ice cream in a churn that had a handle which she turned over and over. The ice-cream cone was the first we ever saw and the first we ever ate.

The second time we saw Eula Mama was when she came to our house six years after she left us. She gave us two dollars each. That was the only time she came to see us, and the money we received from Eula Mama was all she ever gave to all of us.

I was eight years old when we next talked to Eula Mama during the years when we lived in Romulus. We went to the city of Tuscaloosa to see the Freedom Train. We rode on the school bus to Tuscaloosa City to the AGS Railroad Depot where the Freedom Train stopped.

This train displayed pictures of famous Negro people. There were documents that described many of the acts related to the freeing of the slaves. The Constitution and other Acts of Congress and federal laws were displayed. The Bill of Rights and amendments that had been passed, to date, were shown. Many United States flags adorned the outside and inside of the train. Everything was covered in red, white, and blue colors.

After visiting the Freedom Train, we walked up Greensborough Avenue to the Birchfield Hotel where Eula Mama worked as a housekeeper. We went into the rear servant's entrance. Lois, our oldest sister, asked a person working in the laundry if Eula Bailey was working there. Eula Mama came to the back door of the hotel. She quickly ushered us out of the door and away from the entrance. She gave Lois a quarter and told us to hurry away for fear that she might get fired. The older girls cried, being frustrated with the aborted visit.

When I was ten years old, I was walking home from my cousin's house one Sunday afternoon and saw Eula Mama at a house not far from our farm. Even though she was within half a mile of our house, she did not come to see us.

A Mother for Daddy's Children

When Grandma Annie Bailey realized that Eula was gone for good and that she would be required to help take care of Daddy's children, she implored Daddy to ask Annie Lee Hood, a spinster woman, to marry him.

Annie Lee Hood was in her thirties and lived with Grandma's brother, Uncle Louis, whose wife was Annie Lee's aunt, Sally. Annie Lee's mother, Aunt Sally's sister, died and Aunt Sally took the sister's children home with her, including Annie Lee. By the time Aunt Sally was deceased, she and Annie Lee had finished raising her siblings. Although the siblings were grown-up and moved away, there was still one child left to raise. She was the daughter of Annie Lee's sister. Annie Lee was willing to leave Uncle Louis and the child and marry Daddy.

Annie Lee was delighted with Daddy's proposal. Daddy and Annie Lee had been pretend boyfriend and girlfriend when they were children. Daddy genuinely liked Annie Lee but did not love her. He was still in love with Eula. Annie Lee knew the truth but was willing to marry Daddy anyway. She was in love with him from the beginning. Daddy was a handsome man. He was well-liked by Negro and white people alike. Daddy was six feet, one inch tall, slim yet well-built with muscular arms and shoulders. Daddy had a great sense of humor. He told stories that were hilarious, and he played jokes on his brother and cousins that were remembered for years. Annie Lee loved this handsome, humorous man.

Annie Lee was not beautiful. In truth, she was of average appearance, short of stature, and muscularly built. However, she was gentle, kind, hardworking, and caring. Years later, when we had grown into adults, Annie Lee Mama told us that we seemed to be her birth children, except she could not remember giving birth to us.

Upon marrying Daddy, she took charge of feeding us, cutting up her own clothes to make clothes for the older girls, protecting us from every evil that came our way, and teaching us right from wrong. She taught us that we should never speak evil of our birth mother, Eula, and that we should continue to call Eula mama. She invented the names Annie Lee Mama and Eula Mama so we would not forget Eula.

I Remember Well
(At Nine Months Old)

Annie Lee Mama told us that we were too young to understand what had happened. She told us, "What happened was not all Eula's fault. Some of it was your daddy's fault." Annie Lee Mama said we children did not know what happened between our birth mother and our daddy. But we knew a lot about what happened. Even I knew and remembered that when I was nine months old, I was the only child left with Eula Mama. We lived with Aunt Estelle. I remember the house in which we lived. I since have described it to my sister Gladys by asking her to describe the house first. She said that it sat upon a hill. Then I asked, "Did it have a high back porch with long steps going down into the backyard?"

She said, "Yes, it did."

Then I asked if it was tall enough for chickens to go under. She said, "Yes, and we could go under it too." Then I knew that I remembered the house.

I also remember going to the cornfield with Aunt Estelle's teenage children. She told them to "go get some fodder for the cows." I did not know what the words meant, but I remembered what she said and was able to interpret the words later when I saw the children get some cornstalks. I also remember that it had rained that day and the clouds were gray and blue.

It was on this trip that the big boy carried me on his shoulders. I was allowed to stand in the sand at the end of the cornfield. I saw my footprints in the sand and was able to discern how small my feet were. They were the size of a small baby's feet. I remember my cousins talking to me in baby talk. "See your peeties?" they said as I made several prints in the sand. I was just learning to walk, yet I recognized the world and I still remember it all.

I Saw the Moon

When I was eleven months old, I awoke in a dark cavern, lying on a ledge, suspended above a bottomless blackness of swirling mist. Out of the mist protruded a long stem with a circular head that shone in the ambient light. Although the walls on either side of my enclosure were solid, I could see through the top half to what lay beyond. As I became aware of my surroundings, I realized that I was alone.

The last I remembered, I was home with Eula, my mother. She had given me my bottle and put me to bed. Before I slept, Aunt Playdell, Uncle Moody, and another male figure came into the apartment in which we lived. Now I was in a strange place in the dark and alone.

I sat up, nudging against the supportive back of the seat upon which I sat, fearful that I would fall into the endless darkness. My blanket and bottle lay beside me. Feeling the coldness of the enclosure, I reached out for the blanket in an attempt to spread it across my legs. The hands that reached out were walnut size, clumsy little fists that were able to pull the blanket forward but unable to spread it across my knees. I located my bottle. Using two hands to secure it, I lifted it to my mouth and emptied its contents. I was cold, hungry, and alone.

Terror gripped my being. I began to cry out of fear, hunger, and with the hope that my mother would come to rescue me from this dreadful place. I cried, screamed, and searched from side to side of the cavern.

On the right side of the enclosure, I could hear a tinkling sound that went round and round and round. Accompanying the sound were circulating colors that swirled round and round in time with the tinkling sound. The sound and the colors blended in their circular rotations, becoming one image of sound and color combined.

Soon, the color and the sound began to run down, washed out in pastels of pink, yellow, and blue. The image covered my right-side view. From end to end, from side to side, my tears washed the colors down.

Suddenly, a light filled the enclosure, emanating from my left, and it washed over my body and warmed my spirit. I sought the source of the light, feeling that it may have been my mother returning. I knew not the difference between the source of good feelings as all good feelings, heretofore, had been generated by my mother. It was not her.

It was something large, round, and shining. It floated high above me, surrounded by a blue expanse that covered my left view from end to end. Accompanying the large round object were many specks of light that sparkled and twinkled. My mind ceased to register the sound from the right and forgot the colors that had washed down my right-side view.

My attention was riveted on the large, round disc floating above me. It came to me that my mother had shown me an object like this one and she had said to me, "See the moon? It's winking its eye."

I watched as See the Moon looked back at me. It smiled and winked its eye. I cooed at it, hoping that it would come inside the dark enclosure to stay with me until my mother returned.

To my disappointment, a white sheet floated across See the Moon and obscured its face. I was alone again, afraid and ready to cry. The sheet moved on, and I watched as See the Moon reappeared. It smiled at me and winked its eye. I remained at my station for some time, cooing and smiling back at my friend, until I felt safe, warm, and sleepy. The tinkling sound continued in the background. I took one last look to my right and saw the colors still going round and round. I lay down upon the seat, pulled my blanket up, and cuddled my bottle. Gradually, everything faded away.

My mother's voice awakened me as she returned to the truck. She wore a pink dress with a pink bow in her hair. She smelled of dampness and excitement. It was she and others who had made the circular motions to the tune of the tinkling sound.

"I told you it was all right to leave the baby in the truck by herself. She didn't even wake up while we were dancing," Uncle Moody said to my mother. Mama had brought me along as she undoubtedly had been unable to find a babysitter.

I could not dispute my uncle as I was only eleven months old and could not talk in full sentences. Yet I knew that he was wrong. I had awakened while they were dancing. I had been terrified by the darkness. This and more, I remembered. Years later, I told Daddy about this event. Tears filled his eyes as he said, "If I had known where you were, I would have come and got you."

Vignette: In My Mind's Eye

In the year 2011, my husband and I looked for the place where the truck had been parked and where the café was across the road in the west end of Tuscaloosa, Alabama. In my mind's eye, the location was on the northwestern corner of intersecting streets as the moon appeared in an easterly direction.

We rode around the community where I learned that a café had existed in the early days. Suddenly, I stopped the car. I closed my eyes and allowed my spirit to get in contact with the night when I was left alone in the truck.

I said to my husband, "This is where I was." I could feel the same distress and the same fear. We drove around the west end community again and returned to the same spot. The feeling returned. I now know for certain where I was when I was left alone in Zeke's milk truck while my mother went dancing.

Daddy Gathers His Children Home

It was early morning. Dew dripped from the purple trumpet flowers on the morning glory vines. The sun had risen above the trees but had not warmed the earth where I chased the chickens out of the yard. It was one of those days in Alabama when the earth sparkled like a diamond. Everything was clean and shining after a rain the night before. This was a beautiful morning when I felt safe and wanted. Daddy had found me at Uncle Preston's house and had brought me home. Annie Lee Mama had refused to take a baby at first but had warmed to me and we were bonding fast.

In addition, I had four sisters. One of whom, Gloria, was my playmate.

It was comforting to know that my family was intact and that we were together with Daddy. He had striven to obtain custody of us and to gather us under one roof.

I knew how I had come home. It had been a heartrending journey for a child who was less than two years old. It was so difficult that I remembered every detail.

Daddy was a single father. He received custody of four girls when Daddy and our birth mother, Eula, divorced. I was not given to him as I was a nursing baby. Her pregnancy with our brother was not obvious, and Daddy did not know that she was expecting a child.

The judge stated in the decree, "If the mother puts the baby down and the father picks her up, she will belong to the father." Eula, the mother, found a way to put me down so that Daddy could pick me up.

My Birth Mother Puts Me Down

I knew more than Annie Lee Mama thought I knew. I remember the night Eula Mama put me down. I was nineteen months old at the time.

When the headlights of the Model T Ford were extinguished, darkness enveloped the car. I grabbed my mother's arm in one hand and her dress in the other, trying to anchor myself to her in the darkness.

The car stopped somewhere along a long winding road that took my mother, Uncle Moody, Mr. West, and me far from our two-room apartment in Alberta City. Eula had moved from Aunt Estelle's house to live in her own apartment. When we left home, it was daylight, now it was night. "This is it. Parker's house is through those trees," Uncle Moody said.

"I know. It sure is dark. I can't see my hands before my eyes," my mother retorted in a shaky voice.

She slowly emerged from the car. I clung tenaciously to her side, not daring to lose contact. Somehow, she was able to disentangle herself from me long enough to climb through a wire fence. Uncle Moody lifted me over the fence, and Mama eased me down on the other side.

We started walking through a forest "blacker than a hundred midnights."[22] The wind, whistled through the trees, sounding like a thousand voices whispering secrets in the dark woods. A howling sound came from afar. "Awooo! Awooo!" The howling was repeated. "What's that, Mama?" I asked.

[22.] James Weldon Johnson, "The Creation"

"Oh, that's just an old dog, baby," Mama replied.

Mama gave me a paper sack, which I carried with difficulty as my hand was very small. I was fearful but trusting of the firm hand that held onto my hand as she carried my baby brother in her right arm.

Although the howling and the whispering continued, I was only slightly afraid. I have remembered every detail of that nighttime experience.

I realized we were no longer in total darkness. I looked around for the source of illumination and found a path of blue light, duplicating the path upon which we walked, shining far above the trees. Little sparkles of light twinkled in the blue path. The blue-studded path above us allowed me to see where to walk and to ascertain that it was truly my mother's hand I held.

We walked in two different lanes of the road. Grass grew between the ruts. I learned later that this was a wagon road where the two ruts were worn bare by the wagon wheels and the grass was left to grow in between. Often, I stumbled on the grass. Since I was not yet two years old, I found it difficult to match my mother's stride. I skipped or ran to keep pace. Just as I was ready to drop from exhaustion, my mother, my little brother, and I emerged from the forest. The trees ended and a startling sight appeared.

There before us lay a sandy stage upon which dancing figures made of straw pirouetted here and there. Rustling rhythmically, attuned to the breeze, they made their own music to accompany their dance.

The moon flooded the dancing floor and gave light to our eyes, long jaded by the forest gloom.

I held back. Sensing my uneasiness, my mother said, "Those are just old cornstalks looking like they are dancing in the wind."

I knew about cornstalks from having been taken to gather fodder for the cows by Aunt Estelle's children. Aunt Estelle was Eula Mama's sister with whom she lived and who babysat me after my four sisters had been sent back home with my father. With my remembrance of cornstalks and my mama's explanation, I was relieved and stood transfixed to the spot, watching this beautiful sight. Adding to my joy, high above us, the moon smiled down on us and winked its eye. I was content.

"Yoohoo," called my mother. To whom she was calling, I could not imagine as I knew not where we were going or whom we would visit.

A clamor arose on the opposite side of the cornfield where I glimpsed a faded light amid the trees. "It's Aunt Eula!" the voices exclaimed.

Running footsteps could be heard coming in our direction. I hid in my mother's skirt. Peeking out from behind my mother, I saw children running toward us, their arms flailing about and their voices all chattering at once. It seemed as if there were a hundred children with twice as many arms and legs flying about as they came near. I was terrified.

One of the larger girls took the baby from Mama's arms, allowing her the freedom to pick me up. I clung to her neck and would not let go when the children asked to hold me. The children ran back from whence they came. As we followed, I could hear running water. It was a creek that flowed under a footbridge made of two wooden planks laid across the expanse. My mother navigated the wooden pieces and stepped on the other side with ease.

It may be of interest to relate that this house, stream, and farm were taken from Grandpa William Bailey by the white store owner, Mr. Patrick, for seeds and fertilizer. It was now being rented to Uncle Parker, Mama's brother, on a sharecropping basis.

A flickering light could be seen through the trees. I espied the source from which the light came. It was a kerosene lamp sitting on an old table beside a tree in the yard of a tall house. In a large chair sat the biggest man I had ever seen. He was half again as tall as my mother and twice as broad. When he stood up to hug her, he towered so far above her that his head disappeared into the branches of the tree, or so it seemed to me. This was Uncle Parker, my mother's brother. He looked like a white man with a curly black beard that covered his face and extended down his chest. His head was covered with long, curly black hair. He had a chest as big and round as a barrel, which rose up and went down when he spoke. Then he laughed. I screamed. His laughter was as loud as thunder and seemed to come from his belly and rush out of his mouth in a blue fog. Years later, I heard Uncle Parker's laughter from three miles away.

When I was eight years old, Uncle Parker came to our house at night. I was in bed, asleep. Uncle Parker and Uncle Spergin came to talk to Daddy about going to Mississippi to work on a plantation in the Delta. As they talked, Uncle Parker laughed. His laughter terrified me so that I awoke screaming.

The night of our visit with Uncle Parker, my mother held me in her arms and I held tightly to her neck. There I clung until everything began to fade away. The sound of droning mosquitoes, the children's playful laughter, the conversation of the adults, and even Uncle Parker's thunderous laughter faded, and faded, and was gone.

When I awoke, it was early morning. The morning light had yet to penetrate my surroundings which were foggy, misty, and gray. I could tell that I was in a large room. However, my vision was limited to the bed upon which I lay. There were two children on one side of the bed and an adult female on the other.

I sat up to see where I was and to ascertain with whom I had slept. The last thing I remembered, my mother was holding me in her arms.

Perhaps this adult person was her. An urgent matter took hold of me and I said, "I got to peepee."

The adult person picked me up by one arm and swung me over herself to the floor where the pee bucket was under the bed. She pulled the bucket out, and I sat on it and urinated. By the time my bladder was relieved, I had determined that the adult person was not my mother. I began to cry and ask, "Where is Mama? I want my mama."

The adult person said, "Go back to sleep. Your mama is gone." To which I began to scream and cry as loudly as I could. I continued to call for my mother.

I was helpless and afraid of the strangers in whose care I had been left. I was terrified. My chest seemed to cave in. I felt weak, overwrought, and terribly sad. Although I did not know then how it feels when one's heart breaks, I later realized that my heart was broken that morning.

My mother no longer wanted the responsibility of children. She had tried to get rid of me on two previous occasions. She had finally found a way to get rid of me.

On one occasion, my mother took me to a woman's house who tried to persuade me to stay with her. Mama wanted to give me to the woman.

As we entered the woman's house, I looked to the left and saw a room with an unlit fireplace. A man sat in a rocking chair before the hearth. He seemed unhappy. He registered displeasure with something that was occurring in the house. Now I realize that he did not agree with his wife taking the baby from its mother.

The woman and a large girl took Mama and me into a bedroom where the bed was filled with dolls. I had never seen such a house, nor had I seen so many dolls. The room was beautifully furnished. A large wardrobe stood on one side and an even larger dresser was on the other. The furniture was dark brown and shining. The bedspread was white chenille, whereupon the dolls lay in splendid profusion.

The woman cajoled and begged me to be her little girl. "Don't you want to be my little girl? If you stay with me, I'll give you one of the dolls," she said. Mama stood by with her arms folded, waiting for me to accept the woman's offer. I looked at the dolls and chose the one I wanted. It was larger than me and was dressed in a white lace dress with a red ribbon belt. A bonnet was on the doll's head and her hair was tied with red ribbons around two sections of dark curls. I attempted to climb up on the bed to retrieve the doll. My legs were too short to get up on the bed, but I was able to reach the large doll's arm. As I pulled her forward, the woman and the girl cried out, "Oh no! Not that one!" The woman explained that I could not have that doll. I could have a small, nondescript doll that I did not like. In addition, she admonished me for climbing up on the bed.

I had no intention of staying with these people. I thought I would be able to take the big doll and go home. When it was made clear that the plan was that I would remain in this house and be given a small doll, I turned and left my mother and the people. I passed the man sitting by the fireplace who looked at me with sad eyes. I went out the door, across the porch, and into the night. My mother came behind me, and we walked home in silence.

The second event included a trip to visit another one of my mother's brothers. His name was Uncle Preston. Uncle Press, as he was called, was as different from Uncle Parker as two brothers could be. He was an average-sized man with a gentle smile. He appeared thoughtful and kind. He was white in color with blond hair and gray-blue eyes. He spoke earnestly to my mother, seemingly trying to dissuade her from whatever she was attempting to do.

We left Uncle Preston's house and went to another house where three girls were excited to see me. They picked me up and carried me around the yard. They laughed and played with me. They seemed to know who I was. There were two adults present, a man and a woman. The man was a tall, handsome individual who cried when he saw me. He picked me up and hugged me tightly. I was not afraid of these people. I felt happy with them.

The man tried to persuade the woman to let me stay with them. She became upset and said, "I didn't plan on raising no baby. When we got married, you told me that I would help you raise your girls. You didn't say nothing about a baby. I don't know how to raise a baby." I didn't know what she meant, but I remembered what she said. I was not left with these people. We drove away.

Now my mother had finally left me. When I awoke in the bed with strangers, I knew that my mother had successfully found a way to "put me down." She had left me at Uncle Parker's strange gray, misty house, under the trees, by the rushing creek, across from the sandy cornfield, near the dark forest. I knew that she was gone.

Aunt Lurley, Uncle Parker's wife, gave me a breakfast of biscuits, ribbon cane syrup, and fried fatback. I refused to eat even though I had stopped crying when told that after breakfast someone would take me to Mama.

When breakfast was completed, two boys took me away from the gray house. The larger boy put me on his shoulders, and the smaller boy ran along beside us as we headed away from the house in a different direction than we had come the night before.

The early-morning dew glistened on the grass and dripped noisily from the tree leaves where small animals scurried in and out of the underbrush. Birds chirped and flew through the trees. The sun shone brightly, obscuring the sadness of the hour. I relaxed while I watched the spectacle of nature as we traveled through the woods.

At the age of nineteen months old, I came to the realization that I would not see my mother at the end of this journey. I had cried all my tears, and I simply would not cry for her again. I never did.

The boys and I arrived at the home of Uncle Press, the one with the kind, gentle face. My uncle, his wife, Fanny, their children, and Aunt Dorothy were there.

Aunt Dorothy resembled my mother although she was not as beautiful. She was sweet and nurturing. I liked her immediately and began to follow her everywhere she went. "Where you going, Aunt Dotty?" I asked.

"I'm going to the pea patch," she replied.

"What you gonna do in the pea patch, Aunt Dotty?" I asked.

"I'm going to pick some peas," she replied; whereupon, I made a song.

Where you going, Aunt Dotty?
I'm going to the pea patch to pick some peas.
Where you going, Aunt Dotty?
I'm going to the pea patch to pick some peas.

I found a small tree branch with which I chased Ol Porto Rica, the dog, around the yard while I sang my song. When Ol Porto Rica could get away from me, he found a comfortable spot under the old oak tree and went to sleep.

At dinner, I asked for some milk and bread. I was told that they did not have cornbread for dinner. Instead, we had biscuits. One needed buttermilk and cornbread to make milk and bread.

Not heeding the adult's advice, I made myself some milk and bread out of the biscuits and sweet milk. The mixture swelled up and began to overflow the glass. I stood up in my chair, took the glass in both hands, and turned the glass upside down to prevent the explosion. The adults laughed at my solution to the problem of expanding milk and bread.

On a personal note: seventy years later, I took my husband, son, and grandchild to this house and showed them where I had turned a glass full of milk and bread upside down on the table where the pea patch had been and where I had chased the dog under the oak tree that had long since disappeared.

Daddy Picks Me Up

At Uncle Preston's home where I had been taken after my mother left me the night before, I resumed my pursuits of following Aunt Dorothy. After supper, we heard a knock on the door. When Uncle Preston opened the door, the tall man I had seen at the house with the three girls and the disagreeable woman came in. He was accompanied by another equally tall man. When I saw the two men, I ran across the room to the one I knew. He picked me up and held me so tightly I could hardly breathe. Tears ran down his cheeks. He continued to hold me in his lap while he and the adults talked.

When he was ready to leave, he took my paper bag and me with him. I was not afraid. There was something about this man that engendered a happy feeling. The feeling remained as we traveled along a rough road in a model T Ford car. I sat on the back seat and looked out of the window in the rear of the car. I could see the moon and the stars. By the moonlight, I could see the fields and houses that we passed. When we arrived at the man's house, it seemed to be the same one that my mother and I had visited. Although I had never been inside the house, everything was familiar. There were three girls and an angry woman.

The woman had tears in her eyes, and she was unhappy. The girls crowded around me and called me by my middle name, Christine. They knew me. I asked, "Where the other one?" Everyone was surprised that at nineteen months old, I could recognize that there should be four girls. The last time I had seen all four of my sisters together was the day they were taken to Uncle OG's house to go home with Daddy. At that time, I was nine months old.

Daddy spoke of this event with wonder, "How did I count my sisters when I was nine months old, remember all four of them for another ten months, and ask about the missing sister at nineteen months old?" Daddy did not know that I started remembering people, conversations, and events at the age of nine months old.

When I was nine months old and just beginning to walk, I suddenly realized that I recognized the world. It was as if I had seen everything before but had fallen asleep, and when I awakened, I knew what words meant, who people were, and what a house was. The sky was familiar to me, and I understood how things related to the areas around them. For example, I knew that the house was tall. I knew that the sky was cloudy gray as if it had rained or was about to rain. I knew what red mud was and how it became mud—it must have rained to make the dirt wet. I knew what sand was. I understood the words cow, cornstalks, fodder, and field. I knew what chickens were, and I recognized the chicken house and the barn where the cows were kept, and I knew the use of the other outbuildings behind the house.

When I arrived home with Daddy, I realized that I had never been in a house with a lighted fireplace and was afraid of the large people I saw flitting about on the walls. I indicated that the big girl on the wall was going to harm me. The youngest of the three girls, Gloria, assured me that I should not be afraid. She introduced me to my shadow. She made our shadows dance and make the same movements as we. I made my shadow do tricks that Gloria showed me. That night, Gloria became my lifelong friend.

The man whom the girls and I called Daddy held me in his lap and gave me a candy sucker. He said something to me that I remembered, but I did not understand until later. He said to me, "You are home now."

I didn't find out where the other girl was until one day she came home. Gladys had been sent to live with Aunt Clyde, Daddy's sister, in Kentucky. After he brought me home, Daddy immediately wrote Aunt Clyde and told her to bring Gladys home.

On the day Gladys came home, we waited impatiently for her to arrive. When we saw Daddy coming back from our grandparents' house, we looked to see if our sister was with him. Sure enough, a beautiful brown girl with long silky braids bobbing on either side of her head ran toward us. We met at the end of the cornfield, formed a circle, and did "ring around the roses." Then we chased each other through the cornstalks. When we caught one another, we hugged. Finally, we became tired and sat down in the grass. We were happy to see Gladys. We felt complete. Now there were five girls, Lois, Mable, Gladys, Gloria, and Christine.

When we sat down with Daddy around the fire that night, I understood what he said and knew what he meant. "I got you all home now," he said to all five of us.

Although we five, who had been born before the divorce, were home, we would find out years later that the baby boy who was born after our parents' divorce was Daddy's son. He never came home. Eula Mama gave him away to a childless woman who changed his name from L. A. Bailey to James Dunnigan and raised him as her own son.

Life with Daddy

The family members had risen from their beds before daylight and had gone their separate ways. My four sisters had gone to school, walking four and a half miles to the colored children's school near cousin Justin's and Uncle Preston's houses. Daddy left home early to chop wood for old man Ed Robinson. Annie Lee Mama had risen early to make breakfast, help the children get dressed, feed and clothe me, and, finally, clean the house.

After combing my hair, she swept the front yard and told me to guard its cleanliness against the chickens that would squirt their feces on the clean sand.

I was busy chasing the chickens when a frightening sight appeared, coming down the road. It was a large white man wearing a model T Ford truck around his waist. The car seemed to be held off the ground by the man's suspenders on his overalls.

Two hound dogs sat in the back of him, seemingly in his back pockets. Another hound dog sat in his right-side pocket. The windshield of the car appeared to be a transparent vest covering his chest. The rear end of the car appeared to be the man's hips protruding backward to accommodate the two hound dogs. Squeezed between the dogs in the rear and the man's shoulders were two large shotguns. It was Ed Robinson, the man with whom Daddy shared crops.

The man's face was beet red. He appeared to have been crying as his nose was still running. His mouth was filled with a white foam that dripped out the side when he spoke. I stood transfixed to the yard, staring at this apparition.

He began to yell, "Ann Lee, come out heah!" He repeated the command until Annie Lee Mama appeared on the porch.

One look at old man Robinson's face alerted her that something was wrong.

"Yes, sir, Mr. Robinson, what's the matter?" she asked.

"Come here, Bay," Annie Lee Mama whispered to me with such urgency that I was awakened from my reverie long enough to scurry to her side. She wrapped me in her apron and began to croon, "Quiet, Bay. I think something's wrong with your daddy. Lord, have mercy."

Annie Lee Mama was so frightened that she was trembling all over. Her teeth were chattering. I was scared more because Mama was not in control of the situation. Blood rose in my ears, and I could barely hear what old man Robinson was saying.

"LS done hit me!" he yelled as spit went flying from his mouth and snot running from his nose. "He done hit me and I'm going to kill him. Where is he?"

"I don't know where he is, Mr. Robinson. I just don't know. Don't kill him, Mr. Robinson. Don't kill him. Lord, have mercy. Lord, have mercy, Jesus," Annie Lee Mama begged and prayed.

"I'll find him. I'll get my Klan brothers to help me. No nigger is going to hit no white man and get away with it. It just ain't done." He swore vengeance as he carried the car down the road.

Annie Lee Mama hurried us into the house and barred the door with the wooden latch. She continued to cry and fell on her knees beside the bed and prayed. I stood by helpless. There was nothing I could do or say as I was barely two years old. Regardless of my young age, I remembered every word of the conversation that took place on that bright beautiful morning in Romulus, Alabama.

We remained inside the house all day. Toward the afternoon, Grandpa came up the lane behind the house. He and Grandma sharecropped on the Robinsons' place the same as Daddy and Annie Lee Mama. They had been forced to work for Mr. Robinson after Mr. Patrick, the white storeowner, had duped Grandpa out of his thriving farm for the price of seeds and fertilizer.

Grandpa came up the lane carrying two buckets of water. We did not have a well. To get water, Annie Lee Mama would have been forced to leave home to fetch water at the well farther up the road.

"Annie Lee," Grandpa began, "you stay in the house and wait for LS. Don't you and the children leave. When the children come home from school, don't let them go back outside. Keep the lights off when it gets dark."

Annie Lee Mama was crying and begging Grandpa to tell her where Daddy had gone and what had happened.

Grandpa was a quiet man, not given to being flustered. He had experienced great stress in his life and was tempered to great challenges. He was born two years after slavery and had remained on the slave plantation for fifteen more years as a servant. He and his children had culled a large farm out of the wilderness and swamp only to lose it. Mr. Patrick called in his debt in the summer instead of in the fall when money from his finished crops would have paid off his loan.

"Now, Annie Lee," Grandpa continued, "LS is going to be alright. He is over at Buddy's house." Uncle Buddy was named WH, another one of Grandma's J. P. Morgan names. "They are talking with Mr. John Graham, trying to get a place for you all to move to in the morning. You know, even the white people around here like LS better than they do old man Robinson. He's so mean that the white folks have turned their backs on him. None of them will help him kill LS."

Annie Lee Mama was quieted by Grandpa's soft, gentle manner and stopped crying. I remember clearly that we had butter beans and cornbread for supper. Grandpa stayed with us while Annie Lee Mama eased out of the door and picked butter beans that were growing near the side of the house. She expanded the few beans by cooking them down to a creamy soup. The beans tasted so good that seventy-three years later, I still cook my butter beans the same way.

Lois, Mabel, Gladys, and Gloria ran the last two miles to reach home after Uncle Buddy met them on the road and told them that Daddy was in trouble. They were told to hurry home and to stay inside until someone came to see about us. When the four girls arrived home, they told Annie Lee Mama what Uncle Buddy said. We hunkered down for the night and Grandpa went back to his house.

Later in the night, when the moon had risen over the trees so bright you could see the colors of the grass and flowers, Uncle Buddy came up the lane in the rear of the house. We heard a low whistle like the sound Daddy made when he wanted us to know he was nearly home. We all ran to the door and cried, "That's Daddy, that's Daddy." Mama held us back for fear that it was someone else. It was Uncle Buddy.

Uncle Buddy reached the house and asked, "You all, alright?"

Annie Lee Mama asked, "Where is LS?" Uncle Buddy assured her that Daddy was safe and that we need not worry. Everything was going to be fine.

"What happened?" Annie Lee Mama cried.

"Well, LS will have to tell you the whole story, but he did hit old man Robinson."

"Oh my god!" Annie Lee Mama exclaimed and fell into a nearby chair. We all huddled around her, and Uncle Buddy put his arms around us all and prayed. His prayers were sound as he later became a minister.

Early the following morning, Daddy came home. He and Uncle Buddy rode in a wagon pulled by two mules. We all ran to embrace Daddy. We cried until Daddy showed us that we need not be afraid. We were moving to become sharecroppers on the Graham farm.

We scampered around, picking up our scarce belongings and placing them in the wagon. By noon, when we were ready to leave, Mr. Robinson drove up in his little truck. He pulled himself from the vehicle and approached Daddy who stood his ground.

"Now, Mr. Robinson, we don't want any trouble. I'm sorry for what happened," Daddy said.

Mr. Robinson interrupted Daddy and began to talk in a begging tone, "LS, you don't have to move. I need you to stay and farm this land. I ain't got nobody else to take this house for the coming year. You can just stay and we will forget about what happened." "No, Mr. Robinson," Daddy continued. "I can't stay no longer. First thing come up, you and I will be into it again. We'd best part company right now." With that, Daddy said, "Giddy up" to the mules, and we headed down the road to the Graham's farm.

We all walked as the wagon was filled with our goods. Daddy held the mules' reins and walked alongside. Each child carried something. Annie Lee Mama carried the two glass lamps while I carried a miniature blue glass lamp that Annie Lee Mama had been given when she cleaned the house nearby after the woman living there died of lung cancer.

Annie Lee Mama gave the lamp to me. I carried it with care and pride as I walked beside my mama and my sisters. At two years old, my feet were unsteady on the dirt road, so one of my older sisters took the little lamp and carried it for me.

When we reached the house on the Graham farm, we were pleasantly surprised. The house had two bedrooms, one with a fireplace, a kitchen, and a side room that was used as a pantry. There was an outhouse at the end of the backyard. There was a well in the front yard, which meant we would no longer have to go away from home to get water. The girls would no longer be tormented by someone like Josie Lou Allen when our family tried to draw water from someone else's well. Now we had a well of our own.

Before they unloaded the wagon, Annie Lee Mama scrubbed the floor with lye water and swept down the cobwebs. When Daddy and Uncle Buddy finished unloading everything, Annie Lee Mama cooked dinner, and we settled in to live and work on the Graham farm for the next three years. Later, as we sat by the fire, Daddy told us what had happened between Mr. Robinson and him.

Daddy promised to cut firewood for Mr. Robinson for which he was to be paid for a full day's work. The time of year was late fall when everyone cut and stacked wood in preparation for the winter. Daddy lived on the Robinson farm as a sharecropper. The crops were in for the year, and Daddy had agreed to stay on another year. This made him available to Mr. Robinson for daywork.

An argument ensued between the two men as to the amount of pay Daddy was to receive for his day of work. Mr. Robinson offered to pay Daddy fifty cents for the day. Daddy disagreed saying that a piece of salt pork from Mr. Robinson's store would cost more than fifty cents. He had a family and could not spend a whole day working for a small piece of salt pork. Mr. Robinson told Daddy that the wood belonged to him and that Daddy would want to cut some of his wood for himself. From Mr. Robinson's point of view, he would be paying Daddy for his physical labor, which was estimated as being worth fifty cents for the day.

It was early in the morning and Daddy figured he had already done enough work for fifty cents. Daddy lodged the axe into the wood-chopping block and told Mr. Robinson that he could get someone else to cut his wood and he wanted his fifty cents.

Mr. Robinson called Daddy several names, including "lazy, good-for-nothing black nigger," whereupon Mr. Robinson kicked Daddy in his backside. Daddy swung a haymaker with his right fist, upward under Mr. Robinson's chin which connected, knocking Mr. Robinson into the pile of wood Daddy had already cut.

Daddy was known for his strong arms. He was stronger than most men as his long arms gave him leverage to lift and support weight. This was a Blackburn trait, visited upon generations of descendants. One of my sons and I inherited this trait.

Due to Mr. Robinson's three-hundred-pound weight, he had difficulty righting himself and getting up. Daddy was so angry by now that he stood over Mr. Robinson, demanding that he get up and fight like a man, "Get up, get up, come on." Daddy held his fists ready to knock Mr. Robinson down again.

Mrs. Ellen, our Negro neighbor, was washing clothes for Mrs. Robinson and witnessed the altercation. She recovered faster than Daddy did and began urging Daddy to run, "Run, LS! Run away! Save yourself. Remember those five little girls and Annie Lee. They need you. Run!"

Soon, Daddy heard Mrs. Ellen and turned and ran across the road into the woods. He went to Grandpa's house and asked him to go see about us. Then he ran farther through the woods to Uncle Buddy's house. He and Uncle Buddy prayed and discussed what should be done. Finally, Uncle Buddy suggested that they go and talk to Mr. and Mrs. Graham. Mrs. Graham liked Daddy since he was a boy. He worked for her husband as a mule skinner (driving a mule). The white folks were amused at how Daddy, at the age of eleven, could get the mules to snake logs out of difficult places and how he drove the wagon to Northport without any trouble.

Daddy said the mules had more sense than him. He would get on the wagon, head the mules toward Northport, and fall asleep. The mules would keep a steady pace toward town on the one-lane dirt road. If they passed another wagon or truck, the mules would pull over into the ditch to let the other vehicle pass. Then, they would pull back onto the road and continue their journey. Daddy would awaken when the wagon stopped moving, indicating that they had arrived at the sawmill in Northport.

Mr. Robinson, on the other hand, was not liked by many of his race. He was an angry man who had grown up shortly after slavery and had lived through the Reconstruction period after the Civil War. Had he been a slave owner, he would have been rich and prosperous like his father. He was born too late, and slave ownership was denied him. His father had sold off much of the vast plantation that the family owned, leaving Mr. Robinson nearly broke and bitter. The best he could do was to contract with sharecroppers who would bring a little of the glory days back.

Mr. Robinson treated his sharecroppers like slaves if the family was weak enough to allow such treatment. One of the sharecroppers on the Robinson farm allowed Mr. Robinson to kick his children and to treat his family as if they were still in slavery.

Daddy was different. Had Grandpa's farm not been stolen from him, Daddy would have been a landowner and as well-to-do as Mr. Robinson. Even as a sharecropper, Daddy had pride and he had social standing in the community. He was the grandson of Romeo Blackburn Sr., the pillar of Negro society in Romulus, Alabama.

We settled into the house on the Graham farm that was comfortable and warm. The Grahams were more kind to their tenant farmers than old man Robinson.

"Tho Me In De Bri' Patch"

Daddy and Annie Lee Mama had worked for two years on the Graham farm by the time I was four years old. When the crops were in and the work in the fields was finished for the year, the older children went to school.

The Negro children walked to school. Instead of catching a bus, my sisters caught the crowd of children who lived farther up the road. Lois, Mabel, Gladys, and Gloria would wait on the porch until the Negro children came walking down the road. My sisters would join in the group that swelled to include every child living on or near the Big Road.

In the afternoon, they reversed their pick-up order. When the children reached their house or turnoff, they left the group. The children who lived farthest away went home alone. The white children had bus transportation. They were fortunate to ride to and from school and the Negro children were unfortunate in that we had to walk to and from school in the rain, sleet, or snow and in the hot sun. The white children added to the Negro children's misery by spitting on us or throwing wads of paper out the windows and calling us niggers.

When the white children's bus passed, the Negro children hurried off the road to a convenient place at the edge of the woods, up an embankment, or into a field to place distance between ourselves and the dust showers, the spit, and the names that were hurled in our direction.

When the crops were in for the year, each morning after breakfast, my sisters left for school and I remained with Annie Lee Mama who worked around the house. Usually, Annie Lee Mama worked for white people on Saturday when my sisters were available to babysit me. One day, however, Annie Lee Mama was asked to clean a white woman's house during the week and had no one to babysit me. I was taken along.

Annie Lee Mama was uncomfortable taking me to work with her as this was not proper practice. When paid for work, it was expected that she would give the duties her undivided attention. She apologized for my presence and told me to sit in a high chair and not say a word. Instead of being upset, the white woman talked about what a *pretty* child I was and chucked me under the chin.

Telling me not to say a word was a slippery slope as I was very verbal and talked all the time. Not only did I talk a lot but I had also taught myself to read and had an open mind. Daddy said that when I was four years old, I taught myself to read one day in about an hour. I think I knew how to read and count long before I was four. I had demonstrated that I could count by counting my sisters but had not had an opportunity to demonstrate my ability to read. While Daddy sat on the porch smoking a cigarette, I took Gloria's schoolbook, went out into the yard, and sat under the oak tree. When I returned to the porch where he sat, I told him I could read. Daddy said he tried to dissuade me from thinking I could read until I read the entire book to him.

The process of reading was simple. I knew my alphabet, and I knew the letter sounds. When I looked at the words in the book, it was obvious to me what each cluster of letters said. After I read to Daddy, I read everything I could find. I read my sister's books, cans, scraps of paper, and labels, and in the next two years, I learned to read the Bible. The Old Testament was too hard to read, but the New Testament was not prohibitively difficult. However, by eight years old, Mable and I read Revelations, the last book in the Bible. It scared us to death.

There I sat in the white woman's kitchen in a four-year-old child's body with a mind full of wonder. I read everything on the woman's kitchen walls—the clock, the calendar, and little sayings hung in decorative frames.

After what seemed hours of sitting in the chair but was only about thirty minutes, the chair became uncomfortable. I squirmed and made noises to which Annie Lee Mama gave me a cautious look.

The white woman saw my dilemma and asked me if I wanted a biscuit. She could not have known how much the offer of a biscuit touched me. I had not had a biscuit for a long time.

It was 1939, during the Great Depression. Flour was scarce and unavailable to those of us who had no money. We were victims of the Great Depression, wherein we ate what we grew. Our bread consisted of cornbread made from the cornmeal ground from the corn we grew and stored in the barn for the winter. The syrup we poured over our cornbread for breakfast was made from the sorghum and ribbon cane that we also grew. Without hesitation, I responded to the woman's offer, "Yes, ma'am, I would like a biscuit. We had cornbread for breakfast, but I ate it though." I not only talked a lot but I also spoke correct English.

Annie Lee Mama gave me the angriest look I had ever seen on her face. She was ashamed of feeding her family cornbread for breakfast. She did not want others to know how poor we were. Annie Lee Mama and Daddy had pride and went to great lengths to cover up our poor living conditions.

The pastor of Holly Spring Missionary Baptist Church, who was also poor, used his celebrity status to ensure that he ate at least one good meal each week. He would invite himself to the home of the parishioners and tell them that he wanted fried chicken for dinner. Each family strove to provide the requested menu.

Daddy and Annie Lee Mama had not provided their family with fried chicken for many months. We had only several chickens that laid a few eggs for Annie Lee Mama to make a fried egg for Daddy's breakfast or sweet bread or a small cake for Sunday's dinner.

On the day Reverend Long came to dinner, Annie Lee Mama killed one of her hens and fried it.

Reverend Long arrived at our house and immediately sat at the table, ready to devour the food that he expected to have placed before him. The platter of fried chicken was placed on the table in full view of Gladys, Gloria, and me who stood in the doorway of the pantry. We were so hungry and starved for chicken that we stood there crying and clutching each other for physical and moral support. We wanted a piece of chicken as we had been eating nothing but salt pork for our meat.

Sometimes, we did not have any meat for our meals for days on end.

Reverend Long hailed the fried chicken with such reverence you would have thought it was the Second Coming.

"Suster Annie Lee, that chicken looks mighty fine," he said as he placed two pieces of chicken on his plate. He devoured the first two pieces and reached for the third piece. "Suster, that was mighty fine chicken," he said.

We three small children in the doorway of the pantry held on to one another for dear life. Our stomachs were aching, and we were crying and whispering to one another, "He is eating all the chicken." Tears and mucous were running down our faces. The reverend did not seem to notice or care.

After eating the third piece, Reverend Long said, "Now, Suster, that was the best chicken I ever ate. I'll just have one mo' piece." As he reached to stab the fourth piece of chicken with his fork, Gladys could stand it no longer. She screamed, "Don't eat all the chicken. Leave some for me!"

When Gladys screamed, she reached out in a begging motion with both hands, entreating Reverend Long to have mercy on us poor hungry children who had not had chicken for months. As she did so, she broke the hold we had on one another, and Gloria and I fell through the doorway and sprawled onto the kitchen floor, under the table where the few remaining pieces of fried chicken lay in jeopardy on the platter.

I was four years old. I remember the incident up to our falling on the floor as if it were yesterday. I must have blacked out from hunger and the stress of seeing the chicken devoured before our eyes. I could never remember what happened next.

We were so poor that we declared ourselves "po." Even though the nation was in a Depression and most families were suffering, we were in more distress than the average poor family. When Daddy heard about the relief that was being offered to citizens, he went to town and stood in a line to get some help. He stood in the line all day in freezing weather. He was emboldened by the armloads of goods he saw people carrying away from the relief counter.

When he reached the counter where he expected to receive needed items, such as coats and shoes for his children and, hopefully, something for himself and Annie Lee Mama, he was sorely disappointed. The woman behind the counter looked at him as if he was an interloper. Daddy began to list what he needed. "Ma'am, I need some winter clothes for my five children," he began.

"I don't have any winter clothes to give you. Take this dress," said the counter woman as she reached under the counter and handed him a small blue-and-white summer dress that would not fit any of us. "That's all I have for you," the counter woman said as she dismissed Daddy as if he were not standing there, cold and hungry and in need of some relief. Daddy said that he never stood in a relief line again. We weathered the Depression and ate cornbread and syrup for breakfast.

Now I had exposed our extreme poverty to the white woman who asked me if I wanted a biscuit. My answer had revealed just how poor we really were. We only had cornbread to eat for breakfast. When we left Annie Lee Mama's work location, heading for home, Annie Lee Mama told me that she would never take me with her to work again. She was so angry that she proposed to punish me for talking to the white woman and letting her know how poor we were.

"You're going to school with your sisters next time I have to go to work on a school day. I can't take you with me, again. You talk too much," Annie Lee Mama said with tears in her eyes.

I was hurt that Annie Lee Mama was angry with me as I tried very hard to please her. However, the punishment of sending me to school was greatly appreciated as I wanted so desperately to go. Had I known about Uncle Remus's Br'er Rabbit, I would have said, "Thow me in de bri' patch. Thow me in de bri' patch."[23] School was the place for me.

[23.] Joel Chandler Harris, published in book form in 1881 (a journalist in post Reconstruction) en.wikipedia.org/wiki/Uncle_Remus—Cached

Daddy was pleased about me going to school although he tried to hide his pleasure from Annie Lee Mama. He had observed me learning to read. He told the story with pride.

The next time Annie Lee Mama had to go to work during the week, I was packed off to school. I was dressed in my Sunday clothes, and my hair was combed and braided afresh that morning. I was so excited my teeth chattered.

Finally, the other children came down the road. We walked four miles to the schoolhouse. As we passed each house, the Negro children joined us, swelling our ranks and joining cousins, friends, classmates, girlfriends, and boyfriends in the parade.

As we walked, Lois fussed at me all the way to school. She was afraid she would be blamed for bringing me. She told me that Mrs. Melton, the principal, would be very angry and that she might get a whipping for bringing me to school. This saddened and sobered me for the long walk.

When we arrived at school, other Negro students joined us on the playground. Suddenly, a cowbell began to ring. "Ba-lam, ba-lam, ba-lam," it clanged. The entire student body rushed to their assigned locations and lined up in orderly rows.

Standing upon the cement steps, above the older students, was a large Indian-looking woman, over six feet tall (as tall as my daddy), with long braids hanging down the front of a big gray dress. She was an imposing figure, standing upon the steps and clanging the cowbell with such ferocity that the students shook in their shoes. She did not smile; instead, she looked angry as if determined to terrorize the student body. Lois stood there trembling. She shoved me behind her so that Mrs. Melton could not see me. "That's Mrs. Melton, the principal. Be quiet and stand still," Lois admonished me. I wanted to get a good look at the large woman and peered out from behind Lois each time she reached to push me back.

Suddenly, the cowbell stopped clanging. Everyone stood silent and as still as they could muster. I continued to stick my head out to get a better look at Mrs. Melton.

With a booming voice, Mrs. Melton said, "Whose beautiful, big-eyed child is that?"

Everyone in line pointed at Lois and eagerly divested themselves of blame by declaring, "That's Lois Bailey's little sister." I could feel Lois's knees buckle. I felt sorry that I had gotten Lois into trouble with this fearsome woman.

"Come up here, little girl," Mrs. Melton said to me. Lois tried to defend me. Mrs. Melton repeated in a gentle voice, "Come on." She smiled. Lois went limper.

I walked to the tall cement steps, climbed upon the steps, and stood before Mrs. Melton. She turned me around in front of her large gray skirt, put the cowbell in my hands, placed her hands around my hands, and continued to clang the bell, this time in a marching rhythm. The students marched into their respective classrooms. I grinned from ear to ear.

Mrs. Melton took me by my hand and walked me to the little children's classroom. On the way, she asked my name. I told her, "My name is Christine Bailey."

"How old are you?" she asked. I told her I was four years old but would be five in December.

She asked me why I had come to school today. I told her that my mother had to work. I didn't mention the biscuit. When we arrived in the classroom with the little children, she introduced me to the teacher, Mrs. Wade. I knew Mrs. Wade as she lived in Romulus and attended Holly Spring Missionary Baptist Church.

Mrs. Wade did as she was directed by the principal but scolded me for coming to school as I was too young. "The county superintendent will not let you come to school. You must be six years old before you can start school," she informed me.

The first time I entered a classroom, the world appeared to open before my eyes. The room was large with windows that spanned the left side of the room and extended nearly to the ceiling. Sunrays came through the windows, sending the chalk dust streaming across the room on golden threads. There were books on the shelves and on the children's desks. There were pictures on the wall. Writing was everywhere.

Mrs. Wade interrupted my reverie and told me to sit down on the far left side with the smallest children. They were six years old. I could tell they didn't know what they were doing.

They couldn't even color within the circles on the paper on their desks. Mrs. Wade gave me a circle and a crayon. I colored it before she reached the other side of the room. For a while, I sat and watched the dust travel across the room on sunbeams that shone through the tall windows and turned the room to gold. This was a golden room. A room where I could learn all the things my mind was ready to absorb. It occurred to me that the children on the right side of the room were reading. Mrs. Wade sat with them as they took turns reading from their books, *See Spot, See Spot Run*.

Some children read fluently; others had difficulty. I thought, *I can read better than that. I read the* See Spot *book a long time ago. I've read books and things harder than that. Why am I coloring circles? I should be reading.*

Without hesitation, I raised my hand. Mrs. Wade said, "You be quiet over there, Christine. Put your hand down. You are just visiting."

I said, "But I know how to read. I can read." I insisted.

Finally, Mrs. Wade said, "Well, come over here and show me." Wow. Up I jumped and was at Mrs. Wade's side in a flash. She gave me the *See Spot* book. I read all the pages and handed the book back to her. She reached on the shelf and gave me a harder book. I read the book *See the Postman*. Mrs. Wade pulled a chair into the circle and said, "Sit down." In less than an hour, I had graduated from the pre-primer to the first-grade class. I skipped the primer class altogether.

That afternoon, Mrs. Wade told Lois to bring me to school every day. On Sunday, she told Daddy that he was to send me to school. Mrs. Melton had agreed to get approval from the county superintendent to allow me to start school at four years old. Daddy was very pleased and proud.

Our stay on Graham's farm ended when Mr. Graham, with whom Daddy sharecropped, died of consumption. His wife died soon afterward. That left the daughter and her husband to be the landowners and to provide for the sharecroppers.

The son-in-law had proven to be a poor farmer. He did not have the resources to support our family through the year in anticipation of payment when the crops were harvested. Nor did he have credit at the grocery and seed store to provide food during the winter and to buy seeds for planting in the spring, which was the standard practice of sharecropping. The landowner either had a store or formed an account at another white man's store from which the worker could get food and planting seeds on credit. The white landowner had to stand for the Negro workers' debts until the crops were harvested.

At the end of the harvest, the landowner and the store owner contrived to increase the debt to more than the crops were worth. They also contrived to report the cash derived from the crops as being less than had been received. This was the method by which Negro farmers were held in servitude no matter how hard they worked.

The Grahams' son-in-law told Daddy he could not keep the bargain made by his deceased father-in-law and that we would have to move. Daddy was released from his share-the-crops agreement with impunity.

The son-in-law joined the Army and took his family along. Tragically, within the year, his spouse, daughter, and son drowned in a swimming accident, each trying to save the other. We moved to the farm of Clifton Burroughs and continued sharecropping.

We Are Our Brother's Keeper

Mrs. Julia, a member of Holly Spring Missionary Baptist Church, was missing from her home. When she was found missing, her husband intimated that she had probably gone crazy and ran into the woods.

What made the husband relay such a message was that one of his brothers was mentally ill and the husband had shown some signs of mental illness in his day. However, his wife had no history of mental illness in her family.

People said that the brother had conniption fits. There was no medical diagnosis of the brother's illness, yet it was apparent that something was wrong by the mania that took hold of the man and caused him to run and howl like an animal. The husband's family took care of the brother during the week. On Sunday, after church, different families from the community would "sit up" with the brother to give the family respite. To make him presentable to the visitors, he was bathed, his hair cut, and he was dressed in a long white gown. On a Sunday that Daddy and Annie Lee Mama joined the care group, Uncle Buddy, Aunt Angie, and their children came along. Some of the adults sat in the house with the ill man and the others sat on the porch.

Any time a group of our people came together, there was laughter and storytelling. This occasion was no different, and talk and laughter could be heard emanating from the house and from the porch. We children were outside, playing in the yard. The ill man was tied to a chair with a blanket draped over his lap. Under the blanket, the man worked his bonds free. Suddenly, inside the house, an earsplitting howl was heard.

The ill man leaped from his chair, ran over the people in his way, and sped out of the house, across the porch, and into the yard. The people in his wake scrambled to grab the man but failed to hold him back. People ran out of the house, jumped off the porch, and were left to chase him down.

I stood in the man's path as he came barreling down the lane. I could not take my eyes off his pink feet and how fast they were moving. Annie Lee Mama and Daddy were screaming, "Get the baby! Get the baby!" My sister Lois whisked me out of the man's path just in time for him to swoop past. As he passed, our encounter was so close that I felt the wind from his gown.

The man ran so fast that his pink feet did not seem to touch the ground. He sped down the lane toward an abandoned well that was overgrown with bramble and berry vines. Inattentive to the barrier that separated him from the well, the man continued into the brambles and became impaled upon the vines. His feet continued to run even though he was held fast. When the visitors reached the man, they took great care to extricate him from the vines, causing as little damage as possible. It was too late to reduce the damage to the man's body, face, and arms. He was severely scratched and was bleeding throughout the front of his body. His gown was torn and stained with blood. The neat, clean man in the white gown no longer existed.

Years later, when Mrs. Julia was found missing, her husband wanted the community to believe that she had run from the house because she was crazy, the same as his brother.

Where Is Mrs. Julia?

We were chopping cotton, and Daddy was plowing in the cotton field at the Burrough's farm when cousin Willard Blackburn came to tell Daddy that Mrs. Julia had gone missing. Daddy was encouraged to come and help look for her.

Mrs. Julia's husband had whipped his mule into a froth as he hurried to his closest neighbor's house. "Help me!" the husband cried to his neighbor. "My wife is gone."

"Where has Mrs. Julia gone?" the neighbor asked. "I don't know. We went to bed last night, and when I woke up this morning, she wasn't there. I looked everywhere, and I can't find her. She didn't take her clothes or nothing. She must have gone crazy and run into the woods." The husband was out of breath and spoke in a harried tone.

Mrs. Julia's spouse had shown signs of having some form of mental illness that was present in his family, but Mrs. Julia was not heir to her husband's family traits. However, when she was found missing, her husband tried to convince the community that Mrs. Julia had run into the woods in the same way his brother ran from the house into the briers and brambles, around an old well, on a Sunday that members of the church were helping to care for his brother.

A lone woman lost in the woods at the edge of their farm and around the bend in the Black Warrior River was of grave concern. These woods were dense and old as no one had traveled through them since the American Indians had left or had been carried away from the area. Hunters did not go into these woods for fear of getting lost. Snakes abounded along the banks of the river and spread their offspring into the woods. If Mrs. Julia was in these woods, she was in a terrible plight. She had to be found before she wandered too far away as she might never come out again.

The husband and the neighbor decided that the situation was so dire that they would need assistance from other people in the community. The neighbor had an automobile. He volunteered to fetch some of the Holly Spring Missionary Baptist Church members to help look for Mrs. Julia. A relay system of communication existed in the community as no one had a telephone. As each person heard the news, the ones with cars carried the message on their assigned leg of the journey, thus covering the entire community.

Daddy left his plow in the field, put the mule into the barn, and rode with his cousin to the lost woman's farm some four miles away. There, Daddy joined the other men who had left their farming and gathered at the family's home.

The collection of Holly Spring Missionary Baptist Church members converged upon Mrs. Julia's farm. From there, they spread out over the land and into the woods. They traveled in groups of threes and fours, ensuring their own safety and their ability to bring Mrs. Julia home if or when she was found. The searchers carried shotguns to protect themselves and to sound blasts that could be heard if they became lost.

Three days went by with no sign of Mrs. Julia. Every day, when the men returned to the house, they sat on the porch and reported where they had been and which section of the farm and the woods they had covered. They drank water from the well that was situated at the end of the backyard. The water was cool and fresh and much appreciated after a hot day of searching in the fields and in the woods.

On the third day, as they sat on the porch comparing notes from the day's search, one of the imbibers spoke of the water not being as fresh as the day before. Also, he noted something soft attached to the bucket. Upon closer inspection, he realized that a piece of rotting flesh was stuck to the bucket that had been let down into the well to fetch the water that they were now drinking. He screamed out loud, "I found her! I found Mrs. Julia! I know where she is! She's in the well!"

Everyone jumped to their feet, scrambled to the well, and looked down into the water. The well was obscured in the darkness that no one could see the bottom. "What shall we do?" they inquired of one another.

Daddy was the first to speak, "We'll have to go get Parker Reed. Send him down to see if she is down there." Uncle Parker was Eula Mama's brother, the huge laughing man I met the night Eula Mama abandoned me.

It was agreed that Uncle Parker, having inherited his father's ability to dig wells, would be the most likely person to go down into the well in search of Mrs. Julia.

Uncle Parker was fetched. He drank a pint of his homemade whiskey and brought another pint along to bolster his courage. He also brought his well-digging ropes and rappelling devices.

Uncle Parker descended into the well. Everyone waited with bated breath. Suddenly, Uncle Parker's booming voice was heard coming out of the well. "She's down here," he said. Uncle Parker brought Mrs. Julia up and out of the well where she had floated during the three days while the church members looked for her and enjoyed drinking the cool fresh water drawn from the well.

It was a sad occasion, finding Mrs. Julia dead. She had been a contributing member of the Romulus community. She was a kind, gentle woman whom the people were fond of. She was a member of the Holly Spring Missionary Baptist Church. Given to laughter as easily as Daddy and his acquaintances were, they could not help laughing at each other as they started jumping up and down, flailing their arms, stomping their feet, and coughing and spitting. They were trying to disgorge the water from their bodies that they drank from the well during the past three days. Daddy said he coughed and spat for three months in an attempt to relieve himself of the well water he drank that was tainted with Mrs. Julia's rotting body.

When the story of Mrs. Julia's death was told, it was surmised that her husband expected people to think that Mrs. Julia was mentally ill and had run away like his brother. However, since Mrs. Julia was not mentally ill, the community decided that her husband had faked the disappearance of Mrs. Julia and that he knew where she was all along.

In keeping with the way in which crime among Negro people was treated by white law enforcement officers, there was no investigation into the death of Mrs. Julia.

According to the cemetery marker, Mrs. Julia was born in 1888 and was quietly buried in the Holly Spring Missionary Baptist Church Cemetery in the month of September 1940. There is no evidence that her husband was buried beside her.

Daddy, the Family Man

Daddy had moved us to Cliff Burrough's farm two miles further from school and church. We had settled in a small house in the midst of farmland where we found Indian head arrows and remnants of the Red Man when he roamed free in Alabama.

When many men were leaving their children with their mothers and going away to greener pastures or less frustrating lives, Daddy was raising his five girls, working hard, and maintaining a family. Daddy was determined to hold his family together, even living in the country on a farm, where the only way to survive was to work for a white landowner and take the unfair treatment that resulted.

Daddy typified the survival of the fittest by his stature, his muscular strength, and his endurance. These traits were bred into African Americans who survived during slavery. Slaves who survived had to be able to lift, push, pull, jump, twist, turn, and bend. Twisting, turning, bending, and pulling were abilities needed in picking cotton. Pushing and pulling were abilities needed in plowing. Lifting was required in picking up bales of cotton and other produce needing to be carted away from the slave plantations.

Daddy's strong muscles aided in his ability to stand, sit, and walk easily. Without modern forms of transportation, Daddy walked everywhere he went.

Daddy was an intelligent man with a great store of wisdom and common sense. He could look at a problem, whether natural, mechanical, man-made, or accidental, and figure out a solution. He could read and write better than many in his age group, both white and black.

Daddy knew that many of the white men to whom he said "yes, sir" and called mister were unable to perform tasks that came easily to him. On occasion, Daddy was required to show his boss how to perform tasks and often taught white people how to perform jobs for which they were paid more to do than he.

Daddy knew how to survive. He knew that he had to be careful of all white men, but especially those who wore overalls with one strap over one shoulder and no shirt or shoes. These were the type of men who were poorer than their Negro counterparts. They were eager to call a black man a nigger and to announce that they were white. If Daddy had not appeared subservient to these men, they would have taken their misery out on him.

Daddy knew that racial prejudices ran deep in the South and were taught to the small children.

White children were taught that black people were beneath them and black children were taught to show respect to white people. The notion of black and white differences was so deeply instilled in both groups that small infractions could result in beatings or hangings.

Near where we lived was a community composed entirely of white people where everyone living there was mentally retarded as a product of incest. Mental retardation was so rampant in this community that a county mental health center was built to serve the inhabitants. The only person with near-normal intelligence was an eighty-year-old grandmother.

Daddy and Annie Lee Mama were digging sweet potatoes from the garden beside the big road. The eighty-year-old grandmother, who was walking down the road, stopped by the garden fence and said, "Lord, I wish I had me some good old sweet potatoes. I ain't had no sweet potatoes for many a year now." She was ashamed to ask Negro people for a handout.

Daddy took several potatoes and handed them over the fence to the grandmother. She tried to give Daddy a small package of cornmeal that she took from her apron pocket. "Here, take this meal. I got it from the county welfare. I got plenty. They don't give us no sweet potatoes." Thus, she tried to mitigate the gift that Daddy had given her.

Daddy refused the cornmeal by saying, "That's alright, ma'am. I got plenty of meal." The old woman dropped her head and walked slowly up the road.

One Sunday, as we were returning from church dressed in our Sunday clothes, Annie Lee Mama called out, "LS, look over there in the barn. Them crazy boys are milking our cows." There in front of us were a pair of mentally retarded twin brothers from the same community. Their bodies were crippled and gnarled, their arms hung loosely by their sides, and they walked with a loping gait as if one side of each body was shorter than the other side. They were identical in their appearance and in their mental deficient condition.

Daddy yelled at them to leave our cows alone. "Get out of that barn. Leave our cows alone," Daddy yelled. When they would not leave, Daddy picked up several pieces of gravel and threw toward them to run them away.

Even though the boys were severely retarded, they knew that we were black and that they were white. The difference between the races had been taught to them, and they considered themselves superior to us. "Don't you hit us, nigger. We white. Nigger don't hit no white folk. You git in trouble. Nigger, nigger, nigger," they said as they loped down the path toward the pasture. They knew that the word *nigger* was derogatory and hurtful to us.

Mrs. Clara, the white farm owner's wife, caught the boys stealing her pears. She tried to run them away. Instead of leaving, they threw pears at Mrs. Clara until she had to retreat inside her own house.

"You leave us 'lone, you old wai-itch," the two shouted over and over until Mr. Cliff, Mrs. Clara's husband, came outside and ran them away. They did not call Mrs. Clara a nigger because they knew that she was white. Instead, they used *witch* as a derogatory and hurtful term to Mrs. Clara.

Daddy navigated the black and white world with dexterity born of years of intimidation and fear. He maintained *his place* in the racial hierarchy because of an acute understanding of each situation that presented him with a choice to challenge or to acquiesce.

During the spring and summer, we slaved in the fields. Daddy plowed the fields and chopped and picked cotton when the plowing was over. In the fall and winter, he worked in the woods as a lumberjack and at the sawmill sawing lumber. The lumberjack jobs were far away from where we lived, and Daddy was required to find transportation to the work site any way he could. One year, the only job he could find was eight miles away. To arrive when the whistle blew, at eight o'clock in the morning, he would leave home at two o'clock in the morning and walk all the way to work in the freezing cold. He told of the weather that was so cold that the dirt road was frozen solid. He told how he would arrive just as the whistle blew to begin work. He would work all day, and if he could not find anyone driving in his direction, he walked all the way home only to repeat his trek the following morning.

For a long time, Daddy provided our punishments. Sometimes, we realized that Daddy was not only punishing us for something we did, but he was taking out his frustrations with life on us. At these times, Annie Lee Mama would step in and say, "That's enough, LS."

During the first years of their marriage, whenever we did something that Annie Lee Mama thought required a whipping, she told Daddy when he came home or referred us to him if he was home at the time.

After a while, Annie Lee Mama realized that Daddy's striking out was partly because of what we had done and partly because of his frustrations with life. She began to punish us herself. I believe that she whipped us with a switch so that Daddy would not whip us with his belt. She often showed benevolence in that way.

One day, Gloria and I got into trouble for something and Annie Lee Mama administered her first real whipping of us. I was seven and Gloria was nine years old.

At every house we lived in, there was a "switch tree" located at the edge of the yard. This tree was usually a bush that had no name. It had long limbs that grew just the right size with which parents could whip children. The first time Annie Lee Mama decided to whip Gloria and me herself, she wrung a switch off the switch tree and told us to come to her so she could whip us.

Gloria and I looked at each other and decided that it was best not to go near her. We began to run away. We ran for our lives—out of the yard and down the hill.

We reached a small gully that ran parallel to the yard. Gloria led the way down into the bed of the gully. I followed as fast as my little legs would carry me.

Annie Lee Mama was in hot pursuit of us as we sped deep into the gully. As we felt her breathing down our necks and the switch swooshing behind us, Gloria decided to leave the bottom of the gully and rise to the lip of the gully that ran on her side.

I realized that I was still in the gully alone with Annie Lee Mama. I did not want to be the only one in the gully with Annie Lee Mama. I scrambled up the lip on my side. Annie Lee Mama rose up on the top side with Gloria who fell back into the gully without losing a step. Even though Annie Lee Mama was not up on my side, I did not want to run away alone. I fell back down into the gully alongside Gloria, just in front of Annie Lee Mama.

This up-and-down running by Gloria, Annie Lee Mama, and me soon began to make Annie Lee Mama laugh. In addition, she began to tire before we did. As her tiredness and laughter soon rendered her unable to run as fast as we, she began to lag behind. We wondered why she was slowing down.

As we looked back, we saw her doubled over. We thought we had made her ill and that she was in pain. We stopped and gradually walked back to her to see what was the matter. We found her doubled over with laughter.

Annie Lee Mama explained to us that she had to punish us for what we had done and for running away from her. In this way, we would not repeat our behavior nor would we ever run away again. We agreed as she tightened our skirts around our hips and hit us a few times each with the switch from the switch tree.

Working in the Fields

The cotton fields were heavily laden with dew that had fallen on the cotton and corn and the grass that grew between the rows. We were drenched with sticky moisture which made our legs and arms itch. Big caterpillar worms feasted on the cotton leaves and stung us with their rear stinger whenever we failed to detect their presence in time to avoid their painful sting. Daddy, Annie Lee Mama, and us five girls worked on the farm. I was eight years old when I started working full-time in the fields.

During the late spring, the summer, and early fall, our family worked in the fields on the farm from early morning to late afternoon. We started working when the sun appeared over the treetops in the eastern sky. We toiled until just before the sun went down, leaving enough daylight to fetch the water from the spring, bring in the wood, slop the hogs, milk the cows, help cook supper, do our homework if we thought we might go to school the next day, eat dinner, wash the dishes, wash our feet in the wash pan, say our prayers, and crawl into bed. Early before sunup, Daddy called us to start all over again. During this time, we only went to school on rainy days when it was too wet to work in the fields.

There was one respite during the day when we had an hour at noon to eat dinner. After breakfast, Annie Lee Mama left peas or beans boiling on the stove, rendering them almost done before the wood fire went out. When she arrived home before twelve noon, she stoked the fire, and by the time we came from the field, she had finished cooking cornbread and frying salt pork. We arrived home at twelve noon, ate hurriedly, trying to leave ten to fifteen minutes to lie down on the porch to rest. Daddy would rouse us by saying, "Alright, it's time to go back to the field."

Once, Daddy needed us to pick a thousand pounds of cotton in one day as the price of cotton was up. He told us if we picked two bales of cotton before sundown, our usual quitting time, we could go free for the remainder of the day. We all exceeded our usual poundage of cotton. Gloria and Gladys picked two hundred pounds each, Mable and I picked one hundred each, and Daddy and Annie Lee Mama picked three hundred pounds each. Lois had already married. It was around three o'clock when we weighed up and found that we had exceeded the thousand pounds Daddy needed. We jumped for joy as we knew that we could play for the remainder of the day.

Instead of giving us the freedom to play and run free for several hours, Daddy told us it would not look right for Mr. Cliff, the farm owner, to see us at leisure during the work hours. We had to continue picking cotton until it was normal quitting time. We were devastated.

As sharecroppers, no matter how hard we worked and no matter how many days we missed school, we ended up owing more to Cliff Burroughs than we earned. We were held on the land to try to get out of sharecropping debt another year.

Daddy and Annie Lee Mama worked extra for Mr. Cliff, trying to earn enough credit to make the necessary difference. Annie Lee Mama worked for Mrs. Clara, Cliff's wife, two Saturdays each month. On those days, she was not paid. Her salary was supposed to go toward working off our debt. In truth, she was an unpaid slave.

Daddy did extra work for Mr. Cliff on Saturdays when he was not working in our fields. He also had us work for Mr. Cliff when asked, hoping to accumulate enough credit to make the difference when they settled up at the end of harvest. There was always hope as Daddy thought he could overcome the debt that never ended.

The Color of Freedom Is Red

One year, on the fourth of July, when we thought we were free to celebrate the holiday, Mr. Cliff told Daddy he would give him credit if we hoed out his cotton patch. We worked in our own fields five days each week and had not anticipated this request. We felt free to enjoy the day released from working in the fields.

Mable had a friend who lived two miles farther down the road from Holly Spring Missionary Baptist Church. The church was six miles from where we lived; adding two more miles made the journey eight miles one way. We were used to walking everywhere we went and thought nothing of walking sixteen miles in one day. Mable's friend had invited us to her house to eat dinner. She had promised to have fried chicken and cake. We would walk anywhere for fried chicken and cake.

We four sisters (Lois was married) got up early that morning, did our chores, and got dressed to walk to the house of Mable's friend. We hurried away from home, knowing that work was always present around the house and if we didn't hurry, something would show up, needing our attention. We took the shortcut through the woods and over two creeks where snakes were known to inhabit the wetlands. We ran the first mile, chasing one another and relishing our freedom. Suddenly, we heard a shrill whistle. It was Daddy's signal that he used to call us from a distance of as far as three miles. We grabbed one another and began to cry. We knew our freedom was short-lived. Daddy was calling us back to the house.

First, one of us suggested that we could continue on our journey and tell Daddy that we did not hear him. Our sense was that Daddy would harness the mule and ride us down. We would receive a terrible whipping for not having heard him. Reluctantly, we turned back. Over the creeks and through the woods, we traversed our journey no longer free but bound to whatever lay before us. We trudged back up the hill to the house. Daddy met us at the door and said, "Change your clothes. Mr. Cliff wants you to hoe out a patch of cotton today." It was obvious that Annie Lee Mama had tried to dissuade Daddy from calling us back as she was sullen and quiet when we returned.

We changed into our work clothes, old shirts, and torn dresses and headed for the field. By the time we arrived in the field, the sun was already high up in the sky and it was as hot as blazes. We cried as Mable, Gladys, and Gloria talked about how mean Daddy was to take our one day of rest and fun and make us work for the white landowner.

As it turned out, neither our work nor Daddy's and Annie Lee Mama's work made a difference at the end of harvest. According to Mr. Cliff, we still owed more than we made. While we toiled, hoeing the grass from under and around Mr. Cliff's cotton stalks, evading the big horned caterpillars that inhabited the leaves, and feeling demoralized and unloved, we observed Vivian, Cliff's daughter, as she emerged from the big house. We became angrier as we were hoeing out her cotton. It seemed to us that she should be in the field doing her own work.

Instead, Vivian yelled something back at the house, jumped into her red convertible Ford, and sped off down the dirt road. I watched her as she drove fast, evading the dust swirls that chased the car in its wake. Her speed was sufficient to keep the dust at bay. She seemed to be escaping from something that would, if she did not move fast enough, hold her in bondage. She sped along like a bird, flying free. I longed for that freedom. I wanted to fly down the road and away from the cotton field.

We learned in school that the fourth of July is a federal holiday in the United States that commemorates the adoption of the Declaration of Independence that occurred on July 4, 1776.[24] Vivian was a recipient of that freedom; obviously, we were not.

[24.] en.wikipedia.org/wiki/Independence_Day

We continued to hoe until the middle of the afternoon when Daddy came to the field and told us that we had done a good job and that we could rest.

I never forgot that event. From that day on, I envisioned the metaphor for freedom as a red convertible flying down the road, outrunning everything that could hold it back. To me, *the color of freedom was red!*

Sister Lois

We were all good students. Lois was a top student in the ninth grade when she fell in love with a young man who came to Romulus to visit his father. His name was Willie D. Burton. Daddy was not entirely pleased with Lois choosing Willie D. as Lois was only sixteen years old and Willie D. was a fun-loving young man who loved to dance and spent every weekend in a dance hall either in the country or in town. Lois attracted Willie D.'s attention as she was pretty, petite, and intelligent.

She had an adultlike style of behavior. Daddy finally allowed Willie D. to call on Lois, and he bought a living room couch and chair to decorate a section of the front bedroom.

One night, when the suitor was leaving, Lois tipped out of the door to have a little extra time with him. Gloria went along to ensure that Daddy did not suspect Lois of any improprieties, but she stayed out of sight. Daddy took this event to mean that the two lovers had engaged in improper behavior even though they had not. Lois and Willie D. got married. Lois was in love.

Daddy tried to help the two newlyweds make the marriage work. In the end, it fell apart after the couple had two children. Daddy took responsibility for Lois who came back home.

After Lois's two children graduated from high school, Lois went back to high school in the ninth grade, graduated from high school with a 4.0 average, and received a scholarship to Southwest College in Los Angeles, California. From there, she received another scholarship with a 4.0 average to Dominguez College. She graduated with a BA degree in English and became a high school teacher at the age of forty-five. She taught school until she was in her seventies, during which time she acquired a master's degree in school administration.

Mable

Mable was also a good student, very athletic and strong. She played basketball, could turn cartwheels, and could plow a mule. Mable protected us from bullies and snakes. She would fight all comers and would kill all the snakes we ran into. Mable was Lois's protector.

Josie Lou Allen lived in the house where Lois and Mable had to get water from the well when we lived on the Robinsons' farm. She bullied Lois and Mable, frequently preventing them from drawing water from the well. Often, Daddy had to go to the well and make Josie Lou refrain from intimidating the two girls.

When Daddy moved us to the Graham farm, we had our own well. However, Josie Lou continued to bully Lois and Mable on the way to and from school.

Daddy had intervened on several occasions. Finally, Daddy told Lois and Mable that they would have to fight their own battles and that he would not continue to stop Josie Lou from bothering them.

Lois was eleven, and Mable was nine or ten. Josie Lou was sixteen years old. One day, Lois and Mable decided that the time had come to stop Josie Lou from bothering them. They stayed home from school. Mable took the ax and cut limbs off a tree and fashioned cudgels with which to beat Josie Lou. They decided that Lois would take on Josie Lou and that Mable would take on her fourteen-year-old brother, Fred.

The colored children could be heard returning from school. Those who lived beyond our house came walking up the road. Lois and Mable waited in the bushes near our house. Daddy and Annie Lee Mama went up the hill beyond the house and hid in the pine grove so that they could monitor the fight but not intervene. Gladys and Gloria got the smoothing irons and waited on the porch. I was three or four years old and was just in the way.

Josie Lou and Fred were unaware of what awaited them when they came by our house. Lois was the first to step out from the bushes and accost Josie Lou. "You said you were going to beat me up. Well, here I am. Let me see you beat me up," Lois said.

Josie Lou was stunned by this small-statured, attractive, smart girl standing there with a large stick ready to take the larger, ugly, dumb Josie Lou on. Mable collared Fred and held him back. Lois swung with all her might, hitting Josie Lou in the head. The fight was on. Lois continued to swing her stick, never allowing Josie Lou to attack her. Mable, bigger and stronger than Lois, simply beat Fred at will. Gladys and Gloria ran from the porch and held the smaller siblings out of the fight.

Soon, Josie Lou and Fred had had more than enough. They started running up the road. Mable, who could throw a rock with great accuracy, picked up large gravel rocks that had been laid down by the WPA workers when they repaired the roads and threw them at the two fleeing combatants. Gladys entered the fray and joined Mable in "rock battling" the two fleeing teenagers.

Although Lois received punishment from Mrs. Melton, the principal, at school, she was praised by Daddy and Mama for taking care of herself.

Several years later, Josie Lou and Johnny Harper fell in love and were married. Johnny was the son of Deacon Harper, the man who looked like a white man and resembled a later-famous colonel. He was one of the leading citizens in Holly Spring Missionary Baptist Church. Although Johnny was an attractive boy, he was not desired as a boyfriend by the girls in the community. Johnny was mentally retarded.

Josie Lou became pregnant, and people wagged their tongues, wondering if something would be wrong with the baby when it was born. She became ill during her pregnancy. It was in the dead of winter, and it was raining and sleeting. Josie Lou's family was unable to figure out what to do to help the sick woman.

When Annie Lee Mama heard that Josie Lou was very sick, she told Daddy to go by to see how Josie Lou was feeling. Daddy found her nearly dying. Daddy knew what to do. He walked a half-mile in the rain and sleet and got cousin John D. (the same person who brought Daddy to get me) to take Josie Lou to Stillman Hospital. Unfortunately, it was too late for the baby as the baby had died in the womb. Josie Lou died the next day.

Years later, to prepare for the third Sunday in May homecoming, Annie Lee Mama and I went to the Holly Spring Missionary Baptist Church Cemetery to clean the grass from her mother's grave. We also cleaned the grave of Josie Lou and her infant child as no one had cleaned the forgotten grave for years. Annie Lee Mama cried.

Mable and the Snake

Mable worked hard in the fields, plowing and doing work that was considered man's work. She was a good student who was eager to go to school. Like all of us, she attended school when it rained and stayed home on sunny days during the crop-growing season.

One day, Mable and I were hoeing out the cornfield near the creek where snakes were often found. Mable espied a snake in the weeds between the corn and sorghum fields. She could not tell how large the snake was, nor did Mable care. She liked killing snakes—the bigger the better.

In contrast with Mable, I was so scared of snakes that when anyone told of seeing a snake nearby, I began to hallucinate and could see snakes everywhere.

Mable kept her eyes on the snake and called for me to bring her some rocks. Instead of bringing Mable a rock, I ran into the sticker patch in my bare feet. My feet were full of stickers; I was scared, and I could see snakes everywhere. I was no help to Mable who was left staring down the snake. Mable's cries for me to bring her some rocks were heard by our cousin who was planting corn across the creek.

Cousin Boykin Leonard Stewart secured his mule and plow and ran across the creek to see what Mable was screaming about. He found the snake in front of Mable, staring back at her. Boykin took one of our hoes and killed the snake which turned out to be one of the biggest snakes we had ever seen. He coiled the snake inside his corn planter bucket and drove his mule up to our house to play a joke on Annie Lee Mama.

"Cousin Annie Lee," he called, "I brought you some corn for your chickens." Annie Lee Mama came outside to thank him for the corn. She looked inside the corn bucket and saw the very large snake. She took the broom and ran Boykin Leonard all over the yard.

Mable saved the snake for Daddy to see. He said it was truly a large snake, but it was not the largest he had ever seen.

Daddy repeated the story about the larger snake that he saw in Pickens County while he was cutting logs. A log lay on the ground that seemed to have been cut long ago but had not been hauled off to become lumber. When the noon whistle sounded, the loggers stopped to eat their lunch. They sat around on the logs that lay nearby. One logger sat on the old log, which began to move. He jumped up and realized that he had been sitting on a very, very large snake.

The First Graduate in Our Family

Mable graduated from the ninth grade in Romulus. She was the first in our family to go to high school in the tenth grade. She attended Tuscaloosa County Training School in Northport, Alabama.

The colored high school students who lived in the county did not have a bus to take them the thirty miles to school. One of the citizens who lived in Romulus had a truck. He nailed tin on the sides and on the top. He made a tin door in the back of the truck. Two benches were placed inside along the sides. Students, tenth grade and above, traveled to and from school in this contraption. They were embarrassed to ride onto the schoolyard. However, they had no choice but to take this vehicle to school. Mable attended thus for one year.

The following year, we moved to the city of Tuscaloosa where we attended Industrial High School. Mable was a good student who studied hard and did well in all her subjects. She sang in the school choir.

In her twelfth-grade year, Mable was sent by Daddy to North Carolina to care for Lois and her two children. By then, Lois was married to a paratrooper at Fort Bragg who was abusing her and her children. Mable took on the soldier, attacking him with a butcher knife and saving Lois from a severe beating. Lois was hospitalized. Mable brought the two children home, and Lois caught the bus home the day the doctor released her from the hospital. When Lois left home, she weighed 140 pounds. When she arrived home from North Carolina, she weighed 98 pounds. Mable returned to school the following year and was the first person in our family to graduate from high school. Mable married and moved to Detroit, Michigan. It was there that I traveled and lived with Mable, her husband, and child after I graduated from high school at the age of seventeen.

When Daddy died, Gladys's family accounted for fifteen of Daddy's nineteen great-great-grandchildren. Gladys asked that I don't share her stories in this book.

Gladys

Gladys and Gloria were in the same grade due to the failure of Aunt Clyde to send Gladys to school when she lived in Kentucky. Daddy had allowed his sister, Clyde, to take Gladys to Kentucky when Eula Mama sent the four oldest sisters back home with Daddy. Aunt Clyde preferred Gladys because she was pretty and dark-skinned. She looked more like the Blackburn/Bailey family than either Lois or Mable.

While Gladys was living with Aunt Clyde, she abused Gladys and treated her like a servant. At six years old, Gladys was made to babysit Aunt Clyde's baby, wash dishes, and clean the house. She was not allowed to play or go to school. When she did not do a chore, Aunt Clyde would beat her.

When Gladys came home, she was different from us. She was fearful and suspicious of everyone. Her survival tactics consisted of working to please the adults and to tell them whatever she thought they wanted to know. Daddy tried to make amends to Gladys for having sent her to stay with Aunt Clyde. He realized that she had been abused.

As she grew older, she was the most industrious child who worked to please Daddy. She could cook, sew, iron, and curl our hair. She became the best cook any of us ever knew.

Gladys married at seventeen and had six children. She raised her children with the determination that we all had—never to leave our children as our mother had left us.

Gloria

Gloria was a different kind of person from anyone I knew as a child. She was her own person, did her own thinking, and questioned everyone's opinion. She always had an explanation for her behavior. Her activities did not follow general logic, but they made sense to her and sometimes to me. It was this determined spirit that made Gloria a successful businesswoman who owns her own beauty salon, twelve rental properties, and a palatial home.

From the first night when I came home, I had become Gloria's sidekick and tagalong friend. As time went by, I slowly began to question her logic, but not until we had spent years running up against the adults at home, our adult relatives, and the teachers at school. Daddy called the two of us "those two little devils" until he was well into his nineties and we were in our seventies.

The Bouncing Underpants

We still remember the day when Gloria chose to outfit herself and me in basketball attire. Gloria wanted to play basketball like Mable who played on the Romulus Colored School Team. On a Saturday when Annie Lee Mama was working at Mrs. Clara's house, Gloria and I played basketball in the yard.

We did not have a ball. Gloria made one out of rags. Of course, it would not bounce. To dribble, she passed the rag ball from one hand to the other as she skipped around the yard. She kept the ball away from me as I tried to intercept it. She made a basket out of a fruit basket. She was afraid of tearing the bottom out as we only had one fruit basket. She danced around the yard while I scrambled to take the ball.

Soon, she became concerned that we were wearing dresses and needed to be wearing basketball shorts. She wanted something that would bounce like Mable's trunks did when she played basketball at school.

Suddenly, Gloria had a brainstorm. She bid me wait until she returned. She even gave me the ball to play with while she was gone.

When she returned, she had two pairs of Annie Lee Mama's Sunday underwear which Annie Lee Mama called step-ins. They were made of soft, pink material that would jiggle just right. She brought two large safety pins which she used to put the pants on each of us and to drape them securely around our thin waists.

We began to play in earnest as we had "trunks" that swished and swayed as Gloria made baskets and I tried to intercept her and the ball.

A loud voice boomed from the edge of the yard, "What are you two doing in Cousin Annie Lee's underwear? She is going to kill you for wearing her drawers and letting everybody see them." It was our cousin Boykin Leonard, the one who had killed the snake for Mable. He knew that Annie Lee Mama was a private, shy person and would be mortified if her underwear was seen by an outsider.

Just then, Annie Lee Mama appeared around the hill in front of the house. As she entered the yard, she passed the switch tree. She wrung two switches off the tree, took her underwear off our bodies, pulled our skirts tight around our hips, and wore us out.

Three Holes in One Head

It appeared that Gloria did not learn from these events. I was about to get the message. Each time Gloria thought up an activity, I started to dissect the fun from the punishment. We were going to town! Daddy told us that if we picked a bale of cotton in one day, he would take us to town. We picked a bale of cotton. At nine years old, I picked one hundred pounds; Gloria and Gladys each picked two hundred pounds, and Daddy and Annie Lee Mama picked about three hundred pounds each. Mable was not a good cotton picker, but she was able to plow. She fell in the line of cotton picking somewhere between Gloria and me. This was the second time Daddy had coerced us into picking a bale of cotton in one day.

Gloria and I were selected to go to town and were told to climb into the cotton truck on top of the cotton. Daddy and Annie Lee Mama told us to stay seated and not to stand up in the truck. They informed us that if we stood up, we could fall off the truck and get killed.

As we traveled up the road, we had to pass our nearest colored neighbors—the Leatherwoods. Gloria wanted the Leatherwood children to know that we were going to town. As we rounded the curve in the road, we could see the children playing in the front yard.

As we came near the edge of their yard, we passed under an old oak tree with dried limbs that had been broken off by the wind. Gloria was facing backward and did not see the tree coming. At the very moment that we were passing under the tree, Gloria stood up and waved. She yelled to the children, "We are going to town!" An old broken limb of the oak tree caught Gloria in the back of the head and dragged her to the end of the truck bed. She was buried deep in the cotton. I was afraid to get up and help her, yet I crawled over the cotton and unearthed her. I found her head bleeding, and she was in a state of shock. I pressed cotton into the wound and tried to stem the blood.

When we reached our cousin's house farther on, Daddy was told that the cotton prices had dropped and that he should wait to sell his cotton another day. We went home.

When we arrived back home, we got out of the truck on the big road. Gloria and I sneaked off the back of the truck and ran to our house in the woods. Lois tended to Gloria's wound and we did not tell Daddy and Annie Lee Mama about the incident.

Gloria has three holes in her head to this day. The second one occurred when Mable threw a stick into the mulberry tree to dislodge the fruit. When the stick came down, it stuck straight up in Gloria's head. The third stick that was stuck into Gloria's head occurred at Aunt Lucille's house. We were riding on the flying ginny. A flying ginny is made of one large plank affixed to a stump by a large bolt. The bolt is screwed into a stump. The plank is held loosely so that it can turn round like a flat propeller.

When the flying ginny was mounted, the small children were seated near the fulcrum and were held by one of the bigger children. The two oldest boys would sit on the ends of the flying ginny and would run sideways until it was put in motion. Everyone would hold on tightly and have the ride of their lives.

Gloria chose not to be one of the small children even though she was probably the lightest weight of all, owing to her thinness. When the flying ginny was loaded, Gloria jumped on the very end. No one saw her climb aboard as the boys propelled the riders to a fast spin. When the flying ginny sped up to its fastest speed, Gloria flew off the end, was airborne for fifty feet, and landed in the pigpen. As she landed, a stick was waiting to pierce her in the head.

No one knew what to do about the bleeding and was afraid to tell the adults. Uncle Herbert would have whipped the boys with the buggy whip.

Lois took dirt and plugged up the hole in Gloria's skull. Fortunately, Daddy had driven the wagon to Aunt Lucille's house and Gloria was able to lie down in the wagon on the ride home.

The Mule in the Bedroom

When Gloria was a preteen, she strove to spend time away from home as often as she could. The notion that she could spend the weekend with Grandma or one of our other family members resulted in a constant search for someone with whom she could visit.

The last person in the world that Mama and Daddy should have allowed Gloria to visit was Trick. Trick was the child that had been left in the house with Uncle Louis when all her aunts and uncles, including Annie Lee Mama, married and moved away. After Aunt Sally died, no one claimed Trick and no one tried to rear her in a reasonable way. As she grew older, her teenage years found her as wild as an animal in the woods. She was wily enough to fool Uncle Louis at every turn, and without anyone else to check her actions, she ran wild and fully amok.

Somehow, Gloria chose to visit Trick and Uncle Louis. She begged to go until she was given permission to do so just to shut her mouth. One Sunday, after church, Gloria left with her hosts to spend the night with Trick and Uncle Louis

Unfortunately, the big house that Great-Grandpa Romeo Blackburn built had burned down one night as Uncle Louis and Trick lay asleep. A fire started in the kitchen and burned the house to the ground. Trick and Uncle Louis escaped the flames with the clothes on their backs. Everything was destroyed.

Now they were living in the three-room house that he had built for himself and Aunt Sally when they were first married. Later, the house was used to store cotton, corn, and other belongings. After the fire, Uncle Louis cleaned the house as he saw fit, and he and Trick moved into two rooms.

When Gloria and Trick reached the house, Trick embarked upon chasing a chicken to kill for dinner. The two girls neither changed from their Sunday clothes nor did they enter the house. The chase of the chicken took precedence over normal conventions that Gloria would have experienced at home, such as changing her clothes, and dinner was caught and killed. Trick took care not to be seen by Uncle Louis as he never killed a chicken to eat. He ate salt pork for every meal.

When the chicken had been run to the ground, Trick tried to silence its cries, wringing the chicken's neck by holding on to its head and twirling the chicken's body through the air. The chicken was too heavy for Trick to twirl the body around easily. The chicken would not die, whereupon Trick turned the chicken loose. It went wobbling around the yard with its head held to one side. She finally caught a smaller chicken, held it by its head, and twirled its body around until she had wrung its neck and the chicken went limp. She laid the twitching chicken on the wood-chopping block and dispatched its head.

Gloria could not believe the speed with which Trick plucked the chicken, chopped it into four pieces, and placed it in a skillet. Gloria noted that when Annie Lee Mama killed a chicken, she boiled water, dipped the chicken in the hot water, and plucked the feathers with care to render it clean. Trick neither used hot water nor cold water. She skipped water altogether.

When the two girls entered the house, Trick made a fire in the iron stove. The stove was designed with iron eyes that could be lifted with an iron poker to reveal the fire beneath. Trick used the open fire to singe the feathers off the chicken. Then, to speed up the cooking of the meat, she placed a skillet on the open fire.

While the chicken was cooking, Gloria had her first opportunity to view her surroundings. She heard a noise of rustling and moving about in the room next to the kitchen. She had seen Uncle Louis outside walking in the field. It could not be he in the next room. "Who lives in that room?" Gloria asked, pointing to the adjacent room.

"Mule," Trick answered.

"Mule who?" Gloria asked.

"*The mule*," Trick repeated with emphasis.

"You mean a mule lives next door?" Gloria inquired.

"Yes, Uncle Louis took the floor out and put the mule in there. When we moved in, he didn't move the mule out," Trick revealed. The existence of the mule explained the smell of manure that permeated the kitchen.

Gloria became afraid that the mule was close to where she had to spend the night. She wondered what would happen and what she would do living in a house with a mule next door.

When the chicken was cooked, Gloria had difficulty eating it. First, it had not been plucked or washed. Second, it was half cooked. Third, the mule was next door. Fourth, the kitchen smelled of manure and mule urine.

Upon realizing that the family was nearby, the mule began to bray and kick the walls. He ran around the room and smashed into the walls at every turn. Trick explained, "That old mule wants to eat."

Uncle Louis was heard talking to the mule, "Stop that noise. Here's some hay and water. Now you settle down." Gloria hoped the mule would settle down or be placed outside. Neither happened. The mule became more active, brayed more loudly, and made noise eating, drinking, and rustling around in the hay.

As time went by, Gloria became more afraid than she had been initially. She wondered if she could walk home before dark if she left at that moment. Walking outside, she realized that the sun was almost down, which meant that she would not get to the main road before dark.

There was a path over the mountain between her location and our house that provided a shortcut. She had never traveled that way, but she was almost willing to try it.

It was summertime. The path across the mountain would be treacherous and abounding with snakes. Also, there were wild animals and hunters on the mountain. That way was not an option. She was trapped.

When bedtime came, Gloria realized that she would sleep in the room with Trick and Uncle Louis and the mule would occupy the other bedroom.

Gloria was terrified by the appearance of Uncle Louis who had become crippled and gnarled from his rheumatoid arthritis so that he appeared less humanoid and more befitting the appearance of a gnome. Dressed in his nightshirt, he looked like an elf ready to do magic.

Uncle Louis had a bed on the outer side of the bedroom near the window. Trick's bed, which Gloria would be required to share, was located on the wall next to the mule. Gloria lay down on the backside of the bed. She would have chosen the front side had it not been for the sight of Uncle Louis. As she lay down near the wall, the mule turned its back, reared up on its front feet, and kicked the wall just above Gloria's head with both back feet. Dust fell from between the planks as they bent toward Gloria's bedside. She screamed. Uncle Louis yelled at the mule, "Shut up and lie down. Cut out that kicking." Trick laughed until she cried. Gloria just cried.

The mule continued to bray, fart, urinate, and defecate. The smell of each bodily action permeated Gloria's wall and sickened her empty stomach. She could not sleep.

Soon, she heard Uncle Louis snoring, and Trick was asleep as well. Gloria said her prayers over and over. She cried in her pillow.

The mule would not go to sleep, and even if he did, Gloria knew he was still next door. She held her breath and waited for each move the mule made.

Finally, the mule did go to sleep. It snored, farted, and made animal noises in its sleep. Gloria could not escape from the smell or from the sounds. She wished she was home in her own bed.

At the first light of day, Gloria got out of bed and dressed in her clothes from the day before. She sat in a chair in the kitchen and waited for daylight. When the day was light enough to see outside, Gloria headed home. She walked through the woods to the big road, turned right, and walked the four miles home. When Trick and Uncle Louis awoke, they found that Gloria had gone.

It was sometime before Gloria told the story of the mule in the bedroom. It was after she had sufficiently healed from the traumatic experience that she was able to talk about her sleepover visit with Trick, Uncle Louis, and the mule. This story was the source of much laughter, and it cured Gloria from asking to sleep over at the home of our relatives for a long time.

Southern Justice

According to public records, black-on-black crime has existed for a long time. The punishment for crimes committed by and against Negro people has long been met with indifference in the Southern criminal justice systems. Even when the assailant and the victim are both in clear evidence, the police in Tuscaloosa, Alabama have been known to look the other way.

An example of this Southern justice was in evidence when a colored man named Mr. Floyd discovered that his wife was having an affair with Mr. Washington. Truth be known, his wife was having affairs with many men. However, Mr. Washington made no secret about his affair with the wife and did not hide his feeling for her. Day after day, Mr. Washington came by to visit Mrs. Floyd. He even came by on days when Mr. Floyd was home.

For some time, Mr. Floyd endured the affront in silence until he found that he could not take it any longer. One day, Mr. Washington was sitting on Mr. Floyd's porch along with several other men. Mr. Floyd loaded his double-barreled shotgun and tiptoed around the house. He approached Mr. Washington from the rear and fired both barrels of the gun into the suitor's back at close range. The victim's body was blown into pieces.

The men who had been sitting with Mr. Washington ran for their lives. Neighbors came to look at the carnage. The police were called. Upon arrival, they found Mr. Floyd still holding the shotgun and Mr. Washington's body scattered all over the porch and the front yard.

You would think that Mr. Floyd would have been hauled off to jail and tried for the obvious murder. Not if it was a black-on-black crime in Tuscaloosa, Alabama in 1943.

After surveying the scene of the crime and ascertaining that the victim was a colored man, the police told Mr. Floyd that he had twenty-four hours to get out of town. Mr. Floyd went to California. Later, his daughter went to live with him. The daughter married my husband's brother, who, in turn, encouraged us to come live in California. In death, Mr. Washington did not receive justice. However, his death was the catalyst for the westward migration of many generations of our family members.

If a crime involving whites was not obvious and the police did not know who was involved, on their own, colored people would keep the information to themselves as evidenced by another story of Southern justice at play.

It was early evening, about dusk, when a white man drove slowly down Twenty-Seventh Avenue in the colored section of town. He drove past the colored café. Patrons were beginning to arrive for the Saturday-night festivities of dancing, drinking, gambling, fighting, and having sex. One colored patron stood against a building that was situated beside a dark alleyway where many of the sexual encounters took place. The white man stopped, rolled down his passenger side window, and called to the man standing beside the alley.

"Hey, boy. Do you know where I can find me a colored gal?" the horny white man asked.

Before the white man could pull his head back into his car, a soda bottle came out of the alleyway as if shot from a cannon and hit the white man square in the face. That was before plastic was invented when soda bottles were made of thick green glass. The bottle exploded and shattered into splinters, tearing the man's face to shreds.

A one-second glance by the bystander revealed a white man's face intact; the next-second glance revealed a bloody mass of broken bones and torn flesh.

After the white man's face was turned into a bloody mess, the few patrons who had assembled around the café ran home. Everyone who had planned to frequent the nightspot that night stayed home. The colored people took off their fancy dress clothes that they had planned to wear to the club and dressed in their old work clothes to ensure that they would not be accused of going out on the town.

The injured man managed to get to the police and tell enough of his story to implicate some unknown person in the colored community.

The police came to the neighborhood. They rode down the street; they knocked on doors and asked if anyone had seen someone throw a bottle that hit a white man. "No, sir. We ain't seed nothing. We been at home all day. We don't know nothing." That was the answer every colored person gave.

The police went away without ever finding out who was behind the green soda bottle that came out of the darkness. They knew that the colored people knew something because everyone who was questioned answered with the same talking points, "No, sir. We ain't seed nothing. We been at home all day. We don't know nothing."

The police never found out who had injured the white man who was seeking sex in the colored neighborhood.

A third case of Southern justice occurred when our cousin Susie Lee died. It was said that Susie Lee fell and hit her head, causing her death. The colored people understood more than they were willing to express. As quietly as it was kept, she was murdered. The death of our cousin did not come to the attention of the police.

Burying the Dead and Killing the Living

On the day of our cousin Susie Lee's funeral, Annie Lee Mama told Gloria and me to get on the school bus, go home, go to the spring and get the water, get the wood in, and wait inside the house. Gloria and I were told not to light the lamp for fear that we would set the house on fire. We were assured that our parents would be home before dark.

Lois, Mable, and Gladys were told to go to the funeral so they could sing in the school choir since the choir was on the program. The oldest girls dressed in their Sunday clothes, styled their hair, and wore their best shoes. Gloria and I, on the other hand, were not dressed for church but rather wore our old school clothes and shoes. Our hair was not freshly combed. We did not wear bows in our hair. We were prepared to go to school and return home, perform our chores, and wait until our family came home.

The school bell rang and the older children started walking to the church, which was two miles farther down the road. When the school bus came, I went to get on board. As I climbed onto the bus, Gloria asked me, "Where are you going?"

I replied, "I'm going home and get the water and the wood in like Annie Lee Mama told you and me to do."

Gloria informed me that she had no intention of going home. She said, "I'm going to the funeral. This is our cousin, and she would want us to come."

It did not matter that Gloria had never seen cousin Susie Lee nor she Gloria.

Gloria, on the other hand, did not need to go to anyone's funeral. During the last funeral we attended, Gloria sat in the back of the church with the other girls, one of whom had some chewing gum in her mouth. Gloria asked if she could chew the gum for a while. All during the funeral services, Gloria and several girls passed the chewing gum around, each chewing it for a while until the next chewer insisted on taking her turn at chewing the same gum.

I tried to convince Gloria that we would be in dire trouble if we did not go home. Daddy would kill us. She was adamant that our cousin wanted her to come to the funeral. I informed Gloria that Susie Lee was dead and would not know if we came or if we did not come. Gloria would not be persuaded to go home.

I was traumatized by the prospect of going home alone. I reluctantly followed Gloria to the church. When we caught up with the older girls, they tried to make us go home. Mable gave her dire prediction, "Daddy is going to kill you both." By that time, the bus had gone and we could not walk the six miles to the house in time to do our chores before dark.

We all took the shortcut through the cemetery to the church. Gloria and I arrived on the church grounds in the exact spot where Daddy had hitched the mules and the wagon. "What are you two doing here?" Daddy and Annie Lee Mama asked simultaneously. The bravado that Gloria had exhibited at school faded away. Neither she nor I were able to say why we had come.

Our parents were extremely angry with us for not doing as we were told and because Daddy was the only person who could get the wood and water in the dark. They talked to us between clenched teeth. I knew that we were going to get a whipping to remember.

Daddy made us get in the wagon and told us to stay there until the funeral was over. Afterward, we would be dealt with.

As we climbed into the wagon, we realized that we were sitting directly in the sun, without shade, on a very hot day. As we sat there sweltering from the heat, our school friends came around the wagon and asked, "Why are you sitting in that wagon? Ain't you going into the funeral? Did your parents tell you to sit there in the sun?"

As they asked their questions, Gloria rose to the occasion. She said, "Daddy don't want us to see no dead people." I knew that was not true. Daddy wanted us to go home and do our chores. He had no compunction about us seeing dead people.

I shrank lower and lower into the wagon. Sweat was running down both our faces and our clothes were sticking to our bodies. Occasionally, the mules at the head of the wagon relieved themselves. Flies lit on the mules' leavings and then lit on us. The mules were hitched in the shade of the pine grove reserved for this purpose. We were sitting in the hot, boiling sun.

When the funeral was over, we rode home in the wagon. As we rounded the hill in front of the house, we came upon the switch tree at the edge of the yard. Annie Lee Mama wrung two switches off the tree and whipped us soundly. She whipped us before Daddy came from the barn as she knew that Daddy would try to kill us.

To this day, black people talk about what happened to Susie Lee, but no one has ever offered to seek justice for her death.

Hunger Knows No Race

There was one white family of sharecroppers on Mr. Cliff Burrough's farm where we sharecropped. The husband and wife were Bufford and Viola, who lived in the old home house where Cliff's parents had lived. Daddy and Bufford were friends, and the two developed an "old boy" comradeship that lasted for years.

Bufford was a handsome white man. He was five feet, eleven inches tall, had dark tanned skin, blue eyes, and dark brown curly hair. His wife, Viola, looked like a witch. She was very thin with a pointed nose that had a lump on the side. Her hair was dark and stringy. She spoke in a creaky voice. Nevertheless, she was friendly and kind.

Mrs. Viola's family lived in the same house as sharecroppers before she and Bufford took possession. Viola's family had many children, big boys and girls, that worked the fields and made good crops for Mr. Cliff. When the large family moved away, Bufford and Viola tried to continue the farming but failed because Bufford would leave home for weeks and not return until he got ready.

Viola looked to her family to help her through these hard times until they ceased to support her. She approached Daddy one day and said, "I.S, me and my children are starving to death. We ain't got no food in the house, and Bufford has been gone for two weeks. What are we going to do?"

Times were hard for both poor Negro and poor Caucasian people. When food and money were scarce for white folk, usually they knew other whites who would help them. Negroes had to scrounge for themselves. We ate what we grew.

Daddy would go to the store and buy flour and sugar, which were hard to come by during the Second World War when we needed ration coupons to buy both. Mostly, we ate cornmeal and sweetened our food with molasses.

Daddy killed hogs in the winter and salted the meat down in a wooden box. We hoed out our garden on Saturday and in the evenings after working from sunup to sundown in the fields. Annie Lee Mama canned fruits and vegetables during the summer in preparation for the winter months. Potatoes and onions were a staple that we ate nearly every meal. Negroes were acquainted with *making do* and *going without*. It was rare for a Negro person to find out that white people were worse off than they.

Daddy told Mrs. Viola to go over to our house, and Annie Lee Mama would share what we had with her and her children. When Mrs. Viola arrived at our little house in the woods, she was welcomed by Annie Lee Mama who gave her some salt pork, dried peas and beans, white potatoes and sweet potatoes, onions, cornmeal, lard, and cabbages from the garden. Molasses and a jar of canned peaches were added to the pile.

Mrs. Viola cried and hugged Annie Lee Mama. She thanked her for saving the lives of her children and herself. Later on, Mrs. Viola found an opportunity to return the favor by providing school lunches for Gloria.

Before Bufford died, Daddy saw him in town. He had just come from the hospital where he was treated for jaundice. Daddy did not recognize Bufford at first. But when Bufford hailed Daddy in a familiar voice, Daddy said, "Is that you, Mr. Bufford?"

Bufford said, "Yes, it's me."

Daddy asked Bufford what had happened to him to which Bufford replied, "Well, LS, I finally turned into a colored man." Daddy noted that Bufford was blacker than him, and that gave them both a good laugh.

Gloria Makes a Plan

Annie Lee Mama had given Mrs. Viola, our white neighbor, food when she and her children were starving. She seemed eager to return the favor when her situation improved.

Lois, Mable, Gladys, Gloria, and I were waiting for the colored school bus on the side of the big road in front of Mrs. Viola's house. The white children's bus came first. The door opened with a whoosh and Mrs. Viola's daughter, Elizabeth, got on. We waited for the colored school bus that did not make a whooshing sound when the door opened. Instead, it opened with a scrape and a clang that took several tries before the door would close.

White children had been riding school buses since 1935, the year I was born. Now I was eight years old and we still walked six miles to school and six miles back each day. That was, on the days that we were not working in the fields. Sometimes, Daddy would meet us in the wagon when the weather was stormy and cold. It was as if Negro people did not have feelings. We did not feel pain, heat, cold, tiredness, or disdain. All of which was untrue. When we were cut, we bled.

We were happy to have the old yellow bus that had been found in the junkyard gassed up and given to the colored children after Daddy told Mr. Cliff that he would not be able to move to his farm as a sharecropper unless he got the Tuscaloosa County school superintendent to give the colored people a bus for their children. Even though Mr. Cliff drove the bus for the white children, he had not thought of requesting a bus for the colored children until Daddy demanded that he do so.

Since Daddy had secured the bus, he thought he could become the driver to make some extra money. Mr. Cliff would not relieve Daddy from his sharecropping duties to become the bus driver. The job went to another Negro man in the community who owned his own farm. Later, our cousin who owned his farm became the bus driver.

As we waited for our bus, Gloria sat her lunch down by the oak tree. An old stray dog suddenly appeared out of the bushes, grabbed Gloria's lunch, and ran away. Gloria set to screaming and crying that the old dog had taken her lunch. "What was she to do?"

Mrs. Viola heard Gloria crying and came out of the house to inquire what was the matter. When she realized what Gloria was crying about, she invited Gloria to come across the road and get a lunch, which Mrs. Viola would prepare for her. Gloria stopped crying and waited in Mrs. Viola's kitchen until she made Gloria a sandwich of peanut butter and jelly on two slices of white bread. She placed it inside a new brown paper bag and told Gloria to be more careful next time.

Gloria highly prized the sandwich as none of the colored children had such fare. Our lunches consisted of a biscuit with apple jelly, homemade preserves, or syrup inside. Sometimes, we had salt pork or salted ham leftover from breakfast. On these days, we wedged a piece of meat inside a cold biscuit. We conserved paper bags, bringing the same one back home each day until it was greasy and torn.

At lunchtime, Gloria made an outward show of letting everyone on the school playground see her new paper bag. She deliberately opened the sack, withdrew the sandwich, and waved it high enough for everyone to see that she had sliced white bread. She opened the bread so that everyone could see that she had peanut butter and jelly inside.

The children crowded around and asked. How could Gloria have such a sandwich when her sisters did not have the same? Why would Daddy and Mama let her have white bread with peanut butter and jelly when Lois, Mabel, Gladys, and Christine had biscuits and fat meat? Also, where did she get that new brown paper bag?

Gloria answered, "Oh, they only had one bag and enough peanut butter and jelly for one sandwich, and they gave it to me."

The children did not believe Gloria, yet they were enamored with the notion that one of us had such a sandwich. Gloria was delighted that it was her.

Gloria was a schemer. The acquisition of a peanut butter and jelly sandwich started her to thinking, what would it take to get Mrs. Viola to make her another sandwich?

A week went by and Gloria had not come up with a plan until one day, the old stray dog reappeared. Gloria placed her lunch against the old oak tree in proximity to the dog. The dog sniffed around. He could smell the salt pork and the biscuit through the torn greasy bag. Mabel ran the dog away and told Gloria to pick up her lunch.

The threat that was always used when someone would not do what was expected was invoked, "I'm going to tell Daddy." Gloria picked up her lunch in time for the bus to come. The plan had not worked.

Day after day, Gloria placed her lunch by the old oak tree, hoping that the stray dog would reappear. Suddenly, the dog appeared and snatched Gloria's lunch. She set up a howling to beat the band.

Mrs. Viola came out of the house and inquired, "What's the matter now, Gloria?" to which Gloria exclaimed that the old stray dog had taken her lunch again. Mrs. Viola knew that Gloria had deliberately given the dog her lunch, but because Annie Lee Mama had been so kind to her when she was starving, she called Gloria over to get another sandwich. "Goody, goody gumdrops," as we often said when things were going well. Gloria sat in Mrs. Viola's kitchen and waited. Surely, she would again have peanut butter and jelly on white bread.

Mabel called out, "The bus is coming." Mrs. Viola hurriedly placed the sandwich that she had prepared inside a new bag, and Gloria rushed out to catch the bus. Gloria was so ecstatic for having successfully concluded her plan that she chose to wait until lunchtime to reenact the dramatization of exposing her sandwich.

Again, the children gathered around her, waiting to see the wonderful sandwich. Their mouths watered as Gloria took her time to expose the contents of the new brown paper bag. With slow, deliberate speed, Gloria opened the bag, withdrew the sandwich with a flourish, and opened the bread to expose the delicious peanut butter and jelly inside. As she opened the sandwich, tears popped into her eyes. The children said, "Eeuuw." Altogether, they asked, "What's that? That ain't no peanut butter and jelly."

Truly, it was not what Gloria had expected. Lodged between two large slices of homemade white bread was a nearly raw egg. The egg white was slightly congealed, but the yolk was entirely raw. Mrs. Viola had attempted to cook Gloria a fried egg to place between the two slices of bread but had been hurried by Mabel's warning that the bus was coming. She had scoped the egg out of the pan and placed it between the two pieces of bread even though it was still raw.

We could eat raw sweet potatoes, raw carrots, raw peanuts, and raw onions, but no one ever ate a raw egg. When the children recovered their senses enough to comment, they said, "Where you get that raw egg? Mrs. Annie Lee didn't make you no raw egg. Your daddy wouldn't let you eat no raw egg." The comments continued as Gloria sat staring into the Cyclops's eye of the egg yolk. "What had gone wrong?" she asked herself. "Where was the peanut butter and jelly?" She wanted to know.

Finally, Gloria regained her bravado and told the children that she liked raw eggs. She began to nibble around the edge of the bread, which was all that was not soaked through with the runny raw egg. Slowly, the children dispersed and Gloria was left with her sandwich.

She cried. She never fed the old stray dog again.

Hot Lunches for Colored Students

The following year, Daddy and other parents had a meeting to discuss how they could work together to provide lunch for the colored children while at school. It was decided that each family would give to the school's food bank those items that they had available. For example, Daddy gave cornmeal, white potatoes, sweet potatoes, and onions. Other families gave meat, eggs, milk, vegetables, and whatever they grew. Uncle Preston and cousin Justin Harper, who lived next to the school, gave fresh greens. Each gift was scheduled monthly, allowing other families that could provide the same items to have opportunities to do so. The school principal brought cheese, powdered milk, butter, apples, and canned tomatoes and beans from the county school board as part of the agricultural surplus that was distributed by the federal government

The parents looked for someone to cook for the children. Uncle Ben's son, Elijah, had recently gotten remarried, after his wife died, to a woman named Carrie. Elijah was one of Uncle Ben Stewart's sons who, like his father, was barely four feet, five inches tall. Unlike his father, he was not a good farmer. His new bride found Elijah a poor provider and unable to obtain food for his family. Cousin Carrie Stewart asked to become the school's cook. She would do so without salary. All she asked was to be allowed to take the leftovers home each day to feed her family.

The students at the colored school no longer carried a biscuit, salt pork, and syrup to school. We now had a full meal in the middle of the day that gave us the strength to perform to the best of our abilities in the learning environment.

Baptism in the Creek

There is a creek that flows through Romulus, Alabama. As it meanders through the woods behind Holly Spring Missionary Baptist Church, it forms a pond at a bend in the creek. The church leaders chose this pond as the baptismal font in which *sinners* would be submerged under the water and raised again with their sins washed away. There, my ancestors and I were baptized, "In the name of the Father, the Son, and the Holy Ghost."

I was ten years old when I joined the church and was baptized in the same creek. I had long ago decided that life would be less problematic if I just did what was right and stayed out of trouble. I began reading the Bible two and three times each day. When I was eight years old, my sister Mable and I read Revelations, the last chapter of the Bible. We were terrified by the prophesies and descriptions of things to come. I began to pray. At first, my prayer was limited to "Now I lay me down to sleep." Then I memorized and prayed the Lord's Prayer.

Throughout the history of the Holly Spring Missionary Baptist Church, revival meetings were held in the fall of the year when the crops were in and farmers could afford to stay up late at night.

During revival, children who were twelve years old were expected to sit on the mourners' bench and listen to the visiting preacher tell them how to become Christians. The mourners were expected to have a religious experience through which they would be converted from sinners to Christians. After confessing their sins, they were accepted as candidates for baptism.

At the age of ten, I asked Daddy and Annie Lee Mama if I could become a mourner. They agreed that I was aware of what I was doing and consented to my conversion.

Daddy borrowed the mules and wagon from Cliff Burroughs, the white man with whom we shared crops. We rode to church each night of the revival instead of walking the six miles to church and another six miles back home for five nights.

The church was dimly lit as kerosene lamps lost their power of illumination five feet away. Even though numerous lamps were brought from the homes of the parishioners, there was never enough light to cover the sanctuary. Those of us who sat on the mourners' bench were privy to more illumination than those who sat in the pews.

I was ushered to a seat in front of the church, facing Reverend Brent, the visiting preacher. He began his presentation with a long, fervent prayer. He asked God to deliver us poor sinners from evil, save our souls from hell, remove the devil from within us, and wash away our sins.

Reverend Brent spoke of his own conversion, citing that it was emblematic of Saint Paul's conversion when he saw a blinding light on the Damascus Road. Reverend Brent was struck down by a blazing sunlight while he was plowing his field. When he came to himself afterward, he began praising God and promising that he would go spread the Gospel. I assumed that Reverend Brent expected the mourners to have a similar experience before we could be declared saved.

The preacher invoked the name of Jesus Christ who died for our sins. He told us how Jesus was betrayed, beaten, and hung on a cross for me, yet He never mumbled a word. I felt so sorry that Jesus had done all that for me. I wished that I could have been there to stop people from treating Jesus in such a manner.

When Reverend Brent said that God the Father had allowed the people to treat Jesus that way, I wondered about a father who would let his son suffer. Then I was told again that it was all done for me.

After Reverend Brent had preached a stirring hour-long sermon, the deacons and deaconesses came to us and prayed, holding our hands and urging us to confess and be delivered from our sins.

I recognized that some of the mourners needed all the help they could get. There were children and adults on the bench who stayed in trouble. There were those who sat on the bench year after year and never confessed their sins nor were they knocked down by a blinding light. Each year, they went home "unsaved," only to sit on the bench the following year.

I waited until everyone had finished with their tasks of bringing us to the Lord. After the first night of cleansing my soul, I went forward and sat in the seat where you were to sit when you got saved. I never saw a blinding light, but I was saved when I came to church that night. Daddy and Annie Lee Mama accepted that I was saved and prepared me for baptism in the creek behind the church. The following Sunday, after revival, the congregation met around the creek down in the woods to participate in the same ritual that my ancestors had experienced when they were baptized.

Early in the morning before the baptismal ceremony began, the deacons went to the creek, waded into the water, and beat the water with sticks to run the snakes out of the center of the creek.

Annie Lee Mama dressed me in a white robe with layers of underclothes to prevent a naked appearance when I got wet. The congregation stood on the banks of the creek and sang, "On Jordan's stormy banks I stand and cast a wistful eye. To Canaan's fair and happy land, where my possessions lie."

As each sinner waded into the water, the congregation sang, "Wade in de water. Wade in de water, children. Wade in de water. God's a gonna trouble de water."

The water was cold and deep. I was afraid of water as I could not swim. I was also afraid that a snake or two had defied the deacons' sticks and returned to the very spot where I would be baptized.

Two deacons held my arms and literally carried me to the center of the creek. I hadn't been in a creek since Mable dumped us all into the same creek farther up the stream. On that occasion, we were visiting Grandma who was washing clothes beside the creek near the spring where Grandpa and Grandma got their drinking water.

We were supposed to stay away from the deep end of the creek. It was at a point where the water ran fast and went under a footbridge. The bridge was made of a log that had been split into two halves and laid with the round sides down, forming a flat surface on which to walk across. We sat on the log halves while Grandma and sister Lois washed under several large oak trees.

Mable, who was a daredevil, stood on the bridge and began to rock the log bridge back and forth. We, enjoying the rocking motion, failed to discern the danger that lay ahead. Soon, the log halves were rocking with such a tilt that we all were thrown into the water. Mable and Gladys were carried under the water and down the stream. They soon found their footing and were dragged on land by Grandma.

Gloria and I were sitting toward the end of the log, and we landed in the fern and brambles that grew along the bank. We grabbed fern prongs and any bush we could hold on to along the edge and were rescued by Lois.

Grandma, as always, announced the obvious, "Da now, you done fell in that creek."

She stripped us naked and washed our clothes. I did not mind as I was only two years old, but the older girls were mortified.

Here I was being baptized, being carried fully clothed to the middle of the creek where the water ran fast and the creek was deep. The water came up to my armpits.

The pastor, Reverend Holly, stood waiting for me to reach him and to turn in the correct position to be leaned backward and fully submerged. I was afraid that I would be dropped into the water as the pastor only had one good arm. I was thankful to see Reverend Dave McKenny, the assistant pastor, standing on the other side with two good, long, strong arms.

Reverend Holly said, "I baptize you in the name of the Father, Son, and the Holy Ghost." With that said, he laid his good hand over my face, and together they dipped me under the water. I rose, sputtering and coughing. I quickly grabbed the hands of the two deacons who came to escort me to land. Annie Lee Mama covered me with a blanket and held me close to her as she took me to the area where the churchwomen held quilts surrounding the converts. There, Annie Lee Mama dressed me in my church clothes.

We were carried back to church where I sat on the front row with the newly born Christians. Much was made of us being saved that day.

By the following Sunday, it seemed that everyone had forgotten that we were saved. Expectations were not changed. We were treated much the same as we had always been treated. The only thing I noticed was that adults held me to account at a higher level than others around me. It was often said when I was in the company of children, even those older than me, and some difficulty arose, "Christine, I know you know better."

Daddy Becomes Ill

We continued to share crops with Cliff Burroughs, with Daddy taking pride in the amount of cotton he made with his family of five girls, often accomplishing as much as families with as many boys.

We were still living at Cliff Burroughs farm the year in which Daddy became too ill to work the farm. Mable had to do the plowing. We harvested ten bales of cotton that year, with Mable plowing and Annie Lee Mama, Lois, Gladys, Gloria, and me doing the hoeing and picking the cotton.

It was extremely difficult for Mable to do all the plowing. One day, Gloria, then eleven years old, asked to help. The mule, named Bill, was hitched to the plow. Mable showed Gloria how to hold on to the plow handles and steer the plow down the row. Old Bill would do the rest.

Bill was known by Daddy and other men on the farm as a cantankerous old mule who was difficult to control. He would not allow any of the men to ride him, and if he was not harnessed to Old Sam, the other mule who could control Bill, he might just take off for the shade at a moment's notice. Bill must have realized that Gloria was a helpless, skinny girl who was relying upon him to do the right thing. Bill pulled the plow in a straight row and made wide turns at the end so that Gloria would have no trouble making the turn into the next row. When Gloria lost control of the plow, Bill would stop and stand still until she regained control. Then, he would slowly move ahead.

Gloria's legs were very weak, and they hurt all the time. After days of helping Mable plow, Gloria's legs grew weaker. On this day, when it came time to go home, Gloria could not walk. Mable hoisted her upon Old Bill's back, not knowing that Bill had never been ridden. Bill stood still until Gloria was loaded on. She held on to Bill's mane as he walked slowly all the way from the field, along the creek bed, up the hill, and into the yard at the house.

Daddy came to the door to await Mable's arrival as he, although very ill, would try to help unharness the mules at the end of the day. When he saw Gloria on Old Bill's back, he froze with fright. He dared not say a word until Gloria was safely on the ground. Old Bill had carried Gloria into the yard, stopped gently, and lowered his head, allowing Gloria to slip safely to the ground. Then, he righted his head and stood quietly, awaiting the removal of his harness.

After that year, Daddy made Mable plow alongside him until she was sixteen years old. Then, Mable told Daddy that she would not plow anymore since she had become a courting young woman whose boyfriends were reluctant to court a girl who plowed. From then on, he needed to stop sharecropping and move to the town where everyone, old enough, could get work for which they would be paid.

At the same time, mandatory education had been declared and child labor laws were being enforced. Colored children could no longer be kept out of school to work in the fields.

Trying to Get Out of Debt

Daddy had tried to leave the sharecropping farm many times. Each year, he found himself still in debt to Mr. Cliff Burroughs. Even when he raised record crops, he could not get out of debt. The landowner and the store owner rigged the debt and the income so that the debt was always greater.

Now that Daddy had to leave the farm for want of laborers to bring in the crops, he contrived to overcome the debt he owed. He asked for his farm subsidy check to account for part of his debt.

Farm subsidies were available to farmers as payments from the federal government to people who produced agricultural products that helped to strengthen the national economy. Daddy approached Mr. Cliff to discuss getting his check. Daddy asserted that the farmer was due his share of the subsidy according to the land he farmed and according to the information that had been given to Daddy and other colored farmers by the 4-H Club teacher who came to our parent-teacher meeting at the school.

Mr. Cliff and his son got into an argument with Daddy and Annie Lee Mama over this issue. They declared that the subsidy checks belonged to the landowner.

The argument occurred in the cotton crib at the end of the field near our house. Again, Daddy was tempted to use his fists to assert his belief that he was right in the situation. We children heard the loud voices of the two adversaries and Daddy. Annie Lee Mama did not say much, yet she was ready with her hoe which she used to kill snakes, chase dogs, and work in the fields. She was Daddy's backup.

When we went to the door of the cotton crib and looked in, we saw the fracas in progress. Daddy saw us and realized the trouble he and Annie Lee Mama would be in if they had a fight with Mr. Cliff and his son. Daddy relented and agreed to leave the farm.

Daddy tried to find a way to pay off the debt so that we could move away. He sold nearly everything we had except our clothes, beds, and a few kitchen utensils.

Daddy sold his horse and the living room furniture. He sold the few farm implements that he owned. He also sold our best cow, but we kept Old Cromp, a cow with one horn. Even after Daddy sold everything we could relinquish, we still were not able to go free without debt. The following year, we returned many times to hoe and pick cotton on Mr. Cliff's farm to complete paying off our debt.

We were the last family to leave the Burroughs' farm, which did not continue as one consisting of sharecroppers. When Daddy had paid off his debt and we no longer worked for free, the cost of laborers outweighed the income derived from the cotton. The owners tried to farm themselves, which lasted less than two years. Finding that the venture was not cost-effective, Mr. Cliff's son planted pine trees on all the farmland. The trees could not be harvested for thirty years.

Mrs. Baby Ruth

Ten years after our birth mother left us, she remarried and had a second family of children, five in all. Eula Mama loved her second family with unconditional love. She strove to show her love by ensuring that the children had everything they wanted and always saw her as the best mother. She served her children and attended to their every want. She seemed grateful to have a second chance at being a mother.

My nephew told me a story that described Eula Mama's behavior with her second family.

Some mornings, Eula Mama would dress the girls in pretty dresses and put ribbons in their hair. She would parade the children through the neighborhood to hear people tell her how beautiful they were.

Neighbors who were working in their front yards or sweeping their front porches would stop and stare at the beautiful parade. The neighbors would wave and say, "Good morning, Mrs. Eula. Your children are so pretty." Eula Mama would raise her head a little higher and strut down the street, showing her pride in having such beautiful children.

Another ritual Eula Mama had with the children was to give them money to go to a neighbor's house to buy candy. The children always bought a Baby Ruth candy bar, which caused them to call the candy salesperson Mrs. Baby Ruth.

Usually, Eula Mama gave the children a quarter when she sent her four older children to buy candy, which cost five cents each. The four children always bought a Baby Ruth candy bar each, and Mrs. Baby Ruth always gave them a nickel in change.

On the day my nephew and niece were visiting their grandmother, she sent them along to buy candy with three of her children, making five children in all.

The children gave Mrs. Baby Ruth the quarter, received their candy bars, and waited for their nickel change. When they did not receive the nickel, the children went home and told Eula Mama that Mrs. Baby Ruth had stolen their nickel.

Eula Mama thought her children were better than everyone in the world and that no one should do anything that was not pleasant to them. To have Mrs. Baby Ruth take her children's nickel was tantamount to her saying that the children were no better than anyone else. That was an affront to Eula Mama's sensibility regarding her precious children.

Eula Mama grabbed the baby in one arm and herded the children out the door with the determination that she would go and get the children's nickel from Mrs. Baby Ruth, which would show Mrs. Baby Ruth that she could not treat her children with such disrespect.

"I'll get your nickel. Ain't nobody going to take nothing from my children and get away with it," Eula Mama said as she marched down the street to Mrs. Baby Ruth's house. Instead of knocking on the door, Eula Mama stood in the yard and yelled, "Hey, Baby Ruth, you come out here! Who do you think you are, taking money from my children? You give them back their nickel."

Mrs. Baby Ruth tried to explain that she did not owe the children a nickel. They had given her a quarter, and she had given them five candy bars. Eula Mama extolled her children's virtue, "If my children say you owe them a nickel, you owe them a nickel. They don't tell lies. I'm here to make sure you give them their nickel."

By this time, Mrs. Baby Ruth had given up trying to explain her side of the story. She said in a soft voice, "You wait right here, Mrs. Eula. I'll go get your nickel." Mrs. Baby Ruth turned and entered her house.

Eula Mama shifted the baby up in one arm, put her other hand on her hip, and stood as tall as she could, awaiting Mrs. Baby Ruth humbly bringing her the nickel. The children gathered around Eula Mama's legs, enjoying the power which their mama was demonstrating, making Mrs. Baby Ruth do their bidding.

Suddenly, Mrs. Baby Ruth reappeared. Standing high upon her porch, she held a double-barreled breechloader shotgun in the crook of her arm. She inserted two large shotgun shells into the gun, snapped it into firing position, and leveled the barrel at Eula Mama and the children. Mrs. Baby Ruth said in a grave voice, "I got your nickel. Here it is." She looked down at the site of the gun and offered its contents as the nickel.

When my nephew told me the story, sixty years had passed. Yet, he said that the two barrels of the gun still appeared to be the two biggest black holes he had ever seen in his life.

Eula Mama turned and tried to escape. Her path was blocked by the children who, upon looking up the barrel of the shotgun leveled in their directions, ran to Eula Mama for protection. Once they grabbed her around the legs, she could not escape.

When the group realized that they had to disentangle themselves to get away, they moved apart and tried to run. The fleeing group ran over Mama, who ran over the children, who ran over one another. When they were able to untangle themselves, they ran for their lives.

The mother and children, who often paraded down the street displaying beauty and grace, now fled up the same street in total disarray. Neighbors, working in their front yards or sweeping their front porches looking on, had no time to comment on the children's beauty. The unceremonious retreat left the neighbors' mouths gaping and their greetings unuttered. The neighbors watched as skirts flew tumultuously in the wind. Silken plaits bounced to and fro as hair ribbons unwound from the children's lovely heads. Erstwhile, graceful strides were replaced by loping gaits that gave way to spurts of running and scrambling to gain traction upon the path that led home.

Eula Mama led the way—up the street and on to her porch. The fast retreat left everyone, especially Mama, out of breath. As she fell onto her porch, she exclaimed, "Y'all ain't never going to buy another bar of candy from Baby Ruth. *And* don't nair one of you never tell me nothing about no *nickel*."

We Move to Town

After returning to work for Cliff and finishing our school year in Romulus, we were free to live in the house with Grandma and Grandpa in the suburbs of the city of Tuscaloosa, Alabama.

Daddy, along with Grandpa, tried to farm on the twenty-eight acres of land that came with the rented house. For the first year, we were often kept out of school and required to chop and pick cotton. When it became obvious that Daddy could not work away from home and succeed at farming, we were allowed to go to school every day.

Daddy applied for jobs at BFGoodrich and the paper mill. He had been injured in his youth, and one of his legs was slightly shorter than the other. This impediment prevented him from being employed in these two factories. He found work at the box factory and later at Druid City Hospital. He retired from DCH with a pension.

Annie Lee Mama continued to work for white families as a housekeeper. She worked for the Lee family who paid her $1.75 a day.

Unequal Education for Negro Children

Students in Tuscaloosa, Alabama, attended segregated schools. Negro students were provided inferior resources in all areas, including books, instructional materials, furniture, and facilities. For many years, Negro teachers were paid lower salaries than Caucasian teachers.

Even as a child, I realized that the educational resources for Negro students were limited on purpose. We received books that had been used, torn, and filled with graffiti. Books and desks were sent to our school after they had been discarded by the white schools. Desks had *nigger* carved in the wood by white students, and *nigger* was written on page after page of our books as if the white children knew that we would eventually become the recipient of these materials.

No one thought to eliminate the books and desks that were so inscribed and to send us only the clean ones. It was as if no one cared or no one thought that we cared. We did care, and we felt offended and lower-rated by these inscriptions in the books and on the desks that were sent to us by the white school superintendents.

We did not receive books in series either. Information that was taught in one book and should have been continued in the next did not reach us. I read the first half of the story of Peter Pan in one of the third-grade readers. I was devastated, being unable to find out what happened in the second half of the story. It was not until I was in high school that I was able to find the story of Peter Pan in the school library and read the final chapters.

I required a great amount of information to quell my appetite for learning. I was born with a superior ability to learn and an avid thirst for knowledge. At nine months old, I began to understand what was said and even recognized nuances in conversations. I had a photographic memory for anything I saw, especially everything I read. I could remember the page number on which a particular statement was written. I could remember numbers in a series. I memorized long epic poems word for word and could recite them without error.

Our teachers taught us everything they knew, which, unfortunately, was not everything that Negro students needed to know to compete with the white students. Our teachers had, themselves, been educated in inferior schools and were limited by what they had learned.

White students had the best learning environment that money could buy. Their schools were much larger and more accommodating. White teachers were highly trained and well paid to provide the best preparation for students to enter the workforce or college. White students had bus transportation starting in 1935. We walked to and from school until 1943.

With limited resources, we were required to find our own motivation to learn and to succeed. Our parents and relatives were the role models we emulated to become strong, hardworking adults.

My sisters and I idolized our daddy as standing between us and the world. He even stood between us and God. When storms ravaged our tin-roofed house, Daddy would get on his knees beside our bed and pray loud and long until the storm passed.

We identified with our ancestors and living relatives in our efforts to behave as upstanding citizens in Romulus. Still, we needed other role models to achieve success in the greater world community.

We tried to emulate such famous Negro people as Tuskegee Institute College founder, Booker T. Washington, and scientist George Washington Carver; Mary McCloud Bethune, the founder of Bethune Cookman Negro College; Marion Anderson, Lena Horne, Billy Holiday, Sarah Vaughn, Paul Robeson, Billy Eckstein, and Nat King Cole, all famous Negro singers; Joe Louis, the heavyweight boxing champion of the world; James Weldon Johnson, Langston Hughes, and Paul Lawrence Dunbar, all famous Negro poets, and later, Jackie Robinson, the first black major-league baseball player.

We took what we learned at home and in school, added what we knew about these famous people, and tried to create ourselves in their image. We sang like our idols, wrote and recited poetry, and excelled in sports. We believed that we could "pull ourselves up by our own bootstraps."[25] We believed that we could become successful people by our own efforts. We were told by our teachers that we had to be ten times smarter than white students just to stay even. We worked hard to be ten times better with ten times fewer resources. This oxymoron was drilled into us year after year, so that we strove to be better than we knew how to be.

[25.] en.wikiquote.org/wiki/Booker_T_Washington

Industrial High School

By 1948, when I entered Industrial High School in Tuscaloosa, Alabama, less than ninety years had passed since whites and Negroes lived on the same plantations, intermingling their daily lives as one communal entity, notwithstanding that the whites were free and leisurely and the blacks were slaves who did all the work; the two groups lived inseparable lives.

Historical accounts and personal knowledge of my people declare that during slavery, few Negroes were educated. Those who received schooling are accounted for in the annals of history as having stolen their education, obtained education in secret, or those who were beneficiaries of well-meaning white persons who promoted the teaching of reading. Any promotion of reading for slaves was associated with the slaves' need to read the Bible. Fear of the dissemination of abolitionist material led to the creation of laws prohibiting slave education in the Southern states, especially in the prevention of writing. The Nat Turner Revolt in Southampton County, Virginia in 1831 bolstered the slave owners' need to keep the slaves ignorant and isolated.

One area in which slave education was promoted was in the field of skilled labor. Slave owners gained prestige from owning slaves who were carpenters, joiners, barbers, hairdressers, and bankers. For another one hundred years, the approval of Negro education in industrial skills continued to be emphasized in Negro schools.

Until integration became the system of education in the state of Alabama, separation of the races was enforced in all schools. White and Negro children attended different schools and rode separate buses, that is, after Negro children were provided buses.

As a continuation of the slavery-time idea of training slaves in industrial activities, the names of the schools implied that Negro schools emphasized the industrial arts and the white schools emphasized the liberal arts. Our school was Industrial High School while the white school was Tuscaloosa High School. The Negro high school in the county was Tuscaloosa County Training High School while the white school was Tuscaloosa County High School.

My sisters and I enrolled in the colored Industrial High School located in Tuscaloosa, Alabama. I was in the ninth grade, Gloria and Gladys were in the tenth, and Mable was in the eleventh grade. Lois was married.

During our first year at Industrial High School, we were kept out of school frequently to hoe and pick cotton grown on our newly rented farm. Even when I missed days in school, I could stay ahead of the class in all subjects that relied on reading and writing. Mathematics and chemistry required that one attend school every day. When we were able to go to school every day, my classes became extremely easy.

I would have profited immensely from a program of liberal arts and not the industrial arts. I failed my industrial arts ninth-grade home economics class which required that I make a dress of the same pattern given to two other students. Both girls were extremely overweight, and I was slim without girlish curves. I did not finish my garment by the end of the semester and received a failing grade.

Although Industrial High School was not adequate to serve my needs for continued education, it was more advanced than the Negro school in Romulus where books were few and teaching was limited to the rudimentary forms of education. Industrial High School had a library filled with books from wall to wall. I read every book in the Industrial High School library. I checked them out and took three and four books home each week, returning them on Friday in exchange for another armload of books that would be devoured by sunlight, at dusk, and by lamplight. I was such a voracious reader that I read *Gone with the Wind* in one week and *War and Peace* in another. *A Tale of Two Cities* took one weekend. I learned to read two and three books at one time. (I still continue this practice.)

I read subjects as wide as the library afforded. The area of mythology was new to me. It challenged my sensibilities as it included stories about gods and their exploits that were similar to the religious acts in the Bible and predated the religious stories upon which my religious faith was based. I devoured every book that spoke of gods and goddesses. I read *Ulysses* by James Joyce and the *Iliad* and the *Odyssey* by Homer.

History was fascinating. My history and social studies classes only scratched the surface of historical events to date. I wanted to know everything that had happened throughout the world. I fell in love with stories about India, China, and Africa. Egyptian lore was especially fascinating as I considered the pharaohs my ancestors.

I read works by American and English writers. I greatly admired Edna St. Vincent Millay,[26] the American poetess and activist. Shakespeare's plays and sonnets were strange and exciting to read, and I memorized many lines from the bard's works.

I learned many of the poems written by Negro writers, such as Paul Lawrence Dunbar, Langston Hughes, and Phyllis Wheatley, and would recite them at school assemblies. My recitations resulted in being chosen as the school's orator, winning the county oratorical contest, and participating in the state contest in Tuskegee, Alabama.

I was most interested in the library book located on the shelf by the front door and saved it for last because it had French words that needed to be pronounced and understood. The book was *Les Miserables*. I read it twice. Books had become my life. Books were my reason to hurry and complete my chores, finish my homework, or do any other task so that I could have time to read.

By the end of my eleventh-grade year, I had read every book in the library. Not knowing where to find additional books, I asked Ms. Pool, the librarian, if the principal, Mr. Hughes, could request books from the city library. Ms. Pool promised, with a tearful smile, that she would ask Mr. Hughes to do so.

Little did I know that the city library was for whites only. Negro children, such as I, would not be allowed to lay hands on the books

---

[26.] http://www.poemhunter.com/edna-st-vincent-millay/

that were to be read by whites. I never heard if the request was made as I never received additional books. I could not understand how anyone could call Negro people ignorant when, with very little of the resources that others had, we achieved so much. Look at what we could have achieved had we been given an equal chance.

When I was in the eleventh grade, the Industrial High School student body was administered an intelligence quotient (IQ) test. A male student and I tested in the genius category, far above all the other students in the school. Meanwhile, my teachers told me that they could not teach me anything more as I knew as much or more than they did. To fulfill my time in school, I became the substitute teacher for teachers who were out ill.

With the loss of teachers to guide me and the loss of books to read, it seemed that the air had gone out of the world and that life had ceased to have meaning. The intensity of my quest for learning was stymied by finding that there was no one to mentor me and guide me through learning and exploring the world.

This was a mournful time in my life as my quest for knowledge was equivalent to that of slaves who were denied rights to an education. My soul cried out for learning as if it knew the liberation that comes with knowledge; as if it knew the power of reading, writing, and arithmetic; as if it felt the uplifting of song and art; as if it could be emboldened by understanding science, history, and politics; as if it could be set free by the enlightenment that comes with knowing all that books can teach.

Albert Lewis Jr.

At the age of sixteen, I did not have time for boys or social activities. I did not go to football games, which prevented me from knowing the handsome football captain who had won the hearts of all the girls in the school. I was a bookworm.

During my physical education class period, the football captain whose name was Albert Lewis Jr. came to the girls' PE class to obtain basketballs for the boys' PE class. As he entered the room, he saw the girl students lined up, heading out the opposite door. Many girls turned toward him and giggled. I turned to see the attraction. Seeing none, I turned back and exited the door. In that instant, Albert said he saw me from behind and fell in love. When I turned to look back, he was instantly convinced that I was the girl for him. Standing in the doorway, he said to himself, "That girl will be my wife someday." (We were married for 62 years at the time of Albert's death.)

Without books to read, I had time to fall in love. I finally saw the athlete that several male students had told me about when Albert came to the biology class where I was substituting for Mr. Washington, the biology teacher, who was out ill that day.

Albert and I became inseparable. I was sixteen and he was seventeen. Albert was an outstanding athlete. His ability to play both basketball and football preceded him from grade school. He became a varsity team player when he entered high school in the ninth grade.

Albert's prowess as an athlete is described in a story that has been told for sixty years by members of our Industrial High School football team. Even now that only two or three team members are still alive, whenever they meet, one of them will say, "Remember that time when Albert Lewis ran three ninety-nine-yard touchdowns in one game?" The telling of the story will start amid great laughter.

It happened one night when the Industrial High School football team went to play a game in Mississippi. Industrial High was known as a winning team, and the team they were to play that night was known for losing its games. The Industrial High School team traveled to Mississippi with great anticipation that this would be an easy game that would add another win to their record.

The team members were well-dressed city boys who displayed class and sobriety wherever they went. They were outfitted with matching football togs and jerseys that displayed the dragon logo that was the symbol of the school. The Dragons were proud of themselves and their accomplishments. Most of all, they were proud of the outstanding athletes on the team, of which Albert Lewis was the fastest running back in the history of the school.

The Industrial High School Dragons left home early in the morning. They rode west in one of the best school buses to which the colored students had access. The bus had been washed and readied for the trip. Towels were washed white and stored on the front seat. Football jerseys and togs had been cleaned and readied for the occasion. Jars of water and bottles of soda lay in blocks of ice in the coolers. Baskets filled with fried chicken, potato salad, and sweet potato pie, prepared by the school cafeteria workers, made the trip seem more like a holiday picnic.

The student body waved and cheered as the players, coaches, ball boys, and Mickey (the Mascot) rolled out of the yard of Industrial High School.

The Dragons enjoyed the outing on a sunny school day morning. They were free from the cares of school and were going to enjoy playing their favorite sport—football. After a long ride, the bus entered Eastern Mississippi. Before their eyes lay a bountiful green landscape with moss-draped trees and endless fields where cotton and corn had been grown during the spring and summer months.

The bus passed large antebellum homes with rolling green lawns where the gentry lived. Colored children and their mothers emerged from small shanty shacks, turned gray with age. They stared at the bus as it went by and surely said or thought, "Uh-oh, them colored boys from Alabama gonna git it!"

The word was out that the Mississippi school staff and the referees had formed a school football team out of the strongest and most aggressive colored men in the area. They were grown men with families who were free to play the football game as their crops were in for the year. These men were farmers who also cut timber in the winter months. They were strong with bodies hardened by years of toil behind a mule, chopping and picking cotton, and cutting down large trees with saws and axes.

The plan was to have each man grab a visiting team member and pummel him so severely that the player would be put out of commission for the remainder of the game. The plan was to physically destroy the team by stealth, not to win by skill.

The year was 1951 before player eligibility required school enrollment, grades, and sufficient grade point averages. If the school said that these were their students, their school enrollment and their right to play the game could not be disputed.

The busload of Alabamians rolled on. The team was oblivious to what really lay ahead.

The bus occupants espied Mississippi State College and thought they had arrived. They saw a stadium with bleachers and neatly groomed grounds. The buildings were large and stately. Sadly, this was not their destination, and they rolled on.

Finally, they rounded a bend in the dirt road where an old building resembling a school stood. The grounds were untended and overgrown, except where a path led to some homemade bleachers standing in a field. Two privies stood beyond the field, one for men and one for women and children. There were no White or Colored Only signs as only Negroes attended this school.

Ninety years after the slaves were freed, Negroes in the Southern states, especially in Mississippi, still carried the personal behavior traits that had meant survival during slavery. These behaviors are still called the slave mentality. Negroes continued to fear white people. They feared their strength in numbers, their white sheets, their ownership of jobs, and the whites' ability to determine their fate.

Negroes behaved subserviently toward whites but were quick to use deadly force against their own race. It was as if aggression toward their own race was tolerated and condoned, giving birth to a black-on-black crime that resulted in killings that were never punished. Into the valley of death rode the Tuscaloosa Industrial High School Dragon football team. They alighted from the bus, well-fed, refreshed, and prepared to vanquish any foe. They donned their uniforms and admired their appearance as ready and able winners.

The Industrial team ran onto the field in jocular style, ready to play. The home team came on the field slowly and stood to face the visitors.

Standing face-to-face were two generations of people. The Industrial High players were young boys, ages fifteen through eighteen. The home team consisted of grown men, ages twenty through thirty. They had beards and mustaches. They were grown men who might never have played football in school but were going to play these young teenage boys.

The heckling began, "Uh-oh, them colored boys from Alabama gonnna git it!" The Dragons also heard home team comments about how they were going to break their legs and arms, grind their heads into the dirt, cave in their ribs, and try to kill them altogether.

The Industrial High School boys, who had never received such a deadly welcome, stood shaking in their shoes.

The visiting team, Industrial High, won the coin toss and chose to receive the ball from the kickoff.

The Mississippi home team had a kicker who could lay the ball between the ninetieth and one-hundredth yard lines every time he kicked. His first kick ended at the ninety-ninth yard line. Albert Lewis caught the ball and began his run toward the other end of the field.

Every member of the home team ran to tackle Albert. As Albert's team members attempted to tackle the home team players, they were easily dispatched by the bigger, stronger, and older men. Albert was left at the mercy of eleven grown men chasing him down the field.

Albert looked back long enough to see a V-shaped armored attack aimed at his back. The front-runner yelled obscenities at Albert as he outran the fuselage of giants thundering after him.

Albert reported that he not only ran for the goal line, but he also ran for his life. The only thing that saved Albert was that he was one of the fastest runners anyone had seen. Albert had a running style that made him appear to be airborne. He ran on his toes, which needed to touch the ground only slightly to propel him forward. His touch on the ground was so instantaneous that it was undetectable. He just flew.

He easily outran the entire team. He ended his run, in style, as he knelt on one knee and held the ball on the ground to signify that he had made a touchdown. The angry men stopped short of the end zone and the kneeling figure.

The referees watched Albert as he flew down the field, untouched, and could not believe their eyes.

The referees were party to the scheme of selecting the Mississippi players to defeat the Alabama team and were surprised that a touchdown had been made on the first play. They thought that the game would be played on the field where the stronger older players would prevail. They never thought of a player who could run so fast that a touchdown could occur without field play. They surmised that some magic had occurred, although they could not figure out what it was, and they had been unable to throw a flag on any play that was wrong. Nevertheless, the referees called the play back and negated the touchdown.

The home team positioned the ball, and the kicker successfully kicked the ball to the ninety-ninth yard line for the second time. Again, Albert was designated by his team members to be the one to catch the ball. Off he went again, heading for the opposite end of the field. Off went the elderly Mississippi home team, en masse, chasing Albert.

This time, Albert knew that he would be injured badly or even killed if he was caught. He ran even faster and reached the end zone in record time.

The older home team players, still tired from their last run, came puffing up to the goal line. Again, Albert fell on one knee to signify that he had made a touchdown. The home team players were inhibited by the rules of the game from tackling Albert in the end zone. However, they made it clear that if they were ever able to tackle him outside the end zone, they planned to kill him.

The referees had not thrown a flag nor could they find anything that was done wrong by any of the visiting players. Nevertheless, they called the play back again and negated the second touchdown.

The ball was called back and the kicker again kicked the ball to the ninety-ninth yard line where Albert was waiting. Again, he caught the ball and headed for the opposite end of the field. This time, Albert said he knew that if he was caught, he would be killed.

This was Albert's third trip down the field in the first half of the first quarter. He was not tired, for he was a runner who could run all day. However, the elderly home team had tired and had grown extremely angry. They pummeled the other players with whom they came in contact and promised them a killing after they had caught and dispatched Albert.

As they say, "Albert's mother didn't raise no fool." This time, Albert not only ran for the goal line but he also ran for the *bus*. Seeing Albert heading for the bus and safety prompted the other players to head in the same direction. The visiting coaches and ball boys had already had their share of threats from the Mississippi fans and the home team bench and knew that their safety lay in catching up with the players.

The Industrial High School mascot, Mickey, was a crippled boy who was unable to play sports but who traveled with the team and helped dispense water and towels. As the group fled, someone grabbed Mickey and carried him bodily onto the bus. The head coach braved the oncoming Mississippians and counted his people to ensure that everyone was aboard. When Mickey rode in on the back of the last person, the coach yelled, "Let's get out of here!"

The bus driver did not need to be told. He already had the bus revved up and in forward gear. He was ready to roll. The bus driver pressed the gas pedal to the floor and headed out of the schoolyard just in front of a phalanx of fans, followed by the players and their wives and children.

As the bus turned onto the road, rocks spewed from under the rear tires of the bus, showering the thundering hoard with gravel that had been placed to keep the road from eroding. The gravel flew like pellets from a twenty-gauge shotgun, pausing the pursuers in their tracks.

The angry mob would not be denied their pound of flesh. Men, women, and children followed the bus onto the road, picked up every gravel rock they could find, and threw it after the bus. There was a displacement of road covering from the front of the school that was piled up at the bend of the road. The visiting team's bus turned the corner on two left wheels, righted itself, and disappeared into the darkness. No one on the bus spoke until they saw the Alabama State Line.

That was the night that Albert Lewis ran three ninety-nine-yard touchdowns in the first quarter of the game. Industrial High School lost the game in forfeit for leaving the field during the game. To this day, the team credits Albert for not only running the three touchdowns but also for saving the lives of his teammates.

On the night of our first date, Albert met Daddy on the road going home. Albert asked the man in the dark, "Mister, do you know where Joice Christine Bailey lives?" The man answered, "I guess I ought to. She's my daughter." Thus started a lifelong friendship between Daddy and his future son-in-law.

Albert asked Daddy for my hand in marriage when we were still in high school. Daddy asked Albert, "You gonna treat her right?"

When Albert said, "Yes, sir," Daddy consented and spoke of the event throughout his remaining life.

We were engaged for three years. During that time, we graduated from Industrial High School. Albert went to West Virginia State College on a full football scholarship.

In 1953, I had graduated from a segregated high school and had received a partial scholarship to Tuskegee Institute, a private Negro college founded by Booker T. Washington. The tuition at Tuskegee Institute was $500 each year. My scholarship paid $250. This form of scholarship required that I work in the tuberculosis hospital to earn the additional half of my tuition. However, I did not have the initial $250 nor did I have clothes to wear and bus fare to travel to Tuskegee, Alabama. There were no student loans available to Negro students during that time.

As my quest for ways to enter college continued, Daddy tried to dissuade me. "You don't need to go to college. Go over to Druid City Hospital and work with Ms. Lee or Ms. Lutz," he said. These were two women who came from Germany after the Second World War. German soldiers were treated in the white-only section of the veteran's hospital. The two women were related to some of the German soldiers and were allowed to stay in Tuscaloosa as white citizens after the war. Ms. Lee and Ms. Lutz became the supervisors of the colored staff in the local hospital and treated the colored people with the same Jim Crow mentality as Southern white people did.

I retorted with disgust in my voice, "Daddy, I can't work for Ms. Lee or Ms. Lutz. I am smarter than they are. I have been teaching school."

Daddy often told that story and always ended by saying, "I left her alone after that."

I was amazed that Daddy had no greater ambition for me than to become a hospital worker. He had been so proud of me when I taught myself to read at four years of age. He marveled at the knowledge I possessed. Yet he made no effort to help me go to college where I could continue learning.

However, after Daddy saw that I was serious about getting a higher education, he told me that he could not afford to help me go to college. He told me that he earned $45 each week at the box factory and that the best he could do was to sacrifice one week's salary, which he gave to me with the proviso that I could take the money to pay for my school class ring and school album, or I could use the money to leave the South.

To this day, I have never gotten a class ring—either for my high school graduation, my bachelor's degree, my master's degree, or for my doctoral degree. Later, when I could have afforded a class ring, I did not buy it. Subsequent buys would not have made up for not having a class ring when I graduated from high school.

The University of Alabama is located in Tuscaloosa. In those days, black students were not allowed to attend the University of Alabama even though our parents paid taxes to support the school. Foreign students from India and Europe could attend the school, but we colored citizens could not. Had I been able to attend the

University of Alabama, I would have worked nights at Druid City Hospital where, upon my return to Tuscaloosa, I was employed as a nurse aide, making $89 a month. I would have been able to pay the $85-semester tuition. I could have remained at home, worked at night, and gone to school in the daytime.

Because this opportunity was denied me and I did not have the funds to attend a Negro college, at age seventeen, I took the money Daddy gave me and bought a ticket on the Greyhound bus. I left Tuscaloosa, Alabama and went to Detroit, Michigan in search of a better life that would, hopefully, include going to college.

Going North in Search of a Better Life

"All aboard for Birmingham, Tennessee, Kentucky, Ohio, Michigan, and all-points North." The ghostly voice emanating from the loudspeaker stirred the waiting passengers in the white-only and the colored-only sections of the Greyhound bus station in Tuscaloosa, Alabama in the fall of 1953.

Breakfast, lunch, and dinner were available to sustain the white passengers while they waited for their buses. The smell of bacon, coffee, or fried chicken, unfettered by Jim Crow laws, floated on the breeze, rounded the corners of the station, and penetrated black noses, causing colored mouths to salivate.

No food was provided on the colored-only side. There was a window on the outside of the bus station where colored people could ask to buy a sandwich. The sandwich might never appear, depending upon the whim of the colored cook or the direction given by the white cafeteria supervisor.

The white-only bus station restrooms were spotlessly clean, having been washed, wiped, mopped, and maintained by colored janitors who were not allowed to clean the colored restrooms for fear of cross-contamination.

The colored-only restroom was one of two facilities in downtown Tuscaloosa where Negro people could relieve themselves. Colored people could not enter restaurants and cafés where restrooms were available to whites only. These colored-only restrooms were cleaned once each week by a part-time janitor who did not work in the white-only areas. By all accounts, they were too filthy to enter unless nature could not be denied.

Whites waited for the Greyhound bus in their comfortable, clean, spacious area and were seated on leather-bound couches and cushioned chairs.

Colored passengers in their waiting room were seated on hard benches, crowded in a tiny area. Those who had no room to sit down stood within the enclosure during cold days, or when the weather permitted, stood outside.

Upon hearing the call to board the bus, the passengers exited their separate locations and stood in separate lines outside the front and the back doors of the bus. Whites entered the front door of the bus and took their seats, going back as far as needed to ensure that they were comfortable and not crowded.

Then the rear door of the bus was opened and the colored passengers boarded, taking the seats behind the back door. Most frequently, the remaining seats were not adequate to accommodate the colored passengers. Even so, when a last-minute white passenger boarded the bus, the colored passenger seated behind the last white person was required to move back into the overcrowded seats and allow the white passenger to be seated comfortably without inconveniencing the whites upfront.

The overhead compartments were too few to hold the colored passengers' packages. They carried their parcels in their hands and were forced to hold them in their laps. These bundles were the survival kits for the colored people, consisting of food and drink, to sustain them until they reached the state of Ohio where they would be free to buy food at the bus station.

These bundles also included a little bit of home. Hams, bacon, and ham hocks were being carried up North to satisfy the Southern palate until every morsel of meat would be eaten and the ham bone boiled in a pot of collard greens or black-eyed peas. The passengers held tightly to their valuables and dreamed of prolonging the effects of their short visits home that had brought back memories of Mama's biscuits, grits, salted ham, and fresh hen eggs for breakfast.

I boarded the rear of the Greyhound bus with the other colored passengers and found a seat near the window. As others crowded in, I was pressed against the wall of the bus with barely enough room to breathe. I was accustomed to being inconvenienced. I had lived in

Alabama all my life as a second-class citizen. Along with my people, I had followed Jim Crow laws. At seventeen years old, I was leaving Alabama, going to Detroit, Michigan, where I hoped to live as a free and equal citizen and, most of all, find a way to get into college.

The Greyhound bus turned north and traveled up University Avenue, through the campus of the University of Alabama. The Detroit-bound bus carried me through places I had never seen. As the scenery sped by my window, I acquainted myself with the towns, cities, and states that I had only seen on the map. I had never been out of the state of Alabama and had been North only as far as Birmingham.

Night came and I got close to the window, squinting my eyes to see as much of the scenery that could be discerned by moonlight. Late in the night, I fell asleep to the swishing sound of the bus's tires and the hum of the motor. When I awoke, we were in Kentucky. I knew of this state as this was where my sister Gladys had been taken by Aunt Clyde.

Around midmorning, I espied the Ohio River, which was spanned by a massive bridge. As we reached the middle of the bridge, a Negro man jumped from his seat and strode down the aisle with his arms spread wide apart. The man exclaimed very loudly, "I'm free! I'm free! We are in Ohio, where I don't have to sit in the back of the bus! I don't have to say yes, sir! I'm a free man!"

Some watched in horror while I and others like me watched with pride and acquiescence.

Vignette: Before Rosa Parks, There Was Gloria

In 1956, before the civil rights movement when Rosa Parks refused to give up her seat on the bus in Montgomery, Alabama, my sister Gloria traveled from Detroit to Alabama and had an experience at the Ohio state line that was the same as Rosa Parks and the opposite to the man who declared himself free.

Gloria remained in the same seat on the bus that had taken her from Detroit and would continue the trip southward. In Detroit, she had found a seat directly behind the bus driver where she continued to sit. In Ohio, the Southern bus driver entered the bus, saw Gloria sitting behind his seat, and refused to drive. "Get up, nigger, and go to the back of the bus," he said to Gloria. "I ain't gonna drive no bus with a nigger sitting 'rectly behind me. Go on back there where you belong."

Gloria, who was naturally stubborn, did not move. She had been riding in the front of the bus, and she did not see why she should leave her seat because the bus was going southward across the Ohio River. She continued to sit and the driver continued to refuse to drive.

Finally, an elderly colored woman came from the back of the bus and spoke softly to Gloria saying, "Come on, child. Come sit with me in the back of the bus. They ain't gonna do nothing but call the police and put you in jail. Anyhow, I got to get home. My children are waiting by the side of the road, and it will be dark soon. Come on and sit by me so we can go home."

Gloria relented and went with the elderly woman. Gloria cried for hours as the bus traveled back down South.

My Arrival in Detroit and Domestic Work Experiences

When I reached Detroit, Michigan in 1953, I learned that Jim Crow had gotten to Michigan well ahead of my arrival. The Southern way of life had either traveled to Detroit by bus, car, train, plane, or on the wind and had ensconced itself in the hearts of white Northerners as soundly as if they lived in Alabama.

The tenets of Jim Crow and its ideas of segregation, subservience, servitude, and white superiority appealed to the Northern whites as being beneficial to their social and economic well-being. They assumed that colored people from the South could be paid lower salaries and would willingly work as servants to the *superior* race who employed them. Northern whites employed colored servants from the South and treated them the same as Southern employers treated their domestic servants.

My foray into the world of domestic servitude had begun with substituting for Annie Lee Mama when she was ill. I worked one day for Mama's employer, who, after a full day of scrubbing and cleaning, refused to pay me the usual $1.75. I was told that I had not cleaned sufficiently to be paid anything.

I believe that I was not paid because of my attitude of nonsubservience. I was given a gallon of milk from their dairy to give to my mother. I did not receive a penny for my full day of work.

That was not sufficient to deter me from domestic work. I worked in Mama's stead for another employer. I was paid this day, but only after the husband made a sexual proposition to me while his wife was outside in the garden. I retorted that I was a good girl and that he should be ashamed for talking to a fourteen-year-old child in that way whereupon he yelled, "Don't you sass me, nigger gal!"

When I reported the incident to Annie Lee Mama, she cried and said, "Well, Bay, you ain't never going back over there again."

Domestic work continued to be the most available employment during my teenage years in Alabama; however, all of which ended badly. I lost job opportunities because I would not go to white people's back doors and would not abide by the white men's advances. I said, "Yes, ma'am" to white adult women the same as I said to adult colored women. Even though we were expected to look down when talking to whites, I held my head up and made eye contact. As it turned out, I was either too well-spoken, too intelligent, too attractive, or not subservient enough to work in white women's kitchens. Once, I knocked on the front door of a little house to which I had been sent for possible employment. A very pregnant woman came to the door and cursed violently at me, "Git off my front porch, nigger. Don't you know you can't come upon a white person's porch? Git round the house to the back door. Who in the hell do you think you are?"

I knew who I was. I was a poor black teenage girl who needed employment but who had pride and respect for myself. I stepped off her front porch and walked out of the yard. I did not go to her back door. I went home.

Years later, my husband and I bought a house that was located on the same street in which the pregnant woman had lived. We bought the house so that our son could live off-campus when he attended Stillman College in Tuscaloosa, Alabama.

By that time, we lived in two houses—a twenty-room mansion in Union Springs, Alabama and a gated estate home in California. When people came to visit us for the first time in the mansion in Alabama, I insisted that they enter through the front door. Afterward, they could enter through the back door, which was most accessible.

I often wondered what happened to the pregnant woman and how she and her child got along living with the changes that took place during the civil rights movement.

When I was fifteen, I worked for an elderly woman who lived on Queen City Avenue. My job was to babysit the visiting grandchildren, clean up after the children, and wash dishes. One day, when I was washing dishes, the overweight elderly husband of my employer chose to circle the kitchen table to pass close behind me. He rubbed his large belly against my hips and went out the back door, smiling. As he disappeared around the house, I fled home. I did not stop to receive my pay. I just ran.

Weeks later, my sister Mable and I went back to get my pay. Again, I refused to go to the back door. Mable and I walked up on the front porch and rang the doorbell. My ex-employer came to the door.

Her hands and limbs were gnarled with arthritis. She walked with a cane. When she saw us on her front porch, she became violently angry. She cursed us using foul language and brandished her cane.

I stood my ground and asked her for my $1.75. She reached in her apron pocket and threw the money in change on the porch and told me to "Git."

We picked up the money, jumped off the porch, and ran down the street, laughing. I believe the woman saw her husband rub against me and knew why I left without saying anything to her. Otherwise, I believe she would not have paid me.

Vignette: The Swimming Pool

During the summer of my fifteenth year, in 1950, when I worked for the woman who lived on Queen City Avenue in Tuscaloosa, my cousin and I were employed to babysit the woman's grandchildren and to clean up after them.

One day, the grandmother and her daughters took the grandchildren swimming at the local public swimming pool. We traveled from Queen City Avenue to a small street that went in the direction of the Black Warrior River. The street on which we traveled wound down the hill and stopped at the river's edge.

When we arrived at the pool, I was mesmerized by the pool house and the large body of water in which people played. I had never seen a public swimming pool before.

The pool house was a round Romanesque structure with a columned portico that shaded the front entrance leading to massive polished oak doors. The building had a dome that was covered with aquamarine glass. Flowers and shrubbery adorned the grounds and made the swimming house the most beautiful building I had ever seen.

Our employers, the children, my cousin, and I alighted from the car and walked up the path to the swimming house. As we came to an intersecting path, my cousin stopped and lagged behind. I continued walking with the group and arrived at the door of the building.

One of the daughters realizing that I was still with the group turned toward me and grabbed the children's bags from my hand. Her face became angry and snarly. "Where do you think you are going?" she screamed at me. "You can't go inside. Niggers are not allowed in there. That's what wrong with you. You don't know your place. Git round there and sit by that fence until we get ready to go. Git!"

I stood stunned. It had not occurred to me that I was not allowed to go inside and watch the children as that was my job. It had not occurred to me that a higher edict would apply requiring me to "know my place." I was being told that my place was outside the building in the shade-less yard, directly in the sun, by the fence, without water, watching White people swim and have fun in the pool that was paid for by taxes from citizens including Negro people.

When my cousin and I arrived at our "place," I saw the swimming pool for the first time. The pool was a massive body of water situated behind the pool house. The water, cool and sparkling, seemed so inviting on this hot summer day. At one end of the pool, a tall diving board extended high above from which big boys and girls dived into the deep end of the cool, clear water. The opposite end of the pool was adorned with a massive oyster shell that hovered over a shallow wading area where small children played. The shell was aquamarine blue at the top. The color blended downward into a creamy pearl color and merged into a peach color underneath the children's feet.

While the young White people swam, dived, and played in the water, the adults lay on lounge chairs and tanned themselves in the sun. My cousin and I could only sit in the sun outside the chain-link fence and watch the tableau unfolding before us.

My cousin chided me for thinking that I could enter the swimming area. She knew better and was amazed that I did not. I thought about going home several times but remained because of my allegiance to my cousin.

Later, after my cousin told my aunt about the incident, my aunt told me, "You ain't never going to be able to work in White folk's kitchens if you don't learn how to act."

At fifteen years old, I knew that this was not what I intended to do. I told my aunt, "I don't plan to work in White folk's kitchens, I plan to go to college."

She laughed and said, "That's your problem. You think too high. Your Daddy ain't never going to be able to send you to no college."

In 1983, my husband, children, and I visited our parents in Tuscaloosa, Alabama. By this time, I had graduated from the University of San Francisco with a Doctoral degree. We were riding in the 1982 SEL Mercedes that my husband had given me for my graduation present. As we often did when we returned to Tuscaloosa, we visited some of the places where events had happened to us during our youth.

When we approached Queen City Avenue, I asked my husband to turn down a small street that led to the Black Warrior River which flows beside the City of Tuscaloosa.

I said, "There is a swimming pool down there."

My husband responded that there was no swimming pool down the river as his father worked on the river and my husband had often come there to play.

I contended that there was a pool down there and insisted that we continue in that direction.

That my husband had not seen the swimming pool demonstrated the inability of the White and Colored people to see each other's worlds. It never occurred to him to look at the pool as it was for "Whites Only." The Black boys swam in the river or in creeks. Many Black boys were drowned in the Black Warrior River each summer because they could not go to the public swimming pool.

I asked my husband to turn left. There on the left, opposite the river, was the swimming pool. The beautiful sparkling building was no more. In its stead was a shambled ruin that appeared as ancient as the Roman ruins I had seen when we traveled to Rome, Italy. The columns on the portico were decayed and splintered. The polished oak doors were weather-worn and loosened from their hinges. The aquamarine skylight in the dome had been broken and had fallen away.

We made our way around the building through the yard, which was overgrown with brambles and tall grass. As my husband and I emerged from the side of the decayed building, we approached the once-shiny chain link fence which was rusted and broken through.

I espied the once-glorious swimming pool. It was empty, except for piles of leaves that filled the deep end of the structure and the kudzu vines that grew over the wall and into the pool area.

Kudzu is a plant, native to Japan and China, which grows profusely in the Southern United States. Left unattended, kudzu covers everything in its path.

The diving board hung loosely above the empty crevasse. The beautiful blue, white, and pink giant oyster shell was unrecognizable. It appeared to be a trellis upon which small trees and kudzu vines grew and trailed down into the area where the small children once played.

The glorious symbol of White superiority had been destroyed by Racial Integration. When it was declared that Colored children would be allowed to swim in the once White Only pool, it was closed. Whites were not willing to share this recreational activity with Colored people.

I suddenly realized that I was standing in the same spot where my cousin and I had sat in the sun watching the White children swim and play in the cool water. This had been my "place," sitting in the sun. The years that had passed between 1950 and 1983 had allowed me to find my place in the world. Or, more befitting to the memory of that day, I had found my "**place in the sun.**"

Everything had changed. I had changed. The swimming pool had changed. Black and White relationships had changed. Nothing remained the same, except **the road still wound down the hill and stopped at the river's edge**.

Domestic Service Goes North

When I reached Detroit, Michigan in 1953, I was still trying to find a way to go to college. Instead of being able to attend school, I was forced back into domestic service jobs. The first job I found was working in the home of a Jewish woman. She was determined to have the Southern type of domestic help.

After one week of working for her during the day, she told me that I would become her live-in housekeeper. She said, "Come Monday, you will start staying overnight. You will wear this red and white striped uniform with this white cap. You will have Sundays and Mondays off." I never returned to her employ.

Fifteen years later, Whites had moved out of the area where I would have been a live-in housekeeper and my two sisters, Gloria and Mable, owned homes on the same street.

Finding that Michigan was no more welcoming than Alabama and that opportunities to go to college were not available, I returned home to Tuscaloosa, Alabama. Even when I was appreciated for my stellar work, I was not appropriately placed as a domestic worker. Back in Alabama, I became a "food server" at the University Club near the campus of the University of Alabama. We were not called "waitresses."

The manager of the Club, a Caucasian woman from Florida, engaged me in conversations on several occasions. She found that I could talk in-depth with knowledge about Literature, Art, world affairs, racial and domestic issues, and that I could perform any clerical task given with great accuracy. Also, I carried books to work and read during my work breaks. Her admonition to me was, "Joice, you are too smart to be working in a place like this. You have to go to college now. You hear me? You go to college."

To which, I replied, "I am going to college. I don't know how, but I'm going." I said to myself, "I plan to find a way to go to college."

Tears filled my eyes as I wondered, "*Where* was the way to go to college and *how* could I find it?"

After several changes in jobs, I finally broke the bond of domestic work and became a Nurses Aid at Druid City Hospital. At DCH, my salary was $89.00 each month. Had I been able to attend the University of Alabama, I could have paid the $85.00 each semester, attended school in the daytime, worked at night, and lived at home. The prize of going to college was still denied me as Negroes were not allowed to attend the University of Alabama. I returned to Detroit still in search of higher education.

Lewis Business College

After a foray into Wayne State University in Detroit where I sought a way to attend, I was persuaded that I needed ready cash for my tuition. I was bereft of any money and had no way of obtaining the funds to go to Wayne State University.

Government loans and grants were not available in those days. Two people told me that I would never amount to anything. One was my cousin and the other was my birth mother.

My cousin, a fourteen-year-old alcoholic, admonished me for trying to enter Wayne State. In an angry stupor, she yelled at me, "You think you something 'cause you smart. You ain't going to Wayne. You ain't never going to amount to nothing."

My birth mother told me this on two occasions. Once, she was angry with me for discouraging one of my sisters from befriending a married man and the other was when I was unable to send $60.00 to her for sorority fees for her youngest daughter. I was struggling, trying to go to school and maintain and feed my family. I did not have $60.00 to give to anyone, especially for fun.

On what basis they had predicted my future, I cannot say. I was determined to "become somebody."

The only avenue for some form of education was to enter Lewis Business College, a small Negro College that taught typing, shorthand, and writing. I worked for $25.00 a week and paid $25.00 each month for my schooling.

The only reward I received from attending Lewis Business was an increase in my typing skills, an opportunity to display my writing skills, the learning of some shorthand, which I never used, and an understanding of what a good secretary looked like. (Years later, as an administrator, I was able to use my secretarial skills to select two outstanding secretaries the first time I saw them. One of the two outstanding secretaries I selected on sight was Marian Graham Jenkins; the other was Mrs. Bertha Clark. I worked with others who were exceptional professional secretaries. One of whom was Jean Freeman Kliever and the other was Barbara Calhoun. Marian and Jean assisted with the publishing of this book.)

While I was attending Lewis Business College in Detroit, Michigan, my fiancée, Albert Lewis, received a four-year football scholarship to attend West Virginia State College. After one year in the cold, snowy climate, he went to California for the summer just to thaw out. He was rewarded with something greater than warm weather; he found that college was practically free in California. One needed to pay only $2.50 to enroll in Los Angeles City College for one-quarter semester. He called me and entreated me to come to California, get married, and we would send each other to college.

Thank God, I found a way to go to college!

California, Here I Come

I arrived in Burbank, California on July 28, 1955, after having flown all night from Detroit, Michigan. As I stepped out of the Burbank Airport building, I sensed that I had arrived in Paradise.

California was crystal blue. The sun shone so brightly that it permeated not only my vision but my soul. Palm trees waved in the warm California breeze. Needless to say, this was my paradise and it included a means to go to college. Albert had gotten a job and was able to send money for my plane ticket to California. I was only nineteen years of age and to be married in California. I needed permission from my parents who were in Alabama. Therefore, immediately after my arrival, we went to Yuma, Arizona to get married.

When Is a Wedding Not a Wedding?

We arrived in Yuma, Arizona and exited the bus at the Yuma station, timidly seeking which way we should go to be married. Suddenly, a little Negro man grabbed Albert's arm and said, "I can tell you two have come to get married." Albert replied, affirmatively, but wondered how this little man knew who we were. As far as we knew, he might take any two people off the bus and marry two strangers who so happened to be traveling through Yuma on the same bus.

The man introduced himself as a minister whose career included marrying people who came to Yuma for that purpose. He indicated that he had been performing marriages for a long time and could tell those who were in need of his services from those who were just passing through.

We were relieved to find someone who could guide us through the process as we did not know the first step to take. The minister, as we now called him, escorted us to an automobile parked on the sidewalk in which a couple was seated. We felt a little less kidnapped as he had corralled another couple, much older than us.

We were taken to the Yuma Municipal Courthouse where we obtained our marriage license. Everything moved so fast that I gave up trying to enjoy the occasion and gave myself over to Albert and the minister.

In the twinkling of an eye, we were driven up a hill, ushered inside an old house, and asked to stand in the middle of the living room. Two elderly people stood in the door leading to the kitchen. It seemed they lived in the house and appeared on cue to witness each marriage.

"Where can I change into my wedding dress?" I asked.

The minister looked askance at me and replied, "There won't be enough time for you to change your clothes. In twenty minutes, I will have to meet the next bus. Now stand right there." To the other couple, he said, "Now, you two stand behind them. After I marry them, you change places."

Thus began the swiftest consensual marriage in the history of nuptials. I looked at the two older people standing in the kitchen doorway to see if either was holding a shotgun.

The minister shortened the marriage ceremony to the most essential words and hurried through as fast as he could. "We are gathered here in the sight of God and man to join these two in Holy Matrimony. Do you Albert take this woman to be your wedded wife, to love, to honor, and cherish, 'til death do you part? If so, say, I do."

Albert responded, "I do."

The minister continued at a fast pace, adding the words "to love and obey" to my vows.

When called upon, I said, "I do." Instead of directing Albert to kiss the bride, we were directed to move back and allow the next couple to emerge. I wanted to say, "*Wait a minute. Is that all?*"

Instead, we moved back and allowed the second couple to be married. Within an hour, we had been taken off the bus, carried to the Courthouse to obtain our marriage license, taken up the hill to the Minister's house, stood beside another couple who witnessed our marriage as we witnessed theirs, and we were taken back to the bus station to return to California. The bus was not scheduled to return to California for another three hours.

Yuma, Arizona is a desert city located on the edge of the Sonora Desert. Yuma has extremely hot summers. According to the Guinness Book of World Records, Yuma is the sunniest place on earth. According to documented evidence, the sun shines in Yuma about 94% of the year. In fact, it is one of the hottest cities in Arizona with an average summer temperature of 107° F. On July 28, 1995, Yuma reached its all-time high of 124° F (51° C). I can attest to the fact that when we got married on July 30, 1955, it was not much cooler.

After Albert paid for the bus tickets, the license, and the ceremony, our funds were depleted. We were very hungry and very hot in the 120 something degree weather. We needed something to drink and eat. Our choices lay in having a doughnut and waiting inside the air-conditioned movie theater, or having a sandwich and a cold drink and waiting on the street with the Indians selling turquoise jewelry. We chose the doughnut and the air conditioning.

We reluctantly left the coolness of the theater when it was time for the bus to leave for California. We had arrived in Yuma as two young people with separate lives. We were leaving Yuma bound together for life. (At this writing, Albert and I were married for sixty-two years.)

The bus was cool and comfortable. We were talking about our future when the bus suddenly pulled over to the side of the highway. The bus had broken down in the middle of the Sonora Desert in July, the hottest month of the year. As if told to flee, the cool air inside the bus swooshed out and the hot desert air entered the bus. The heat seemed to be looking for a cool place in which to hide. Suddenly, we were bereft of the cool air and were swamped by the hot air that permeated the bus.

The bus driver had a walkie-talkie on which he called for another bus. He informed us that the new bus would take two to three hours to arrive as it would be coming from Los Angeles.

Meanwhile, he suggested that we could stretch our legs. I wanted to scream, "What? Stretch our legs outside the bus in the 120-degree heat?" I knew that if I stretched one leg outside that bus, the Sonora Desert would burn it off like a shriveled math stick.

We remained seated trying, to have something to do and to remain cool while we watched the dirt devils swirl around the desert floor, sweeping it clean or just spreading the dirt around. I tried to find a fan with which to generate a small amount of coolness. There was nothing available that resembled a fan, except our marriage license. The first purpose that this document served was to provide a modicum of respite from the heat in the bus in the Sonora Desert.

As the hours passed, we became thoroughly cooked. A fork could have been stuck into us and it would have gone all the way to the bone. We were done.

After three hours of waiting, the bus had become an oven. We were so hot that we could hardly see the large square form coming toward us in the distance. It was misshapen by the heat waves that caused it to be distorted. To us, it could have been a mirage. It could have been a large tumbleweed or a dirt devil whirling in our direction. After sitting in the torrid heat for three hours, we could have been hallucinating. We prayed for the misshapen form to turn into a bus. The distorted apparition came closer. It was a bus. Our bus! It stopped.

There were no shouts of happiness, although we knew that we had been redeemed from hell. We moved onto the new bus and gulped the cool refrigerated air.

When we arrived back home in Los Angeles, at two o'clock in the morning, we were too tired to consummate our marriage.

We made plans for our future. We decided that Albert would continue his schooling full-time in California instead of returning to West Virginia where he had a full scholarship. Albert would work part-time. I would work full-time and go to school part-time.

What we did not count on was that we would start a family the following year when our first son was born. We named him "Al Deric," a name we had chosen while we were in high school. Al Deric was a beautiful baby weighing nine pounds, ten ounces at birth.

As it turned out, Albert was required to work full-time. He worked nights at Los Angeles County General Hospital as a janitor and went to school during the day. He often fell asleep in class or while driving to and from work.

Our second child was a girl whom we had selected the name of Jocelyn Christina while we were in high school. For some reason, this name did not seem appropriate for our daughter. We named her Tamera Desiree. She looks like a Tamera. She is tall and attractive, and she displays exquisite social graces. We are best friends.

Ten years after Al Deric was born, Tari Christophe was born. He is our youngest and last child. At this writing, they are all grownups.

They are hardworking, good people who love their parents. They are all married with a total of eight children. I have 7 great grandchildren. We are blessed.

We were fortunate that our children were born five years apart, which gave me time to continue working and allowed me time between children to make minimal progress in school. I worked fulltime up to two weeks before giving birth to each of our children and returned to work thirty days after each child was born.

After seven years and two children, Albert graduated from California State College with a BS degree in Physical Education. He was hired by Los Angeles City Parks and Recreation, which afforded us the luxury to buy a small house in La Puente, California and a new car for me.

After Albert graduated, I was able to go to college full-time. Within three years, I graduated with a BA in Education and an Elementary teaching credential. It had taken me ten years from the day I entered Los Angeles City College to the day I graduated from California State College with my first degree.

The staff at the school where I did my student teaching insisted that I sign a contract to teach for the Rowland Unified School District after I received my degree. One week before our third child was born, I signed the contract at the Rowland Unified School District office. One month after our son, Tari, was born, I started substitute teaching and continued with daily assignments throughout the second semester of that year. In the fall, I began teaching in the same classroom in which I had done my student teaching.

It had been a long journey from age four when I first decided that I would be a teacher to finally becoming one. The journey had been filled with suffering and disillusionment. The many hardships that I had experienced made me strong and capable of withstanding whatever life threw at me. I felt a kindred spirit with my ancestors who had suffered through slavery, smallpox, Jim Crow, sharecropping, segregation, and poverty. They had survived and so had I.

First, I was not a stranger to hard work. Second, I had been teaching so long in my head that teaching was a cinch. Also, I still lived by the mantra given to me when I was growing up in Alabama.

I had to be ten times as good as others just to stay even.

I was a natural-born teacher. The two supervisors of my student teaching had threatened the principal that if he did not hire me, they would quit. These two teachers had worked together at the Los Alamos Atomic Center in New Mexico and were the top teachers at the school. After I arrived, they remarked that they were learning about teaching from me. I wasted no time before entering the

Master's Program and earned my MA Degree in Special Education. I was able to obtain my Administrative Credential through the State of California Examination Program in a one-day exam.

Albert returned to school and completed his classes for a Teaching Credential. He, too, continued in a Master's Degree Program, receiving his MA Degree in Psychology and an Administrative Credential.

Upon graduating from Cal State, I was offered a Joint Doctorate with UCLA, the first of its kind. I had to decline the offer as my family lived in the East Valley and the University of California at Los Angeles (UCLA) was in West Los Angeles. I had small children in school and I needed to continue working. Instead, I enrolled in the University of Southern California (USC) at night and began a journey that took me another five years, ending at the University of San Francisco where, in 1982, I received my Doctoral Degree in Administration, Organization, and Leadership. It had taken me twenty-six years to complete my college education!

All the years that Albert and I went to school, we never stopped working. We paid every cent of our tuition and school costs. We never applied for school loans nor did we receive assistance to defray our school costs. Notwithstanding, that tuition costs skyrocketed after Ronald Reagan became Governor of California. Nevertheless, we still paid our tuition costs in full.

Vignette: Being Ten Times Better

When I attended California State College in Los Angeles, California, my learning abilities were championed by the instructor of my Children's Literature class and were challenged by the Director of the Department of Psychology.

In my Children's Literature class, I was considered the top-performing student. The instructor asked me to teach her class for two days. I taught Folk Tales including Uncle Remus and Brer Rabbit. As a result of my prowess in the class, I was invited to the home of my instructor to meet several famous writers of children's books. I received an "A" in the class.

I had been the top-performing student in my Master's Degree Psychology class for the entire semester notwithstanding that I was working half-time, raising three small children, and going to school full-time. I had striven to be ten times better than the other students in the class. When I received my grade for the psychology class, I received a "B+." I sought to find out why the instructor had given me a "B+" when I had received an "A" on every assignment and every test. Upon inquiring the instructor as to the reason for a lower grade, she replied, "Don't think that you can come in here and get an A when you are working half-time, raising your children, and taking a full load. I don't want anybody to think that our department is no more rigorous than that."

I replied, "But I made all A's."

The instructor's response was, "But you are getting a B+."

I stood up, walked out the door, went to the Department of Special Education, and finished my Master's Degree. In the end, I was offered a Joint Doctoral Scholarship to UCLA. Sadly, I had to decline the offer as we had bought our first home in the San Gabriel Valley. I needed to return to work full-time, and I had three children to raise.

I entered the Doctoral Program at USC with a strong recommendation from the Director of Special Education at Cal State LA and went on to obtain my Doctoral Degree at the University of San Francisco. Throughout the time I went to school for my doctorate, I worked full-time and continued raising three wonderful children.

When our children were young, I worked in the same school district where they went to school. I would reach home by the time they walked home from school. Together, we would go back to my classroom to complete my classroom cleanup and lesson preparations. Then, we would go home where I would cook dinner, bathe the children, oversee their homework, and go to bed. The next day, we would start all over again. My husband worked at night and took care of the younger children in the daytime until they were at school age.

On payday, the children and I would go out. Most of the time, it was their choice or we agreed on places that we all liked. We would go to dinner or to a drive-in movie. When Father, as we now called Albert, was off work, he would go as well.

The children still remember the meals I prepared and placed in a large blue roasting pan. When we arrived at the drive-in, I opened the roasting pan cover and all the aroma of fried chicken, greens, cornbread, corn, and fried apple pies spilled into the car. They would eat while they watched the movie. Tari, our youngest son, would climb on top of the station wagon, eat, and watch the movie from his lofty perch. Father would fall asleep after dinner.

Albert became a teacher in the Compton Unified School District and then in the Los Angeles Unified School District. He was employed as a P.E. Teacher, an Athletic Director, a College Advisor, a Counselor, and an Assistant Principal/Dean during the twenty-eight years he worked for LA Unified.

As our children were growing up, we traveled. We went to Alabama every year to visit Albert's Mother, my Daddy, and Annie Lee Mama. Every three years, we continued our travels and visited our relatives in Alabama, Georgia, New York, Michigan, Indiana, Missouri, and Kansas. At first, we were not allowed to stay at hotels due to our race. Therefore, we had to stay on the road, cook at rest areas, and sleep in the car. In 1964, while traveling through Nebraska, Albert became ill. I could not drive and I was expecting Tari, our youngest son. I saw a Cattleman's Hotel off in the distance and asked Albert to drive up to it and stop. I went into the hotel and said to the desk clerk, "Madam, my husband is sick. I am pregnant. I have two small children in the car and I don't know how to drive. I need a place for my family to rest."

The desk clerk was a very tall western-looking woman. She bent over the tall counter and said, "Honey, you just go out there and get your family and bring them on in here. I'm gonna put them to bed tonight." That was the first hotel in which we were able to lodge.

Freedom to Travel

Afterward, we traveled by car, bus, train, plane, and ship all over the United States and Canada and to many foreign countries. Our most rewarding trip was to South Africa where we were welcomed home by our ancestors.

When we arrived in Cape Town, South Africa, we were greeted by our African Ancestors with "Welcome Home." Albert responded, "We have been gone for four hundred years. We are glad to be home." He cried.

We thought nothing of deciding to go to and from California or Alabama at a moment's notice. Albert and I would drive for days or enjoy the train and each other. We never tired of being together, talking and laughing.

My professional journey took me from Rowland Unified School District to Los Angeles County Schools where my assignment as Assistant Principal in the Department of Special Education began a career of "fixing" broken schools, school programs, and school districts. I took on the most difficult assignments, the worse the better and within record time, the school, program, or district was in good shape. Comments from my supervisors were, "Dr. Lewis is the best principal." "I didn't think it could be fixed, but Dr. Lewis has cleaned it up in two and a half years." "The school has gone from the lowest test scores in the state to 'Clear Status' in less than three years with a 97% graduation rate." I received awards for many of my accomplishments.

After fourteen years with Los Angeles County Special Education, I received a Fellowship from the State of California and Los Angeles County to Harvard University to attend their Organization and

Leadership Principal's Summer Institute. This was the reward for being one of the first principals in Los Angeles County to graduate from the California Leadership Academy. I was among the first trainees in Los Angeles County Schools to be selected to train others in the academy. These opportunities to train and be trained, further enhanced what I had learned about leadership in my Doctoral Program.

My career grew as I left the Los Angeles County Office of Education to reestablish the Department of Pupil Personnel Services in the Inglewood Unified School District. This assignment allowed me to stretch and be challenged to use all my training and education. Also, the successes in this job prepared me to apply for a position as Superintendent of Schools in Bullock County, Alabama.

Albert and I retired in California in 1994. We packed our furniture on an eighteen-wheeler truck and shipped our two Mercedes cars on another truck. We rented out our home in California and returned to Alabama to help educate children in our home state. We also wanted to be near Daddy as he was getting older. So, we bought a twenty-room mansion and used this home as our dwelling whenever we lived and worked in Alabama.

Retirement Reflections

When I left the Inglewood Unified School District in California, my retirement event, planned by my staff, included people with whom I had worked as far back as twenty years earlier.

During my farewell speech, I spoke of my life's journey that had taken me from the cotton fields of Alabama to the hallowed halls of the University of Southern California, the University of San Francisco, and Harvard University. I had come from a lowly state of a sharecropper's daughter to rise up the career ladder. I had come from a young girl seeking a way to go to college and get an education to becoming a Doctor of Education.

As I was walking across the stage at my graduation ceremony at the University of San Francisco to receive my Doctoral Degree, I said to myself, "I will never have to pick cotton, again."

Lois, my sister, said that my feet never touched the floor and that I floated across the stage at the University of San Francisco to receive my Doctoral Degree. I don't know how I got across the stage. I was having an out-of-body experience. Thanks to God, to Albert, and to the State of California, I had completed a long, hard journey trying to get an education.

I had come from being unable to attend college in Alabama to being able to attend Los Angeles City College, California State College at Los Angeles, the University of Southern California, the University of San Francisco, and Harvard University. I returned to Alabama to become not only the Superintendent of Bullock County Schools but a Chief Financial Officer for the State of Alabama Department of Education and the Superintendent of Macon County Schools in Tuskegee, Alabama. Amidst these top-level positions, I agreed to save a high school by becoming its principal. As a result, the high school went from imminent State take-over to achieving a 97% graduation rate by the end of my three-year tenure.

Finally, I came full circle to return to California and became the Interim Superintendent for Inglewood Unified School District. I ceased to work at the age of seventy-four and wrote this book the year after I retired. It is my goal to complete two more books before I reach my eightieth birthday. The voices of my ancestors still whisper to me, "Be the best you can be." I believe the legacy that my ancestors left me in strength, determination, and perseverance, coupled with my Daddy's tough love and Annie Lee Mama's tender love and rearing practices, prepared me to be the best I could be—whether it was being an educator, a wife, a mother, a grandmother, a daughter, a sister, a friend, or a god-fearing human being.

Vignette: "It Beats Picking Cotton"

On the occasion that we visited Annie Lee Mama when she was a patient at the Druid City Hospital, Daddy pointed out the nurse's aide whom we observed bringing in a bedpan. He asked us, "Do you remember when we lived on Cliff Burrough's farm?" Many years had passed since we were sharecroppers.

The memory of which could not be readily brought to mind. By that time, we were professional women. Gloria owned her own beauty salon and several rental properties in Detroit, Michigan. Gladys was a cafeteria cook for the Oakland, California School District. Mable was a homemaker. Lois was a school teacher in California and I was the principal of a school in California.

"Do you know who that is?" Daddy asked, pointing to a White nurse's aide.

None of us recognized the person to whom Daddy pointed. She was a tall, slightly bent middle-aged White woman. We looked at the nurse's aide who was attending Annie Lee Mama's needs and tried to guess who she was.

Daddy said, "That's Vivian Burroughs, Mr. Cliff's daughter. She is a nurse's aide here at DCH."

I reflected on that 4th of July holiday when my sisters and I were forced to chop Vivian's cotton as she drove down the road in her red Ford Convertible. That day, I had voiced a metaphor, "The color of freedom is red."

As I reflected on the different paths that we all had taken, I said to my sisters, "Perhaps, freedom is not driving fast in a red car. Perhaps, freedom is the drive you get from working as a sharecropper and deciding that there are no limits to how far you can go if you are running from the cotton fields."

My sister, Lois, and I created a mantra, "No matter how hard life's struggle becomes, it beats picking cotton."

The Civil Rights Movement

During the Civil Rights Movement, life began to change for Daddy and Annie Lee Mama. My husband and I were living in California when the movement came to Tuscaloosa, Alabama as marches, "sit-ins," and peaceful demonstrations.

Students left school and marched downtown. They were met by angry White citizens, the police, and the Ku Klux Klan, many of whom chose to beat the children as they marched. The KKK members were robed and incognito. As they beat the children, one girl fell to the ground. A KKK member continued to beat her as she lay there defenseless. She looked up and saw the face of her attacker underneath the KKK hood. She said, "Don't hit me anymore, Mr. Barr." The story was told and retold that the child had identified Mr. Barr as one of the KKK members who were beating children for marching.

Mrs. Barr, the mother of the KKK member, owned the largest grocery store in the Black community. Before the Piggly Wiggly supermarkets arrived, local grocery stores were the only places to buy food. Barr's Grocery Store had prospered for years due to the purchases made mostly by Colored people.

Mrs. Barr did not hesitate to cheat her customers. She was known to place her hand on the scale and press down to make a small piece of meat weigh more. Aunt Luella would watch Mrs. Barr and catch her pressing down on the scale. "Mrs. Barr, take your hand off that scale. That little piece of fat pork can't cost that much," she would say. Sure enough, when weighed properly, the meat would cost less.

After the child reported that Mrs. Barr's son was the one who had beaten her and that he was a member of the KKK, everyone ceased to buy food from Barr's Store. Not one person went into the store. Mrs. Barr would stand in the door of the store and beg Black people (as we were now being called) to come in and buy something. Everyone would say, "No, Mrs. Barr. We can't buy in your store."

The store went out of business. The store building sat empty for many years until it decayed and the city tore it down. The land where the store sat still lies fallow as if it is scorched earth. The closing of the store was a testimony to the defiance of Black people.

The same defiant behavior put the Tuscaloosa City buses out of business. These buses received most of their trade from Black people. After Rosa Parks refused to go to the back of the bus in Montgomery, Alabama, the people in Tuscaloosa, Alabama would not ride the city buses. They walked to work, caught rides from anyone who had a car, or took taxis that would pick up anyone who called as well as those who were seen walking until the taxis were filled to capacity.

Students sat in at the Kress Department Store food counter. Blacks drank water from the "White Only" water fountain instead of the "Colored Only" smaller fountain located nearby.

Vignette: Personal

In 2008, I passed the old Kress Department Store building in Tuscaloosa, Alabama and found that it had gone out of business. The present occupant was a furniture store.

As I passed by, two young African American men came out of the building and walked across a metal plate in the doorway. The metal plate had the name "Kress" emboldened on the floor.

I stopped the two young men and asked them, "Do you know what the name on that metal plate implies?"

They said, "No, Ma'am. We don't know anything about that name. It was there when we started working for the furniture store."

To which I replied, "Let me tell you about your history. This store was the Kress Department Store where the young Black students held sit-ins at the lunch counter and they drank from the 'White Only' drinking fountain during the Civil Rights Movement. Young people your ages helped Martin Luther King, Jr. and other Civil Right Leaders put an end to racial segregation."

The young men looked at the plaque for several seconds. They raised their heads in unison. Tears clouded the eyes of one of the young men. He said, "Ma'am, thank you for telling us that story. We didn't know anything about what happened in this store."

With that, I bade them "God bless" and continued down the street. The encounter brought tears to my eyes. It was disheartening to know that the history of the Civil Rights Movement had not been passed on to the younger African American generation.

The Civil Rights Movement as Seen by White People

During the Civil Rights Movement, domestic workers like my Mother, Annie Lee, began to require higher pay for their day's work or they ceased to work as housekeepers. Many White employees, who had been able to have their homes cleaned for $1.75 a day, now had to clean their own houses as Black women charged more for their services and they were able to get jobs other than domestic work.

During the early days of the movement, Annie Lee Mama worked for the Lee family.

Once, when Annie Lee Mama was ill, she sent me to work for Mrs. Lee in her stead. I worked all day, scrubbing the kitchen on my hands and knees, washing the dishes, sweeping, dusting, and making beds. Mrs. Lee did not alert me to anything I had done improperly. Yet, at the end of the day when I was due to receive $1.75 for my day of work, Mrs. Lee told me that my work had been unsatisfactory and that she would not pay me anything. She gave me a gallon of milk from her dairy and told me to give the milk to my mother. She sent me home without pay.

During the Civil Rights Movement, Mrs. Lee watched as Black people fought for their civil rights.

One day, when Annie Lee Mama arrived at work, Mrs. Lee was crying. Mama went about her duties while Mrs. Lee continued to cry. Since Mrs. Lee and Mama had never behaved as equals, Mama did not feel that it was her place to inquire why Mrs. Lee was weeping. Finally, the crying woman could contain herself no longer. She exploded, "Annie Lee, the Colored folk are marching downtown and sitting at the lunch counters. Don't they know that the counters are only for White People?"

Mama answered, "Yes, Ma'am."

"I hear they're drinking at the 'White Only' drinking fountain. They're going to want to go to our schools. Next thing, they're going to want to be White. Annie Lee, what are we going to do?"

Annie Lee Mama said, "I don't know, Mrs. Lee."

Daddy and Annie Lee Mama realized that the Civil Rights Movement allowed them to live more as equals in their own community. Annie Lee Mama ceased working as a servant. For the first time in her life, she became "just a housewife."

The Death of Eula Mama

When Eula, our birth mother, died, her ghost appeared to Daddy as he rested in the porch swing at his home. Over thirty years had passed since Eula Mama and Daddy had divorced.

Daddy enjoyed lying in the swing with his legs through one end and his head resting on the arm next to the wall of the house. In this position, he could see whoever came down the road that ran in front of the porch.

A car went by. It sped down the dirt road. Dust swirled high, blowing into the porch, obscuring Daddy's view, and filling his eyes with dirt. Daddy closed his eyes against the dust and opened them when he felt that the dust had settled. As he opened his eyes, he saw our birth mother, Eula Mama, standing before him, between himself and the road. Although his eyes felt gritty, he refused to blink as long as he could hold back his autonomic nerves.

Eula stood facing him. She was young. She wore the same pink dress and the pink bow in her hair that she had worn when she left home the first time. She did not smile nor speak. She just looked at Daddy. Finally, he had to blink his eyes. When he opened his eyes again, she was gone.

Daddy extricated himself from the swing and ran into the house. "Annie Lee," he called to his wife, "I just saw Eula."

Annie Lee Mama said, "Was Eula in that car? She couldn't have been in that car. She is in the hospital. She is very sick."

"I know," said Daddy. "She was not in the car. She appeared to me like she was young. She was wearing the same pink dress that she had on the first time she left me and the children."

Annie Lee Mama suddenly understood that Eula Mama had appeared to Daddy as a spirit. "You go and see about Eula. Something is wrong," Annie Lee Mama exclaimed as she helped Daddy change into clean clothes.

Daddy drove away at a fast pace. When he arrived at Druid City Hospital, he found that Eula Mama had died. She was fifty-eight years old.

The Death of Annie Lee Mama

Our step-mother, Annie Lee Mama, had a genetic heart condition. Her mother died from a heart attack while plowing in the field she sharecropped. For years, Annie Lee Mama was under the doctor's care for her heart.

Annie Lee Mama was in a coma when she was in the hospital being tended by Vivian Burroughs, the girl for whom she had worked when we were sharecroppers. The doctor relieved the pressure on her brain by trephine, causing her to lose a segment of her memory. Following the surgery, her conversation consisted of missing words that Daddy filled in. She would continue talking as if what Daddy said was coming from her. They were a team.

Even though Annie Lee Mama had a severe heart problem, she lived to be sixty-nine years old. Just before she died, she had a period in which she seemed to be responding well to her medication. The day she died, she cooked dinner and encouraged Daddy to go to choir practice since he had not gone for some time. When Daddy returned, he called Annie Lee Mama to let her know that he was home. She did not answer.

He found her in her favorite chair by the fireplace. As he stooped beside her chair to kiss her "hello," she grunted and fell forward into his arms. Daddy said that she had waited for him to return before she died. When we came home to Annie Lee Mama's funeral, Daddy confessed how much he loved her. He said that he did not love her when he married her, but he grew to love her more than he had ever loved any woman.

Land Ownership Makes a Man

Daddy lived in the farmhouse until he was ninety-five years old, which was thirty-one years after Annie Lee Mama died.

Daddy lived all his life on someone else's land until 1989 when the farm where Daddy lived was put up for sale. My husband, Albert Lewis, and I got a loan on our California home to buy the farm. By this time, I had acquired a Doctoral Degree and was on my way to attend a Summer Institute on Leadership at Harvard University. On our way to Cambridge Massachusetts, we stopped in Tuscaloosa to see Daddy. The three of us drove to the lawyer's office. I handed the check to Daddy and said, "Buy your own land." He took the check and turned it over and over. He said, "I have never seen so much money in my life." Then, he handed the check to the lawyer and said, "I'll buy my land, now."

The following years were the happiest of his life. He was finally a "man." He owned land. He touted his ownership of the land by telling people, "When you come on this land, you got to come by me."

He remained on the farm we bought for him until he was ninety-five years old. By that time, he was deaf, had poor vision, and had difficulty walking.

Albert and I took Daddy home to live with us in Union Springs, Alabama where I was Superintendent of Schools. He lived with us in a twenty-room mansion until he became unable to walk. Every day, he would sit on one of several porches around the mansion. He would talk to people as they passed by. Sometimes, passersby would come to the porch and sit awhile. Everyone knew and liked Mr. Bailey.

My husband was very close to my Father. Daddy would say, "Son, I love you. I don't know if I ever told you, but I love you."

My husband would say, "I love you too, Daddy." This conversation was repeated many times until Daddy stopped talking.

After Albert had a hernia operation brought on by lifting and bathing him, Daddy asked us to find him a nursing home.

For the remainder of his life, he lived in the Southern Springs Nursing home in Union Springs, Alabama.

Daddy was a snappy dresser. He wore white suits in the summertime and he always wore a stingy brim hat. For his internment, Albert bought Daddy a white silk suit with a matching shirt, tie, and handkerchief. Daddy lay in his bronze casket imprinted with birds flying in the background and "Flying Home" written thereon. He was dressed in his white silk suit and wore a stingy brim hat tipped over his right eye. He still had a full head of white hair and his white mustache was neatly trimmed. He was as handsome as ever.

According to Public Records, Daddy was born in July 1908 and died in April 2009. In July of that year, he would have been one hundred and one years old. He always said that he wanted to "make a hundred." He did.

He was interred beside his wife, Annie Lee Bailey, to the left of his mother and father, William and Annie Bailey, on the front row of the Holly Spring Missionary Baptist Church Cemetery.

Hushed

Hushed was my father's voice. Hushed were my ancestral voices.

Hushed, hushed, hushed. Sleep and rest, my ancestors.

Your voices have been heard. Your stories have been told.

I sat in the silent morning and prayed my childhood prayer.

"Now I lay me down to sleep. I pray Thee, Lord, my soul to keep. If I should die before I wake, I pray Thee, Lord, my soul to take."

Bless Daddy. Bless Annie Lee Mama and Eula Mama. Bless Lois, Mable, Gladys, Gloria, James, and me. Bless my husband, Albert. Bless my children, Al Deric, Tamera, and Tari, their spouses, and their children. Bless my ancestors. Bless each and every heart. Amen.

The voices of my ancestors joined me in prayer. "Amen. Amen."

APPENDIX

The Holly Spring Missionary Baptist Church History

The Holly Spring Missionary Baptist Church has come full circle. Great-Grandpa Romeo Blackburn was one of the church founders. He was the first deacon who led the church from the Brush Arbor Church location toward erecting a church building.

Throughout the years, members of the Blackburn family have continuously participated in the church. The leadership of the church has returned to its beginning. Great-Grandpa's great-grandson, Frederick Blackburn Sr., is the present pastor of the Holly Spring Missionary Baptist Church.

Starting in 1874, Reverend Bobby Edwards, Reverend Alex Brown, and Reverend Robert Morrow were the first three pastors of the Holly Spring Missionary Baptist Church. Records are not available as to the length of each pastor's service.

Reverend Jack C. Mosley was the fourth pastor. He served thirty-one years. During his administration, the church prospered and continued to grow in numbers. Reverend Mosley led the community in setting up a welfare organization known as the Home Mission Society. Uncle John Blackburn was one of the earlier presidents. The purpose of the Home Mission Society was to assist in caring for the sick and burying the dead.

For Daddy's generation, who were the grandchildren of Romeo Blackburn, the gravesites in the cemetery were free. However, payment was required for opening and closing the graves. The grave digging job has been passed down from generation to generation and is presently assigned to cousin Latham (Blackburn) Harris.

Deacons added to the board during Reverend Mosley's service were cousin Robert Wells, Uncle Romeo Blackburn Jr., Uncle Robert Blackburn, cousin Jack C. Foster, Deacon James Knox, and cousin James Wells.

Reverend Henderson Lewis served two years as pastor of Holly Spring Missionary Baptist Church. Reverend Lee Grant Page followed Reverend Lewis and served three years. The Reverend Robert Gilvan was the next pastor called by the church and served seven years. He resigned.

In 1917, the Reverend I. W. White accepted a call by the church and served ten years. During this time, a Baptist Young People's Union and a Young Men's Christian Association were organized to help young people in their Christian development. The Reverend J. H. Martin followed Reverend White as pastor of the church and served only one year. He was followed by Reverend J. W. Shelton who served for four years.

In 1932, Reverend W. J. Long was called to the pastorate of the church and served until 1941.

The membership increased under the leadership of the former pastors to the degree that a more suitable building was needed. The present church was constructed and other improvements were made. Deacons who were added to the deacon board during the pastorate of Reverend Long include the following: Uncle John Blackburn, Deacon Russell Thomas, cousin Thero Blackburn, and Deacon Hosea H. Brown. In 1941, Reverend Frank D. Holly was called to pastor the church. Reverend Holly served as pastor of Holly Spring Missionary Baptist Church for over forty-three years. He served longer than any other pastor in the history of the church. It was he who baptized my sisters and me.

The church programs expanded as new activities were added. Again, the church building was remodeled and enclosed with brick. A two-story annex, including a basement, was constructed to provide space for the various teaching and fellowship activities. The inside of the church building was renovated and made more attractive. The church continued to grow in all aspects.

The deacon ministry under Reverend F. D. Holly's leadership consisted of Uncle John Blackburn, chairperson; cousin Thero Blackburn, church clerk for more than thirty-five years; cousin Justin Harper, treasurer; Brother Willie J. Robinson; cousin Willard Blackburn; Brother Webster Harris; cousin Joseph Foster Sr., Brother Andrew Henderson, Brother Nathaniel Henderson, and Brother Willie Lewis Henderson Sr. served as chairpersons, clerk, treasurer, and trustees of the church. Brother Webster Harris and Otis Henderson served as church clerks later in the history of the church.

Past pastors of Holly Spring Missionary Baptist Church also included Reverend Frank Davis who served from 1983 to 1985; Reverend Frank Lyles who was called in 1986 and served for one year and nine months, and Reverend Virgil A. Harper, great-grandson of Romeo Blackburn, who served as pastor from 1987 to 1989.

Reverend W. E. Pitts was called to serve the Holly Spring Missionary Baptist Church as pastor the second Sunday in February 1990. Since Reverend Pitts became pastor, the following things have been done: installation of a safety gate at the entrance of the church's property, blacktop paving of the parking lot area to park seventy-five or more cars, and installation of a sidewalk in front of the entrance of the dining hall. A new steeple has been placed on top of the church. The old church bell has been placed in a freestanding bell tower and can be tolled during funerals and other services. Underneath the bell, a plaque has been placed that lists the church officers and the dates of exterior improvements. A ramp and handrail are in place beside the steps at the front of the church. City water has been brought to the church. Vinyl siding covers all exterior woodwork relieving the members of the need to paint. The church founders are listed on the cornerstone of the original church.

In November 2004, Reverend Frederick A. Blackburn, another great-grandson of Great-Grandpa Romeo Blackburn, accepted the pastorship of the Holly Spring Missionary Baptist Church. Under his leadership, improvements continue to be made to the church. Most notably, Reverend Blackburn has reinstated the midweek prayer and

Bible study. Monthly meetings are held with deacons and auxiliary organizations. Church services are held every Sunday of the month.

The current deacon ministry consists of cousin Lathan Harris, chairperson, cousin Eddie Lee Blackburn Sr., Brother Otis Henderson Sr., and cousin Cleveland Foster Sr.

The current trustee board consists of cousin Joseph Foster, chairperson; Roscoe Cunningham; Otis Henderson Sr., church clerk; Johnny Lee Henderson Sr.; cousin Lathan Harris; Grady Leatherwood Sr., and Stanley J. Henderson.

The following persons have been church presidents: cousin Willard Blackburn, Webster Harris, and Doris Stewart, with Deacon Webster Harris as director. Currently, Sister Catherine Foster serves as director. The history of the church choir covers many years. Brother Sterling Foster was the first president of the choir. He was followed by Sister Leella Snoddy who served faithfully for more than thirty years. Currently, Sister Dorothy Henderson serves as the choir president.

The following persons have served as pianists and music directors over the years: Rosa Mae Blackburn, Annie D. Holly, and Dr. Cassandra Blackburn. Marcia Henderson is the current pianist and music director.

The usher board of the church is another important service organization. It has been led by the following chiefs: Brothers Frank Davis, Levi Harris, Andrew Henderson, and Sister Helen Harris. Sister Mattie Snider serves as the current president.

The following preachers, who were also members of the church, have acted as assistants to the pastor: Reverend U. S. Wells, (cousin) Dave McKenny, Reverend (Uncle) Lewis Blackburn, and Reverend (Uncle) William H. Bailey.

Throughout the history of the Holly Spring Missionary Baptist Church, various auxiliaries have been established in the church. These auxiliaries and leaders are as follows: superintendent of the Sunday school: Brother Hiter Wells, J. C. Foster, John Harper, Russell Thomas, and Willard Blackburn. Currently, Cleveland Foster Sr. is the superintendent of the Sunday school, which also sponsors a vacation Bible school each year.

The Ladies Missionary Society was established in 1920, and Sister Bessie Wells was the first elected president. Following her presidency were Aunt Hattie Blackburn, Aunt Emma Blackburn, cousin Mary Blackburn, Aunt Glover Hood, cousin Ruby Blackburn, Helen Harris, cousin Queen Esther Harris, Clara Henderson, cousin Racile Blackburn, and Edna Parker. Cousin Lillian Blackburn, the spouse of the present pastor, is the current president.

Along with the adult activities, the Missionary Society sponsors various youth organizations supervised by selected adult leaders. The Baptist Training Union was reorganized after Reverend F. D. Holly became pastor, with Deacon Willie J. Robinson and Sister Alene Taylor serving as directors.

The Holly Spring Missionary Baptist Church Cemetery is located on the west side of the church. According to the dates on the gravestones, Mrs. Rachel Wells, the first wife of co-founder Hiter Wells, was the first person buried in the cemetery. She was born a slave in 1862 and died in January 1892 at the age of thirty years old.

The Holly Spring Missionary Baptist Church and the graves of those buried in the church cemetery stand as monuments to my ancestors who proved the strength and worth of a people that rose up from slavery to create a lasting legacy of hope, love, and family.[27]

[27.] Pamphlet submitted by Pastor Frederick Blackburn, 134th church anniversary, Holly Spring Missionary Baptist Church, Romulus, Alabama, Sunday, October 11, 2009

ABOUT THE AUTHOR

During the Jim Crow era in Alabama, African American children were told by their parents and teachers that they had to be "ten times better than their white counterparts, just to stay even." Striving to be ten times better became the standard behavior for Joice Lewis who achieved success with ten times fewer resources and against ten times greater odds. What sustained her during the most difficult times was the evidence that her people had survived the hardships faced during two periods of slavery: the enslavement of Africans and the era of sharecropping. Raised on a sharecropping farm, she was a gifted learner who had no money to go to college. Joice Lewis, nevertheless, found a way to achieve a doctoral degree at prestigious universities and experience success as a top-level educator. She was married to her high school sweetheart, until his passing for sixty-two years.

www.ingramcontent.com/pod-product-compliance
Lightning Source LLC
Chambersburg PA
CBHW021438070526
44577CB00002B/206